H.L. MENCKEN

GARLAND REFERENCE LIBRARY
OF THE HUMANITIES
(VOL. 776)

H.L. MENCKEN
A Research Guide

Allison Bulsterbaum

GARLAND PUBLISHING, INC. • NEW YORK & LONDON
1988

© 1988 Allison Bulsterbaum
All rights reserved

Library of Congress Cataloging-in-Publication Data
Bulsterbaum, Allison.
  H. L. Mencken : a research guide.

  (Garland reference library of the humanities;
vol. 776)
  Bibliography: p.
  Includes indexes.
  1. Mencken, H. L. (Henry Louis), 1880–1956—
Bibliography.   I. Title.   II. Series.
Z8563.5.B84   1988   016.818′5209   87–36668
[PS3525.E43]
ISBN 0–8240–6634–0 (alk. paper)

Printed on acid-free, 250-year-life paper
Manufactured in the United States of America

For my lovely mother, of course

CONTENTS

Preface	ix
Acknowledgments	xiii
Introducing H.L. Mencken	xv
Abbreviations	xxvii

Part 1: PRIMARY BIBLIOGRAPHY
- A. Major Works
  - i. Full-length Works and Collaborations — 3
  - ii. Pamphlets — 11
  - iii. Essays — 13
  - iv. Magazine Articles — 25
  - v. Newspaper Articles — 45
  - vi. Contributions — 65
- B. Anthologies, Collections, Selections — 71
- C. Letters — 93

Part 2: SECONDARY BIBLIOGRAPHY
- D. Bibliographies — 99
- E. Biographies, Reminiscences, Memoirs — 105
- F. Books and Pamphlets — 119
- G. Chapters and Sections of Books — 125
- H. Articles — 157
- I. Mentions — 217
- J. Dissertations — 237
- K. Forthcoming Works — 241

Author Index — 243
Subject Index — 255

Preface

Where H.L. Mencken's work itself did not touch virtually every major sphere of American life in the first half of this century, his personality and "prejudices" did, so that even if we could hope to turn up all that he wrote, we could never uncover all that has been written about him. A bibliography covering everything that is known to date could not easily be contained in a single volume, perhaps not in two. Even Betty Adler's landmark *H.L.M.: The Mencken Bibliography* and her ten-year Supplement are selective, as is the second ten-year Supplement compiled by her successor, Vincent Fitzpatrick.

This bibliography is also selective, in some respects highly so. My aim has been to hit the high points of primary and secondary Menckeniana, to choose materials according to the criteria of interest, significance, relevance, and, to some extent, intrinsic literary or intellectual value. Whereas Adler's work and the subsequent Supplements have been broad, this volume intends to shrink the range of material to more manageable limits--to separate the wheat from the chaff, as it were. Occasionally I have made silent corrections to entries listed in these earlier works; but as an infallible bibliography often remains an elusive ideal, what mistakes this one may contain are mine alone. The scholar already acquainted with Mencken and his era should by all means consult Adler and Fitzpatrick; the general reader and newcomer to Mencken would do well to begin here.

Part 1 is a selective list of works by H.L. Mencken separated roughly according to length and genre (for instance, full-length studies are separated from essay collections, magazine from newspaper articles, and so forth). Section A iii singles out for annotation Mencken's more significant essays regardless of where they first appeared in print; most of them were subsequently collected in books listed in Section B, and cross-references within brackets [ ] refer the user to those collections. Although Mencken's essays have often been and continue to be reprinted in various anthologies and college readers, Section B includes only collections devoted exclusively to H.L. Mencken. Similarly, Section C covers articles and books of which letters to and from Mencken comprise

PREFACE

a substantial portion (see headnote to Section C for cross-references to other items in this volume which reprint or excerpt individual letters). Foreign translations of Mencken's works have not been given separate entries but have been mentioned within the annotations for the original works.

Part 2 is a selective list of works about Mencken, also divided roughly by length and genre. Here, magazine and newspaper articles have been kept together. No attempt has been made to cover foreign studies, although a few are mentioned. In the interest of space, I have excluded all plays, films, recordings, and other non-print media; such items can be found listed through 1981 in the Adler bibliography and its Supplements.

In Part 1 individual entries are listed first chronologically within each division and subdivision, then alphabetically by title (H.L. Mencken is understood to be the author, editor, a collaborator in all instances); the exceptions to this arrangement are Sections A iv and A v, which are strictly chronological. In Part 2 the arrangement of citations is chronological according to year, then alphabetical by author or title where no author is given. The most recent items included in this bibliography date from Summer 1987; a list of works in progress at this writing appears as the last section of the book preceding the indexes.

For any one item, complete publication information is provided only once, though the work may be mentioned more often; in such instances cross-referencing indicates where publication information may be found. Mencken's major, full-length works are not given descriptive annotations, but the nature of most of these books is suggested in the introductory essay. Those works not mentioned in the essay generally have self-explanatory titles. For individual essays and articles by Mencken and for all items in the secondary bibliography, I have supplied brief, descriptive annotations except, again, where titles are self-explanatory. In these annotations reprint information is usually kept deliberately brief.

Finally, the indexes are intended to be of use to one searching for all items pertaining to a particular subject or to those written by a certain author. The author index also lists the names of such cartoonists, illustrators, and translators as

PREFACE

are mentioned in the bibliography. Numbers refer to citations, not pages.

Throughout this bibliography, "HLM" shall be understood to mean Henry Louis Mencken. *SS* and *AM* shall be understood to mean the *Smart Set* and *American Mercury* magazines. All other periodical titles of more than one word are abbreviated in annotations but not in citations, as is the name of the library housing most of Mencken's own books and papers, the Enoch Pratt Free Library. A list of Abbreviations follows the introduction.

In compiling this volume I have made generous use of various library collections (see acknowledgments); the annual, international bibliography published by the Modern Language Association; the *Essay and General Literature Index*; the bibliographies appearing in works on Mencken; the "Bibliographic Checklists" included in most issues of the journal *Menckeniana*; and finally, the Adler and Fitzpatrick bibliographies. To these last works every scholar of H.L. Mencken must sooner or later be indebted.

Acknowledgments

Surely no one ever wrote a book without help from someone, usually many people. I am indebted to Mr. Neil Jordahl and Dr. Vincent Fitzpatrick of the Enoch Pratt Free Library in Baltimore, Maryland; to the staff of the Main Reading Room and of the Newspaper and Current Periodicals Department of the Library of Congress; to the librarians of the University of North Carolina at Chapel Hill; to UNC Professor Thomas Stumpf; and finally to Rebecca Barnhouse, Lisa Carl, Judith Burdan, Christopher E. Baxter, and Michele Morris, for reasons they understand. And to Karen Moranski I am especially grateful, for her patience, advice, and--of course!--her typing.

Introducing H.L. Mencken

The one-hundredth anniversary of his birth has passed, the thirty-fifth anniversary of his death approaches, and Henry Louis Mencken continues to elude definition. Newspaper columnist and editor, magazine editor, political commentator, literary critic and prose stylist in his own right, humorist, philologian, spokesman for the causes of liberty and individuality, pathologist of human nature generally and American nature particularly: at some point in his seventy-five years he was each of these, and frequently he played several roles at once. Younger newspapermen emulated him. Aspiring writers sought his editorial and critical favor. Students of American speech followed his lead in nurturing their fledgling discipline. The young intelligentsia enjoyed being seen with a well-thumbed copy of his little green journal, *The American Mercury*, on hand. Patriots, clergymen, pedagogues, ladies' clubs, and even a U.S. President (Franklin D. Roosevelt) attacked him. And virtually everywhere, it would appear, Americans read him for the laughs he constantly provoked. "H.L.M.," as he often signed himself, was a national phenomenon.

At least part of the reason lies in timing. Born in 1880, Mencken came into his prime in the 1920s, just when many young, disaffected artists and intellectuals were ripe for loud proclamations of disaffection, hungry for the show of irreverent individuality Mencken's prose personality embodied. Americans were just putting the war behind them, and although they were not devastated, their knuckles were skinned and their ideals bruised. At home they found that Mencken was growing into the pied piper of a cultural elitism that disdained nearly everything America had heretofore been about. That Mencken was a generation older than most of the people he inflamed did not weaken but rather strengthened his position as iconclast *par excellence*, for his experience and wide reading lent credibility to a movement of otherwise feverish groping for the new, the untainted, the untried, and the uninhibited. He sent traditional notions sprawling on all fours, and in the twenties America both loved and hated him for it.

To approach some explanation for the rise to eminence of an H.L. Mencken, however, one must look

INTRODUCTION

a little farther back. The era of his young manhood had been those *fin de siecle* years of prosperity and promise in which the nineteenth century had grown into the twentieth, a time when the nation was smugly certain, at least on the surface, of its destiny as a political and economic world power. Progress was the catchword of the day: the growth of periodical journalism was fast contributing both to the spread of literacy and to the "muckraking" which aimed at political and governmental reform; trust busting and land conservation were underway Teddy Roosevelt style; and the social "sciences" were in their infancy. But to Mencken the cries of the reformers and the cheers of the progressives amounted to the bleating of so many absurd little sheep. Although personally he was well fed and happy, he did not share the prevalent belief that the United States was on the threshold of the best of all possible worlds. Turning thirty in 1910, he had already published books on iconoclasts and truth-seekers Friedrich Nietzsche and George Bernard Shaw. The uncovnentional thought of these men and of others like Thomas Huxley and James Huneker contributed to Mencken's growing skeptical habit of mind, which was also partially inherited from his bourgeois, German-American father, August Mencken.

Casting a wide glance over the contemporary scene, young Mencken realized that popular America had not heard Nietzsche's convincing, to Mencken's mind, proclamation that God was dead--quite the contrary. The Puritan tide of American Christianity rolled through the national life as boldly as ever, implacable in its self-righteous beliefs: that material wealth was a sign of God's favor for a country just as it was for an individual; that literature should not reflect life but uplift it by inculcating Christian and capitalistic values (not in the least perceived as mutually exclusive); that strong drink was usually responsible for social ills like crime and poverty; and that a descendant of Presbyterian ministers in the White House--Woodrow Wilson was elected in 1912--represented just the ticket for keeping America out of a world war or, failing that, for keeping war out of the world ever after. To all this Mencken responded: "Balderdash."

Another by-product of Mencken's reading and of his predisposed skepticism toward the life around him was his aversion to democracy. He thought it

INTRODUCTION

"palpably absurd" that a nation should be governed according to the principle that all human beings are created equal, for to Mencken nothing could be further from truth. Clearly there were superior and inferior mortals born every day, more of the latter than of the former, and it grated him to think that the common mass of American humanity should be allowed to impose its choice of public officials upon the enlightened minority. "Democracy is the theory that the common man knows what he wants and deserves to get it good and hard," Mencken quipped. The trouble was that everyone else got it good and hard, too. At least one tenet of democracy, however, was dear to Mencken's heart: the right of every person to speak his mind. It mattered little to Mencken whether a man's pronouncements were worth listening to--if not, he might be annoying at worst, entertaining at best. What mattered was that ever-present chance that the speaker might indeed say something others needed to know or consider. But as for the rest of what democracy was about, Mencken had little use for it beyond sheer personal amusement. "Why remain here, then?" he was asked when the ex-patriot movement got underway. Mencken's response: "Why do men go to zoos?"

Thus it happened that sacred cows of popular thought and culture abounded by the time Mencken developed a temperament and a style capable of blasting them accurately, and with infectious delight. In the 1920s his position with the Baltimore *Sunpapers* as editorialist and chief political correspondent, along with his joint editorship first of the *Smart Set* magazine and later of *The American Mercury*, provided him the limelight of public worship and denunciation that fed his soul. By the 1930s this light had blinded him, so much so that Prohibition continued to be the chief political bone he wanted to pick when in fact the country had left him behind in its greater concern with economic depression at home and the vague smell of another war abroad. By the 1940s it was possible to meet young people who had not heard of him, although it is also true that readers of philology and of autobiography knew very well he was still going strong. In the early 1950s it was time to lament his passing though he had not died; the voice that might have leveled old-fashioned common sense against a new wave of anti-communism and Red-baiting had been silenced by a severe stroke.

INTRODUCTION

* * *

H.L. Mencken lived in Baltimore, Maryland, all his life, from 12 September 1880 to 29 January 1956. He even remained at the same respectable Hollins Street address all those years excepting the five of his marriage, surrounded by middle-class, Victorian comforts. Mencken's childhood was stable and ordinary, his youthful aspirations hardly more so, his means for realizing them adequate but not remarkable. He performed well in school but he did not care for formal education. He did love to read, so he made his way through Chaucer, Milton, and Thackeray, among many others of the British classics, and through such American writers as Henry James, Stephen Crane, and Mark Twain. He balked at his father's demand that he either learn the family cigar trade or go to college; the youth expressed a preference for journalism, but August Mencken would not admit it as an option. For two years Henry made and sold cigars. The Monday after his father's funeral, however, in January 1899, he sought out the city editor of the Baltimore *Herald*.

Even from the beginning of his career as a newspaperman, astonishing drive and competence were Mencken's strongest traits, closely followed by a sharp sense of humor. Thus in retrospect it is not surprising to learn that he persisted when the *Herald*'s editor showed no immediate desire to hire him; nor that when he finally was hired, his work steadily improved to the point that he was allowed the more interesting reporting assignments and even a column to himself; nor that when real news was scarce, his high spirits led him to make up a little here and there. This was a grand period for him, as he later recalled:

> It was the maddest, gladdest, damndest existence ever enjoyed by mortal youth. At a time when the respectable bourgeois youngsters of my generation were college freshmen, oppressed by simian sophomores and affronted with balderdash daily and hourly by chalky pedagogues, I was at large in a wicked seaport of half a million people ... getting earfuls and eyefuls of instruction in a hundred giddy arcana, none of them taught in schools.... If

INTRODUCTION

I neglected the humanities I was meanwhile laying in all the worldy wisdom of a police lieutenant, a bartender, a shyster lawyer, or a midwife.[1]

The Baltimore Fire of 1904 was the beginning of the end for the *Herald*, so by 1906 Mencken had moved on to the *Sunpapers*, after a short stint with the *Evening News*. Even today many Baltimoreans remember him for his work with the *Sunpapers*, an association that spanned forty years, excepting a couple of leaves of absence. From drama criticism and political editorials in the early days to music and literary criticism, business and cultural commentary, national political convention coverage (all set forth in the "Free Lance" column of 1911 to 1915 and the "Monday Articles" of 1920 to 1938), and finally to numerous miscellaneous articles written all along and as late as 1948, H.L. Mencken found more to say about the national scene than did any other journalist of his era, and on virtually every American interest except sports. Moreover, he said it all better than other journalists could hope to; stylistically he was unmatched.

Man Mencken did not thrive on newspaper work alone, however. As early as 1908 he began writing book reviews for a slick periodical called the *Smart Set*, and in 1914 he began to edit the magazine along with friend and drama critic George Jean Nathan. Through this rather light publication many American as well as British and Irish writers found their way to an audience. James Branch Cabell, Willa Cather, F. Scott Fitzgerald, Eugene O'Neill, Ezra Pound, D.H. Lawrence, James Joyce--the roll call of distinguished literati Mencken and Nathan published in the *Smart Set* could go on. By the time they left the magazine to begin their own *American Mercury* in 1924, they were a notorious pair whose acquaintance and editorial approval formed the stuff of a young writer's best hopes. Nathan did not remain long with the *Mercury*, for he did not care for the wide range of topics Mencken insisted their magazine embrace. Issues, ideas, opinions, events, movements, and, of course, books in all avenues of the

---

[1] *Newspaper Days*, ix. For complete publication information on this and other works cited throughout the introduction, see the bibliography.

INTRODUCTION

national life, America in all her thumping energy and variety: that was what Mencken envisioned for the *Mercury*. Plainly, that was what Americans wanted from it, too, for the magazine quickly became, and remained for the ten years of Mencken's tenure, one of the most prestigious of national periodicals.

Magazine editorship represented for Mencken his strongest position from which he might crusade against those forces of puritanism which the "Sage of Baltimore" had come to believe largely responsible for much that was weak in American letters, politics, and culture. He denounced the influence of traditional American Christianity with humor--"Puritanism [is] the haunting fear that someone, somewhere, may be happy"--and with swift, devastating attacks aimed at writers and critics formed in the genteel tradition, or at such political figures as Woodrow Wilson, "a typical Puritan.... Magnanimity was simply beyond him." Mencken's commitment to the war on irrationally inhibited attitudes held by "the booboisie" even brought him a legal skirmish when in 1926 the secretary of Boston's Watch and Ward Society, J. Frank Chase, pressed for censorship of the *Mercury* after it published a story about a prostitute. The publicity Mencken enjoyed through this "Hatrack" case was only slightly more significant to his cause than that resulting the year before from his coverage of the John T. Scopes "monkey" trial. In Dayton, Tennessee, the advocates of evolutionary theory (led by Clarence Darrow) had met those of creationism (led by populist William Jennings Bryan) to decide what could be taught in Tennessee public schools. With this case Mencken took on the puritan, fundamentalist mindset, blaming it for keeping Southern education, politics, and culture intellectually and spiritually barren.

He had long been addressing the contemporary Southern condition, another of his favorite topics, even prior to the appearance in 1917 of his famous essay "The Sahara of the Bozart." By means of vituperative attack, this article and subsequent ones written in a similar vein goaded Southern writers and editors into action, or more accurately into better work than they had been producing. Encouraging them in his letters and publishing them in his magazines, Mencken aided Southern writers who were trying to break literary ground. Ever at war with the genteel tradition, he also came to the defense of Midwestern writers Theodore Dreiser,

INTRODUCTION

Sinclair Lewis, and Sherwood Anderson. In this way Mencken contributed much to the general unshackling of American letters witnessed especially in the first two decades of the century. A host of other writers had reason to thank him, including many whom he certainly influenced, such as Richard Wright, even when he did not actively campaign in their behalf.

When he was not writing for or editing newspapers and magazines, Mencken was usually at work on his own books. Although several of these (most notably the six-volume *Prejudices* series, 1919-1927) merely collected essays first published in periodicals, others were full-length studies of the men and topics that fascinated Mencken: Shaw (*His Plays*, 1905), Nietzsche (*The Philosophy*, 1908), socialism (*Men Versus the Man*, 1910) women (*Defense*, 1918), democracy (*Notes*, 1926), and religion (*Treatise on the Gods*, 1930, and *Treatise on Right and Wrong*, 1934), to name a few. Still respected for its breadth, depth, and readability is his much-revised and twice-supplemented work of philology, *The American Language* (1919-1948). Still admired for its charm and lucidity is his three-volume autobiography, known collectively as the *Days* books (1940-1943). Besides these works Mencken collaborated on and contributed material to many more. And despite the 8,000,000 or so words he penned for publication, somehow he managed also to write approximately 200,000 letters.[2] True, it was his custom to answer much of his mail with only a few lines typed on a half-sheet of paper, but even so the bulk of his correpondence may well exceed that of any other American figure of his day.

All this, and yet at Mencken's death he left much unpublished material placed under time-lock. Restricted until 1971 was a great batch of letters to and from literary correspondents to add to the thousands already known; restricted until 1981 were a five-volume diary and four volumes of "Letters and Documents relating to the Baltimore *Sunpapers*"; and it will be 1991 before the four-volume "My Life as Author and Editor" and the three-volume "Thirty-five Years of Newspaper Work" are released.

---

[2] Estimated by Douglas C. Stenerson in his introduction to *Critical Essays on H. L. Mencken*.

INTRODUCTION

These days we might call a man of Mencken's prodigious production a "workaholic" (and doubtless he would have liked the word, for he appreciated Americans' boundless ability to expand their vocabulary), but Mencken himself would probably have said merely that he loved his work so much it was play. He did make time for other interests, however. One of them was a young Southerner named Sara Haardt, to whom he was happily married for five years before her death in 1935. His engagement had been announced much to the nation's mirth, for until age 50 Mencken was bachelorhood's funniest and most outspoken defender ("Bachelors have consciences. Married men have wives"). Marriage tamed but did not destroy another important pastime, his weekly gathering of male friends for dinner, drink, and music which they loudly made themselves, Henry at the piano. Mencken was so much the central figure of the Saturday Night Club, as the group called itself, that despite a forty-year history it disbanded soon after his debilitating stroke of 1948.

* * *

As many of the works listed in this volume's secondary bibliography attest, readers of H.L. Mencken do not always agree on which of the man's several careers his lasting reputation will rest. But last it almost certainly will, for Mencken developed a highly readable and entertaining prose style, and on this point even his detractors and champions agree. To illustrate a few characteristics of his style, one might begin with this passage on psychologist William James and educator John Dewey:

> [James's] ideas, immediately they were stated, became the ideas of every pedagogue from Harvard to Leland Stanford, and the pedagogues rammed them into the skulls of the lesser cerebelli. When he died his ghost went marching on: it took three or four years to interpret and pigeon-hole his philosophical remains and to take down and redact his messages (via Sir Oliver Lodge, Little Brighteyes, Wah-Wah the Indian Chief, and other gifted psychics)

INTRODUCTION

> from the spirit world. But then, gradually, he achieved the ultimate, stupendous and irrevocable act of death, and there was a vacancy. To it Prof. Dr. Dewey was elected by the acclamation of all right-thinking and forward-looking men. He was an expert in pedagogics, metaphysics, psychology, ethics, logic, politics, pedagogical metaphysics, metaphysical psychology, psychological ethics, ethical logic, logical politics and political pedagogics. He was artium magister, philosophiae doctor and twice legum doctor. He had written a book called "How to Think." He sat in a professor's chair and caned sophomores for blowing spit-balls. *Ergo*, he was the ideal candidate, and so he was nominated, elected and inaugurated, and for three years ... he enjoyed a glorious reign in the groves of sapience, and the inferior umbilicarii venerated him as they had once venerated James.[3]

Here are the liberal touches of latin or latinate words so often used by Mencken for the purpose of mocking the otherwise elevated idea or personage. Here are the striking juxtapositions of images, their dissimilarities exaggerated for effect--"Sir Oliver Lodge" and "Wah-Wah the Indian Chief." Here are the characteristic sequences of epithets, phrases, and clauses with which Mencken builds up his subject only to undercut it: Dewey was "an expert in pedagogics, metaphysics, psychology," and a number of ludicrous combinations thereof, he was "artium magister" and so forth --yet his book was entitled simply "How to Think" and his daily work consisted of "can[ing] sophomores." Here too Mencken's sense of cadence comes through; he had a sensitive ear for the pleasing rhythms of English just as he had for music: "But then, gradually, [James] achieved the ultimate, stupendous and irrevocable act of death, and there was a vacancy."

Mencken often did some of his best writing when he addressed writing itself, as when he said of Thorstein Veblen's work:

---

[3] "Professor Veblen," *A Mencken Chrestomathy*, 267.

INTRODUCTION

> What was genuinely remarkable about [his ideas] was not their novelty, or their complexity, nor even the fact that a professor should harbor them; it was the astoundingly grandiose and rococo manner of their statement, the almost unbelievable tediousness and flatulence of the gifted headmaster's prose, his unprecedented talent for saying nothing in an august and heroic manner.[4]

Of Warren G. Harding's writing, Mencken remarked:

> It reminds me of a string of wet sponges; it reminds me of tattered washing on the line; it reminds me of a stale bean-soup, of college yells, of dogs barking idiotically through endless nights. It is so bad that a sort of grandeur creeps into it. It drags itself out of the dark abysm (I was about to write abcess!) of pish, and crawls insanely up the topmost pinnacle of posh. It is rumble and bumble. It is flap and doodle. It is balder and dash.[5]

Although Mencken derided Abraham Lincoln's "Gettysburg Address," on another occasion he found the man's prose "as bare of rhetorical element and the niceties of professors as a yell for the police." All these instances reveal Mencken's mastery of several devices that make for clarity--precise word choice, concrete images, and parallel sentence structures.

Mencken knew that when he spoke of a writer's prose style, he also implied something about the man. To him the two were inseparable; he likened a writer's style to his skin, "a living and breathing thing, with something of the demoniacal in it ... [fitting him] tightly and yet ever so loosely .... It is, in fact, quite as securely an integral part of him as that skin is. It hardens as his arteries harden. It is gaudy when he is young and gathers decorum when he grows old."[6] Mencken's own prose

---

[4] *Ibid.*, 269.

[5] "Gamalielese," *A Carnival of Buncombe*, 39.

[6] "On Style," *A Mencken Chrestomathy*, 460.

INTRODUCTION

style and his sense of humor were similarly integrated. Each derived from his sharp eye for balance and imbalance, whether between sentence elements or between the real and the ideal in human behavior. Thus he had a penchant for exposing incongruity wherever he found it, and his vehicles were often the definition and the axiom--for example, "Christian--One who is willing to serve three Gods, but draws the line at one wife"; "Remorse--Regret that one waited so long to do it"; "A man always remembers his first love with special tenderness. But after that he begins to bunch them."

Mencken's joy in incongruity suited his "debunking" approach to nearly everything and everyone. He was fond of attaching bogus titles or degrees to the names of generally respected personages, such as the German "Herr Professor-Doktor" to the name of a U. S. president, which might then be followed by "LL.D." And he often summoned up a host of archaic or fabricated words to describe or name an idea ("pother," "flummery," "buncombe," "brummagem nonsense") or a professional ("mountebank," "wowser," "charlatan") or someone's statements ("pronunciamentoes," "rhodomontades," "laparotomies").

Mencken did have his gentler moods. The tone of his autobiography has often led readers to compare the funny, nostaglic flavor of his writing to that of Mark Twain, whose *Adventures of Huckleberry Finn* Mencken claimed he returned to year after year. Although in general Mencken preferred to join or instigate a lively debate--and he almost always took the offensive--it would appear that he hoped to be remembered as a humanizing rather than an agitating presence in the life of his day. The epitaph he wrote for himself reads, "If, after I depart this vale, you ever remember me and have thought to please my ghost, forgive some sinner and wink your eye at some homely girl."

* * *

A brief introduction does not do justice to the personality and pen that have come to symbolize an important period in America's modern development. The pages that follow, in which I have sketched further background where appropriate, are therefore

INTRODUCTION

intended to guide more thoroughly the would-be
Menckenite along a rich and varied journey into the
man, his world, and his influence.

                              Allison Bulsterbaum
                              Christmas 1987

Abbreviations

ACLU	American Civil Liberties Union
AlR	*Alabama Review*
AM	*American Mercury*
AP	*American Parade*
AtlM	*Atlantic Monthly*
AW	*All's Well*
BBC	British Broadcasting Company
BCR	*Birth Control Review*
BM	*Bohemian Magazine*
CaR	*Catholic Review*
DD	*Double-Dealer*
EH	Baltimore *Evening Herald*
EM	New York *Evening Mail*
EP	*Evening Post*
EPFL	Enoch Pratt Free Library (Baltimore, MD)
ES	Baltimore *Evening Sun*
GaR	*Georgia Review*
HLM	Henry Louis Mencken
HM	*Harper's Magazine*
HT	New York *Herald Tribune*
JT	Baltimore *Jewish Times*
LR	*Little Review*
NAACP	National Association for the Advancement of Colored People
NAR	*North American Review*
NR	*New Republic*
NWW	*New World Writing*
NY	*New Yorker*
NYRB	*New York Review of Books*
PT	*Plain Talk*
RD	*Reader's Digest*
SAQ	*South Atlantic Quarterly*
SEP	*Saturday Evening Post*
SewR	*Sewannee Review*
SLN	*Sinclair Lewis Newsletter*
SR	*Saturday Review*
SRL	*Saturday Review of Literature*
SS	*Smart Set*
ST	Chicago *Sunday Tribune*
TCL	*Twentieth Century Literature*
VF	*Vanity Fair*
WHR	*Western Humanities Review*
WT	New York *World-Telegram*

Part 1

Primary Bibliography

A.   MAJOR WORKS

This list covers HLM's most important works, including those he edited, translated, or co-authored and those contributions he made to the works of others. HLM is the author, editor, a collaborator, or a contributor in all instances. Where given, annotations cover basic publication history, subsequent and foreign editions, and cross-references [ ] to reprintings and other pertinent items located elsewhere in this volume.

The subdivisions of this section are as follows:

A i.   Full-length Works and Collaborations

A ii.   Pamphlets

A iii. Essays

A iv.   Magazine Articles

A v.   Newspaper Articles

A vi.   Contributions

A i.   Full-length Works and Collaborations

                         1903

1   VENTURES INTO VERSE: BEING VARIOUS BALLADS, BALLADES, RONDEAUX, TRIOLETS, SONGS, QUATRAINS, ODES AND ROUNDELS, ALL RESCUED FROM THE POTTERS' FIELD OF THE OLD FILES AND HERE GIVEN DECENT BURIAL (PEACE TO THEIR ASHES). "With illustrations and other things" by Charles S. Gordon and John Siegel. Baltimore: Marshall, Beck and Gordon.
        Only 100 copies of the first edition were printed, followed by 250 copies of a 1960 facsimile edition.

4   Full-length Works and Collaborations

1905

2   GEORGE BERNARD SHAW: HIS PLAYS. Boston and
    London: Luce.
    Reprinted: New Rochelle, NY: Edwin V.
    Glaser, 1969; Brooklyn, NY: Haskell House,
    1976; Folcroft, PA: Folcroft Press, 1976;
    Norwood, PA: Norwood Editions, 1977; Darby,
    PA: Arden Library, 1979. Partially re-
    printed in [422].

1908

3   THE PHILOSOPHY OF FRIEDRICH NIETZSCHE. Boston:
    Luce.
    Issued also in London by Fisher Unwin, 1908,
    which omitted the section "Books and Arti-
    cles about Nietzsche." Second edition was
    only a reprinting. Third edition: Boston:
    Luce, 1913, reprinted: Port Washington, NY:
    Kennikat Press, 1967. Edition of 1908
    reprinted: Folcroft, PA: Folcroft Press,
    1973; Norwood, PA: Norwood Editions, 1977;
    Philadelphia: R. West, 1978. Partially
    reprinted in [422].

1910

4   MEN VERSUS THE MAN: A CORRESPONDENCE BETWEEN
    RIVES LaMONTE, SOCIALIST, AND H.L. MENCKEN,
    INDIVIDUALIST. New York: Holt.
    Partially reprinted in [422].

1914

5   With George Jean Nathan and Willard Huntington
    Wright. EUROPE AFTER 8:15. "With decoration" by
    Thomas H. Benton. New York: Lane.
    This group of sketches of European cities
    first appeared in the SS. Also issued in
    Toronto by Bell and Cockburn.

1918

6   IN DEFENSE OF WOMEN. New York: Philip Goodman.
    Second edition actually a reprinting.
    Knopf brought out another edition in 1918
    and reissued it in 1922 as the sixth volume
    of the "Free Lance" Series. Also issued in

1922 by Garden City Publishing. Knopf published the 1927 revised edition. Reprinted: New York: Time-Life 1963, 1982; New York: Octagon Books, 1977. Foreign editions include the English IN DEFENCE OF WOMEN (London: Cape, 1923; reprinted 1927); the German VERTEIDIGUNG DER FRAU (translated by Franz Blei, Munich: Mueller, 1923); the English language IN DEFENCE OF WOMEN (Leipzig: Tauchnitz, 1927); the Hungarian A NÖK VEDELMEBEN! (translated by Fekete Oszkar with introduction by Juhåsz Andor, Budapest: Révai Kiadås, 1928); and the French DEFENSE DES FEMMES (translated by Jean Jardin with preface by Paul Morand, Paris: Gallimard, 1934).

1919

7 THE AMERICAN LANGUAGE: A PRELIMINARY INQUIRY INTO THE DEVELOPMENT OF ENGLISH IN THE UNITED STATES. New York: Knopf.
Second edition, revised and enlarged, published by Knopf 1921; third edition, revised and enlarged, Knopf 1923; fourth edition, corrected, enlarged, and rewritten, Knopf 1936. SUPPLEMENT I to the fourth edition (Chapters I-VI) published by Knopf 1945; SUPPLEMENT II to the same edition (Chapters VII-XIII), Knopf 1948. This set also published by Routledge (London) and McClelland (Toronto). Fourth edition reprinted by Knopf in 1974; both Supplements reprinted by Knopf in a two-volume set, 1975. THE AMERICAN LANGUAGE, fourth edition and two Supplements, abridged, with annotations and new material, by Raven I. McDavid, Jr., with the assistance of David W. Maurer, published by Knopf 1963 and reprinted 1977. Foreign editions include the English issuing of the second edition (Cape 1922); the German version of the third edition, DIE AMERIKANISCHE SPRACHE (DAS ENGLISCH DER VEREINIGTEN STAATEN), translated by Heinrich Spies (Leipzig: Teubner, 1927); the English version of the fourth edition (Kegan, Paul, Trench, Trubner, 1936); and the Japanese version of the fourth edition and both

Supplements (Tokyo: Senjo, 1962). Braille edition (14 volumes) available in the Library of Congress, Division for the Blind.

1920

8   With George Jean Nathan. THE AMERICAN CREDO: A CONTRIBUTION TOWARD THE INTERPRETATION OF THE NATIONAL MIND. New York: Knopf.
At least the Preface, running to nearly a hundred pages, is HLM's. Preface translated into the German by Tony Noah in DIE GRENZBOTEN 81 (January 28-March 18, 1922): 141-44, 166-71, 203-06, 232-35, 266-70, 294-97, 331-33, 362-65. Revised and enlarged, Knopf, 1922; reprinted: New York: Octagon Books, 1977.

9   THE ANTICHRIST. By Friedrich Nietzsche. New York: Knopf.
Translated and edited by HLM as the third in Knopf's six-volume series called the "Free Lance" Series. Issued as a Borzoi Pocket Book 1923; reprinted 1931.

10 With George Jean Nathan. HELIOGABALUS: A BUFFOONERY IN THREE ACTS. New York: Knopf.
Foreign editions include the German HELIOGABEL: EIN SCHWANK IN DREI AKTEN, translated by Peter Perpentikel (Berlin: Theatralia Verlag, 1920).

1926

11 NOTES ON DEMOCRACY. New York: Knopf.
Foreign editions: the British issue (London: Cape, 1927) and the German DEMOKRATENSPIEGEL, translated by Dora S. Kellner (Berlin: Widerstands, 1930). Reprinted: New York: Octagon Books, 1977; Ann Arbor, MI: University Microfilms, no date.

1930

12 TREATISE ON THE GODS. New York and London: Knopf.
Knopf brought out a revised second edition

Full-length Works and Collaborations 7

in 1946, which was also reprinted in London by G. Allen. This edition again reprinted by Random House (New York), 1977.

1934

13 TREATISE ON RIGHT AND WRONG. New York: Knopf. Also issued 1934 in London: Kegan, Paul, Trench, Trubner; and in Toronto: Ryerson Press. Reprinted by Octagon Books (New York), 1977.

1937

14 With Gerald W. Johnson and others. THE *SUNPAPERS* OF BALTIMORE, 1837-1937. New York: Knopf.
    HLM wrote chapters XI through XVIII and served as general editor of the project.

1940

15 HAPPY DAYS: 1880-1892. New York: Knopf.
    The first volume in HLM's three-volume autobiography. This work began as a series of sketches for the *NY*. See [16,18]. Foreign editions include the Canadian (Toronto: Ryerson Press) and the English (London: Kegan Paul, Trench, and Trubner), both 1940.
    Contains:
    "Introduction to the Universe"
    "The Caves of Learning"
    "Recollections of Academic Orgies"
    "The Baltimore of the Eighties"
    "Rural Delights"
    "The Head of the House"
    "Memorials of Gormandizing"
    "The Training of a Gangster"
    "Cops and Their Ways"
    "Larval Stage of a Bookworm"
    "First Steps in Divinity"
    "The Ruin of an Artist"
    "In the Footsteps of Gutenberg"
    "From the Records of an Athlete"
    "The Capital of the Republic"
    "Recreations of a Reactionary"
    "Brief Gust of Glory"

8   Full-length Works and Collaborations

"The Career of a Philosopher"
"Innocence in a Wicked World"
"Strange Scenes and Far Places"

1941

16 NEWSPAPER DAYS: 1899-1906. New York: Knopf.
    Also Canada (Toronto: Ryerson Press) and
    England (London: Kegan Paul, Trench, and
    Trubner), both 1942.
    Contains:
        "Allegro Con Brio"
        "Drill for a Rookie"
        "Sergeant's Stripes"
        "Approach to Lovely Letters"
        "Fruits of Diligence"
        "The Gospel of Service"
        "Scent of the Theatre"
        "Command"
        "Three Managing Editors"
        "Slaves of Beauty"
        "The Days of the Giants"
        "The Judicial Arm"
        "Recollections of Notable Cops"
        "A Genial Restauranteur"
        "A Girl From Red Lion, PA"
        "Scions of the Boyers Nobility"
        "Aliens, But Not Yet Enemies"
        "The Synthesis of News"
        "Fire Alarm"
        "Sold Down the River"

1942

17 A NEW DICTIONARY OF QUOTATIONS ON HISTORICAL
    PRINCIPLES FROM ANCIENT AND MODERN SOURCES.
    New York: Knopf.
        Selected and edited by HLM, this work, HLM
        writes, began around 1918 as a personal
        collection.

1943

18 HEATHEN DAYS: 1890-1936. New York: Knopf.
        Other editions include the Armed Services
        Edition (New York: Council on Books in
        Wartime) and the Canadian (Toronto: Ryerson
        Press), both 1943.
        Contains:

Full-length Works and Collaborations

"Downfall of a Revolutionary"
"Memoirs of the Stable"
"Adventures of a Y.M.C.A. Lad"
"The Educational Process"
"Finale to the Rogue's March"
"Notes on Palaeozoic [sic] Publicists"
"The Tone Art"
"A Master of Gladiators"
"A Dip into Statecraft"
"Court of Honor"
"A Roman Holiday"
"Winter Voyage"
"Gore in the Caribees"
"Romantic Intermezzo"
"Old Home Day"
"The Noble Experiment"
"Inquisition"
"Vanishing Act"
"Pilgrimage"
"Beaters of Breasts"

1947

19   THE DAYS OF H.L. MENCKEN: HAPPY DAYS, NEWSPAPER DAYS, HEATHEN DAYS. New York: Knopf.
Reprints in one volume all three of the DAYS books [15, 16, 18].

A ii. Pamphlets

1912

20 THE ARTIST: A DRAMA WITHOUT WORDS. Boston: Luce.
    First appeared in the *BM*, December 1909. Subsequent editions include one for the stage in 1917 (THE ARTIST: A SATIRE IN ONE ACT, New York: Lane) and a Spanish translation by Gonzalo G. de Mello, 1926. Reprinted: in the *SS*, August 1916; in all editions of A BOOK OF BURLESQUES [399]; New York: Samuel French, 1920; Folcroft, PA: Folcroft Press, 1969 and 1973; Norwood, PA: Norwood Editions, 1977; Belfast, ME: Bern Porter, 1979.

1916

21 THE CREED OF A NOVELIST. New York: Lane.
    Reprint of HLM's *SS* review (October 1916) of Dreiser's A HOOSIER HOLIDAY.

1917

22 Hatteras, Owen [pseud]. PISTOLS FOR TWO. New York: Knopf.
    An HLM/George Jean Nathan collaboration; opening and closing pages as well as the biographical sketch of Nathan is HLM's. Nathan wrote the biographical sketch of HLM. Reprinted: Folcroft, PA: Folcroft Press, 1977.

1927

23 JAMES BRANCH CABELL. New York: Robert M. McBride.
    Reissued in 1928 in hard cover, illustrations omitted, according to Adler [459].

1935

24 THE ANATOMY OF QUACKERY. Cleveland: William Feather.
    First appeared in the Baltimore *ES*, 12 December of the same year.

25   EREZ ISRAEL. New York: Privately printed by
     B.P. Safran.
     Brings together HLM's two articles on the
     Holy Land first printed in the Baltimore
     ES, 1934; see [338].

1936

26   THE INCOMPARABLE PHYSICIAN. San Francisco: T.W.
     McDonald.
     Reprinted from the *SS* November 1915;
     reissued 1940 and retitled, "The Eminent
     Physician."

1946

27   CHRISTMAS STORY. Illustrated by Bill Crawford.
     New York: Knopf.
     First appeared as "Stare Decisis," *NY* 20
     (30 December 1944): 17-21.

1947

28   VACHEL LINDSAY. Washington, DC: John S.
     Mayfield.
     Reprinted in the COURIER [University of
     Syracuse Library Associates], December
     1962.

A iii. Essays

1917

29 "James Huneker." In A BOOK OF PREFACES [401]. Celebrates Huneker's "genuine gusto" (159) as compared to an entire range of bloodless, simpering critics of the *belles lettres*. Original version appeared in the Baltimore *ES* 7 April 1916, which is reprinted in THE YOUNG MENCKEN [422].

30 "Joseph Conrad." In A BOOK OF PREFACES [401]. Praises the writer's unflinching stance in the face of "the profound meaninglessness of life" (11). Sketches characteristics of Conrad's fiction. Original version appeared in the Baltimore *ES*, 20 June 1916, and is reprinted in THE YOUNG MENCKEN [422]. This essay is not the same as [132].

31 "Sahara of the Bozart." New York *EVENING MAIL* (13 November).
    Notorious attack on the South for its utter lack of culture since the Civil War. Reprinted in PREJUDICES: SECOND SERIES [404], A MENCKEN CHRESTOMATHY [413], PREJUDICES: A SELECTION [418], THE AMERICAN SCENE [420], and THE YOUNG MENCKEN [422].

32 "A Neglected Anniversary." New York *EVENING MAIL* (28 December).
    HLM's infamous "history" of the bathtub; reprinted in A MENCKEN CHRESTOMATHY [413] and THE BATHTUB HOAX [417].

33 "Puritanism as a Literary Force." In A BOOK OF PREFACES [401].
    Asserts that Calvinism and puritanism have taken so strong a hold in this country as to thwart most American artists' attempts to produce works of beauty. A few exceptions include Poe and Whitman; Twain nearly overcame puritan influence, but he could not escape his American heritage.

Discusses such contemporary American writers as Dreiser, Norris, Bierce, and Sinclair.

34 "Theodore Dreiser." In A BOOK OF PREFACES [401].
Looks at Dreiser in the context of contemporary American fiction. Tempers his praise for the author by lamenting Dreiser's penchant for minutia. Reprinted in THE VINTAGE MENCKEN [414].

1919

35 "The American Magazine." In PREJUDICES: FIRST SERIES [403].
Critiques THE MAGAZINE IN AMERICA by Algernon Tassin and improves upon this adequate but unexemplary history.

36 "Among the Avatars." In PREJUDICES: FIRST SERIES [403].
Damns the panegyric tendencies of Will Levington Comfort, particularly where Comfort makes woman second only to God.

37 "The Blushful Mystery." In PREJUDICES: FIRST SERIES [403].
These five brief essays offer interesting and often entertaining insights into contemporary ideas and literature on sex. Portions of these reappear in A MENCKEN CHRESTOMATHY [413].

38 "The Butte Bashkirtseff." In PREJUDICES: FIRST SERIES [403].
Uses Mary MacLane as a springboard for comments on puritanism in American life and literature.

39 "Criticism of Criticism of Criticism." In PREJUDICES: FIRST SERIES [403].
Praises Joel Elias Spingarn, who sees the critic's aim as that of examining what an artist has tried to say and how he has or has not said it. Suggests that the critic is supposed to act as a catalyst, helping to bring about a reaction between reader and text. See "Footnote on Criticism"

[57], in which HLM revises this notion. Originally published in the New York *EM*, 1 July 1918; here much revised. Reprinted in PREJUDICES: A SELECTION [418], in THE AMERICAN SCENE [420], and in CRITICISM IN AMERICA: ITS FUNCTION AND STATUS (New York: Haskell House, 1924; reprinted 1969).

40 "The Dean." In PREJUDICES: FIRST SERIES [403].
    Assesses the work and reputation of William Dean Howells.

41 "The Genealogy of Etiquette." In PREJUDICES: FIRST SERIES [403].
    Considers a variety of American customs and mores as the probable results of basic human fear, especially the fear of being or appearing different. Reprinted in PREJUDICES: A SELECTION [418].

42 "George Jean Nathan." In PREJUDICES: FIRST SERIES [403].
    Explores the work, mind, and personality of his friend the drama critic. Reprinted in PREJUDICES: A SELECTION [418].

43 "The New Poetry Movement." In PREJUDICES: FIRST SERIES [403].
    Comments on the merits and defects of such contemporary American poets as Carl Sandburg, James Oppenheim, Amy Lowell, Edgar Lee Masters, Vachel Lindsay, Robert Frost, Ezra Pound, and others. Comments also on Harriet Monroe's POETRY: A MAGAZINE OF VERSE.

44 "Portrait of an Immortal Soul." In PREJUDICES: FIRST SERIES [403].
    An autobiographical novel sent to him by an untalented but painfully honest writer leads HLM to comment on the dangers of excessive puritanism to the young psyche.

45 "Professor Veblen." In PREJUDICES: FIRST SERIES [403].
    Blasts the thought and prose style of Socialist Thorstein Veblen. Reprinted in

THE AMERICAN SCENE [420] and A MENCKEN CHRESTOMATHY [413].

46 "Six Members of the Institute." In PREJUDICES: FIRST SERIES [403].
"The Boudoir Balzac" praises the late Percival Pollard, literary critic. "A Stranger on Parnassus" evaluates the efforts of writer Hamlin Garland. "A Merchant of Mush" is on Henry Sydnor Harrison, "The Last of the Victorians" on William Allen White, "A Bad Novelist" on American writer Ernest Poole, and "A Broadway Brades" on White DeKansas.

47 "Three American Immortals." In PREJUDICES: FIRST SERIES [403].
Describes ways in which American "Kultur" manifested its misunderstanding or underappreciation of Ralph Waldo Emerson ("Aristotolean Obsequies"), "Edgar Allan Poe," and Walt Whitman ("Memorial Service"). The first and third of these is reprinted in A MENCKEN CHRESTOMATHY [413]. All three appear in PREJUDICES: A SELECTION [418] and THE AMERICAN SCENE [420].

48 "The Ulster Polonius." In PREJUDICES: FIRST SERIES [403].
Explains why the work of George Bernard Shaw so often seems revolutionary when in fact the dramatist is not so much original as he is brave. Reprinted in PREJUDICES: A SELECTION [418].

49 "An Unheeded Law-Giver." In PREJUDICES: FIRST SERIES [403].
Asserts that Ralph Waldo Emerson left little impression upon his own country and that Americans generally misunderstand and misconstrue his transcendental philosophy.

1920

50 "The Divine Afflatus." In PREJUDICES: SECOND SERIES [404].
Attempts "to account for that puckish and inexplicable rise and fall of [intellectual] inspiration" (157). Reprinted in

Essays

A MENCKEN CHRESTOMATHY [413] and THE AMERICAN SCENE [420].

51 "Exeunt Omnes." In PREJUDICES: SECOND SERIES [404].
Looks at the subject of death from several angles, especially with reference to the work of F. Parkes Weber. Reprinted in A MENCKEN CHRESTOMATHY [413] and THE VINTAGE MENCKEN [414].

52 "The National Letters." In PREJUDICES: SECOND SERIES [404].
Famous for its wide look at what is right and what is wrong with American literature and literary life. Reprinted in THE AMERICAN SCENE [420] and THE VINTAGE MENCKEN [414]. Various sections also appear, with new titles, in A MENCKEN CHRESTOMATHY [413].

53 "Roosevelt: An Autopsy." In PREJUDICES: SECOND SERIES [404].
A debunking of Theodore Roosevelt in reaction to recent panegyrical biographies. Reprinted in PREJUDICES: A SELECTION [418].

1922

54 "Das Kapital." In PREJUDICES: THIRD SERIES [405].
U.S. capitalism goes wrong because it is made to co-exist with democracy.

55 "The Dismal Science." In PREJUDICES: THIRD SERIES [405].
On political economy. Reprinted in PREJUDICES: A SELECTION [418].

56 "Five Men at Random." In PREJUDICES: THIRD SERIES [405].
Brief essays on Abraham Lincoln, Paul Elmer More, Madison Cawein, Frank Harris, and Havelock Ellis. The first is reprinted in A MENCKEN CHRESTOMATHY [413] and THE VINTAGE MENCKEN [414].

57 "Footnote on Criticism." In PREJUDICES: THIRD SERIES [405].
HLM revises his earlier idea that the critic is a catalyst; here he comes down firmly on the side of the critic as artist. See [39]. Reprinted in CRITICISM IN AMERICA: ITS FUNCTION AND STATUS (New York: Haskell House, 1924; reprinted 1969) and in THE AMERICAN SCENE [420]. Revised and retitled "The Critic's Motive," serves as introduction to Gilbert A. Harrison's THE CRITIC AS ARTIST: ESSAYS ON BOOKS, 1920-1970 (New York: Liveright, 1972).

58 "Huneker: A Memory." In PREJUDICES: THIRD SERIES [405].
Personal and professional recollections of HLM's favorite American critic. Reprinted in A MENCKEN CHRESTOMATHY [413] and PREJUDICES: A SELECTION [418].

59 "Memorial Service." In PREJUDICES: THIRD SERIES [405].
Presents a roll call of forgotten gods. Reprinted in A MENCKEN CHRESTOMATHY [413] and PREJUDICES: A SELECTION [418].

60 "The Novel." In PREJUDICES: THIRD SERIES [405].
Its chief aim is the depiction of "what actually is true" (205), which is why women, who are more attuned than men to reality, have the potential ability to produce better novels.

61 "On Being an American." In PREJUDICES: THIRD SERIES [405].
Explains why a man of HLM's disposition can be happier in the United States than anywhere else despite this country's generally ridiculous if not stupid public and private life. Reprinted in PREJUDICES: A SELECTION [418] and THE AMERICAN SCENE [420].

62 "Star-Spangled Men." In PREJUDICES: THIRD SERIES [405].
A debunking of the practice of military decoration. Reprinted in A MENCKEN

Essays

63 "Types of Men." In PREJUDICES: THIRD SERIES [405].
Comments on "The Romantic," "The Skeptic," "The Believer," "The Worker," "The Physician," "The Scientist," "The Business Man," "The King," "The Average Man," "The Truthseeker," "The Relative," "The Friend," and "The Pacifist"; all but the last are reprinted in A MENCKEN CHRESTOMATHY [413].

CHRESTOMATHY [413], THE VINTAGE MENCKEN [414], and THE AMERICAN SCENE [420].

1924

64 "The American Novel." In PREJUDICES: FOURTH SERIES [406].
Chiefly historical remarks.

65 "The American Tradition." In PREJUDICES: FOURTH SERIES [407].
... Is chiefly that of Anglo-Saxon puritanism, roars HLM. A section of this appears as "The Anglo-Saxon" in A MENCKEN CHRESTOMATHY [413] and THE VINTAGE MENCKEN [414].

66 "From a Critic's Notebook." In PREJUDICES: FOURTH SERIES [406].
A selection of random remarks on literary criticism.

67 "High and Ghostly Matters." In PREJUDICES: FOURTH SERIES [406].
On religion, faith, and believers. Portions appear in A MENCKEN CHRESTOMATHY [413].

68 "The Husbandman." In PREJUDICES: FOURTH SERIES [406].
Refutes traditional, romantic notions about farmers. Reprinted in A MENCKEN CHRESTOMATHY [413], THE AMERICAN SCENE [420], and PREJUDICES: A SELECTION [418].

69 "Meditations in the Methodist Desert." In PREJUDICES: FOURTH SERIES [406].
Offers a series of skirmishes in the war

against Prohibition. One section, "Portrait of an Ideal World," appears in A MENCKEN CHRESTOMATHY [413].

70 "On Government." In PREJUDICES: FOURTH SERIES [406].
Distinguishes between good and bad government, good and bad types of governors. Reprinted in PREJUDICES: A SELECTION [418].

71 "On the Nature of Man." In PREJUDICES: FOURTH SERIES [406].
Observations on human character, aspiration, behavior, and powers of ratiocination.

72 "The Politician." In PREJUDICES: FOURTH SERIES [406].
Explains why "a good politician, under democracy, is quite as unthinkable as an honest burglar" (130). Reprinted in PREJUDICES: A SELECTION [418] and THE AMERICAN SCENE [420].

73 "Reflections on Human Monogamy." In PREJUDICES: FOURTH SERIES [406].
Refutes traditional views on the game of love as found in life, literature, and history. Portions of this collection of short essays are reprinted in A MENCKEN CHRESTOMATHY [413].

74 "Totentanz." In PREJUDICES: FOURTH SERIES [406].
On New York City.

75 "Toward a Realistic Aesthetic." In PREJUDICES: FOURTH SERIES [406].
Comments on the practice and composition of literature, painting, and music.

1926

76 "Catechism." In PREJUDICES: FIFTH SERIES [409].
HLM's famous quip explaining why he remains in a country he finds ludicrous: "Why do men go to zoos?" Reprinted in A MENCKEN CHRESTOMATHY [413].

Essays

77 "Essay in Pedagogy." In PREJUDICES: FIFTH SERIES [409].
   Offers a lesson on the chief ingredient of a good novel--memorable characters.

78 "Four Makers of Tales." In PREJUDICES: FIFTH SERIES [409].
   Comments on Joseph Conrad, Joseph Hergesheimer, Ring Lardner, and Edgar Lee Masters. "Joseph Conrad" and "Ring Lardner" are reprinted in A MENCKEN CHRESTOMATHY [413] and PREJUDICES: A SELECTION [418].

79 "Four Moral Causes." In PREJUDICES: FIFTH SERIES [409].
   HLM's views on birth control, war, capital punishment, and "comstockery" (puritanism) in literature. Portions of this collection are reprinted in A MENCKEN CHRESTOMATHY [413].

80 "The Fringes of Lovely Letters." In PREJUDICES: FIFTH SERIES [409].
   Offers a variety of comments on writing style, and literary and art criticism, among other topics. Some of these are reprinted in A MENCKEN CHRESTOMATHY [413].

81 "The Hills of Zion." In PREJUDICES: FIFTH SERIES [409].
   Describes a revival meeting held near Dayton, Tennessee, which HLM witnessed from a distance while in the area to cover the Scopes trial. Reprinted in THE VINTAGE MENCKEN [414] and THE AMERICAN SCENE [420].

82 "In Memoriam: W.J.B." In PREJUDICES: FIFTH SERIES [409].
   Famous obituary and dissection of the populist leader William Jennings Bryan, written shortly after the close of the Scopes trial. Reprinted in THE AMERICAN SCENE [420], A MENCKEN CHRESTOMATHY [413], and THE VINTAGE MENCKEN [414].

83 "*THE NATION.*" In PREJUDICES: FIFTH SERIES [409].
Critical acclamation for the magazine HLM prefers over other American weeklies.

84 "On Living in Baltimore." In PREJUDICES: FIFTH SERIES [409].
Praise for his hometown, especially as it compares to New York. Reprinted in PREJUDICES: A SELECTION [418], and A MENCKEN CHRESTOMATHY [413].

85 "Rondo on an Ancient Theme." In PREJUDICES: FIFTH SERIES [409].
... That of women and sex.

1927

86 "Ambrose Bierce." In PREJUDICES: SIXTH SERIES [410].
A slightly different version appears in A MENCKEN CHRESTOMATHY [413] and THE AMERICAN SCENE [420].

87 "Appendix from Moronia." In PREJUDICES: SIXTH SERIES [410].
Includes some ungenerous remarks on the art of filmmaking generally but also the very compassionate portrait of Rudolph Valentino particularly. "Valentino" also appears in A MENCKEN CHRESTOMATHY [413] and THE VINTAGE MENCKEN [414].

88 "Clarion Call to Poets." In PREJUDICES: SIXTH SERIES [410].
Asks that someone write a graceful funeral service appropriate for atheists.
Reprinted in A MENCKEN CHRESTOMATHY [413].

89 "Dives into Quackery." In PREJUDICES: SIXTH SERIES [410].
Of these three essays, "Chiropractic" is reprinted in A MENCKEN CHRESTOMATHY [413], PREJUDICES: A SELECTION [418], and THE VINTAGE MENCKEN [414].

90 "Five Little Excursions." In PREJUDICES: SIXTH SERIES [410].
Includes "The Libido for the Ugly,"

Essays

comments on the city of Pittsburgh, PA, which is reprinted in A MENCKEN CHRESTOMATHY [413] and THE VINTAGE MENCKEN [414].

91 "The Human Mind." In PREJUDICES: SIXTH SERIES [410].
Some startling thoughts on philosophy and its "metaphysicians," suicide, the muddled state of most controversy, and the mistaken beliefs of Socialists. "On Suicide" is reprinted in A MENCKEN CHRESTOMATHY [413] and "On Controversy" in PREJUDICES: A SELECTION [418].

92 "Hymn to the Truth." In PREJUDICES: SIXTH SERIES [410].
HLM sets the record straight on his bathtub hoax [32], but comments that the human mind prefers fiction over truth. Reprinted in PREJUDICES: A SELECTION [418].

93 "In the Rolling Mills." In PREJUDICES: SIXTH SERIES [410].
On the state of American education.

94 "Invitation to the Dance." In PREJUDICES: SIXTH SERIES [410].
On enlightenment and atheism.

95 "Journalism in America." In PREJUDICES: SIXTH SERIES [410].
Describes in characteristically lively fashion journalism's coming of age in this country. Reprinted in PREJUDICES: A SELECTION [418], THE AMERICAN SCENE [420], and A GANG OF PECKSNIFFS [423].

96 "Metropolis." In PREJUDICES: SIXTH SERIES [410].
Praise--but not love--for New York City.

97 "The Pedagogy of Sex." In PREJUDICES: SIXTH SERIES [410].
Where the authors of books on sex lose the very adolescent audience they hope to warn and instruct.

98 "Souvenirs of a Book Reviewer." In PREJUDICES: SIXTH SERIES [410]. Reprints reviews of books on Anthony Comstock (this also appears in PREJUDICES: A SELECTION [418]), "Babbits" (i.e. Americans), witchcraft, bartending, the South, Thomas Jefferson, fundamentalism, and American language.

1936

99 "The American Language." *YALE REVIEW* n.s. 25 (March): 538-52.
A significant essay, often reprinted in college readers. Reprinted also in THE YALE REVIEW ANTHOLOGY, edited by Wilbur Cross and Helen MacAfee (New Haven: Yale University Press, 1942).

A iv. Magazine Articles

The following is a sampling of HLM's work published in magazines or journals, arranged only in chronological order. Several of the more noteworthy book reviews are included, but as his best *SMART SET* reviews are collected in [421], they are omitted here. Except for the first one [211], the *NEW YORKER* articles which led to the DAYS autobiography [15, 16, 18] are also omitted. In citations, *SS* and *AM* stand for the *SMART SET* and the *AMERICAN MERCURY*; for periodical titles within annotations, see Abbreviations, page xxvii.

1899

100   W.G.L. [pseud]. "To Rudyard Kipling." *BOOKMAN* 10 (December): 337.
      HLM's first poem to be published in a magazine, later included in VENTURES INTO VERSE [1].

1900

101   "The Cook's Victory." *SHORT STORIES* 39 (August): 238-47.
      One of HLM's earliest pieces of short fiction; in later years he estimated his total number of stories to have reached 25 before he stopped writing fiction altogether.

1908

102   With Hirshberg, Leonard K. "What You Ought to Know About Your Baby." *DELINEATOR* 72 (October): 592-93.
      First of a series of articles appearing through October 1909 which were ghost-written by HLM, though he did get his facts from Hirshberg. Dreiser's editorship of this periodical meant that these articles were the start of his and HLM's long association. Butterick of New York published the series as a book in 1910.

1913

103 "The American." *SS* 40 (June): 87-94.
Begins a series of articles which ran through February 1914 on the nature of the American and his morals, his language, his aesthetic values, his freedom, and his puritanism. Reprinted in [422].

1914

104 "Newspaper Morals." *ATLANTIC MONTHLY* 113 (March): 289-97.
See also Ralph Pulitzer's "Newspaper Morals: A Reply," *AtlM* 113 (June 1914): 773-78.

105 "The Raw Material of Fiction." *SS* 42 (March): 153-58.
... Is the story, "just as melody is the raw material of music" (153). Reviews Conrad's works to date, particularly the most recent novel CHANCE.

106 "The Mailed Fist and its Prophet." *ATLANTIC MONTHLY* 114 (November): 598-607.
Surveys Nietzsche's impact on Germany.

1917

107 "The Dreiser Bugaboo." *THE SEVEN ARTS* 2 (August): 507-17.
Responds to the "Comstockian" attacks of the critics, particularly Sherman.

108 "Ibsen: Journeyman Dramatist." *DIAL* 63 (11 October): 323-26.
Reprinted in [390].

1919

109 With George Jean Nathan. "Répétition Générale." *SS* 58 (April): 49-53.
With this issue began a monthly department on which the editors collaborated until they left the magazine in December 1923; it included a string of separate paragraphs, epigrams, and "definitions"

chiefly intended to be provocative or even shocking.

1920

110 "The Literary Capital of the United States." *NATION* [London] 27 (17 April): 90-92.
... is Chicago, says the Sage, not New York. Reprinted in ON AMERICAN BOOKS: A SYMPOSIUM BY FIVE AMERICAN CRITICS AS PRINTED IN THE LONDON *NATION*, edited by Francis Hackett (New York: B.W. Heubsch, 1920).

111 "Meditation in E Minor." *NEW REPUBLIC* 24 (8 September): 38-40.
On politics, class, and capitalism. Partially reprinted in the magazine's fortieth anniversary issue, 22 November 1954: 81-82.

112 "Conversations: Set Down by Major Owen Hatteras [pseud]." *SS* 63 (December): 93-98.
This item on anatomy and physiology begins a series of "conversations" between HLM and George Jean Nathan. Subsequent topics include women (January 1921), politics (February 1921), literature (April 1921), dress (May 1921), magazine editing (June 1921), marriage (July 1921), and "the darker races" (March 1923).

1921

113 "A Short View of Gamalielese." *NATION* 112 (27 April): 621-22.
Satirizes President Warren G. Harding's use--or misuse--of the English language. HLM wrote similar articles for the Baltimore *ES* 7 March and 9 September of the same year; these are reprinted in A CARNIVAL OF BUNCOMBE [415].

114 "Release from Puritans, Pedagogues and Anglo-Saxons." *INDEPENDENT* 107 (10 December): 249.

1922

115 "Footnote on Journalism." *NATION* 114 (26 April): 493-94.
Reprinted from the Baltimore *ES*, 3 April 1922.

116 "Maryland: Apex of Normalcy." *NATION* 114 (3 May): 517-19.
Safe and sane though Maryland appears to be, falling as it does along the middle point of virtually any set of statistics, the fact is to be lamented because it suggests that the growing American tendency toward standardization is taking hold of the state. Reprinted in THESE UNITED STATES, edited by Ernest Gruening (New York: Boni and Liveright, 1923).

117 "Mr. Mencken Replies." *BOOKMAN* 55 (June): 367.
Responds to Walpole's "Open Letter" to HLM published in the May 1922 *BOOKMAN*. See [804].

1923

118 Hatteras, Major Owen [pseud]. "Americana." *SS* 71 (March): 59-60.
Until they left the *SS* in December 1923, HLM and Nathan published this monthly collection of excerpts from contemporary American periodicals. A number of them comprise AMERICANA 1925 [407] and AMERICANA 1926 [408].

119 "Calvinism: New Style." *THE OUTLOOK* [London] 52 (29 September): 237-38.
On the means U.S. presidents use, in this case Calvin Coolidge, to insure their own re-election; this is typical of several HLM articles printed intermittently in British periodicals.

120 "Is the South a Desert." *SOUTHERN LITERARY MAGAZINE* 1 (October): 4, 34.
Notes such hopeful signs of a literary renaissance as the criticism being written

Magazine Articles

by Gerald W. Johnson, associate editor of the Greensboro, North Carolina *DAILY NEWS*.

121 "Fifteen Years." *SS* 72 (December): 138-44.
In his farewell to the magazine, HLM looks back over the gradual improvement of American literary life, ending with a call for a valuable history of American literature. Reprinted in H.L. Mencken's *SMART SET* CRITICISM [421].

122 "H.L. Mencken." *NATION* 117 (5 December): 647-48.
HLM on himself as a literary critic.

1924

123 "Clinical Notes." With George Jean Nathan. *AM* 1 (January): 75-78.
This department featured brief commentary by the editors on various topics. By August 1925 Nathan was no longer co-editor but he continued to write the "Clinical Notes," whereas HLM did not.

124 "Editorial." With George Jean Nathan. *AM* 1 (January): 27-30.
The editors set forth their intentions in the founding issue of the magazine. With a few exceptions, every issue through November 1933 featured this department, though it was often titled differently. Several of these editorials were later reprinted or revised for publication in the PREJUDICES books [403,404,405,406, 409,410]. HLM retired from editorship in December 1933. See [195].

125 "Three Volumes of Fiction." *AM* 1 (February): 252-53.
Reviews Sherwood Anderson's HORSES AND MEN, Joseph Conrad's THE ROVER, and Willa Cather's A LOST LADY.

126 "A Modern Masterpiece." *AM* 1 (March): 377-79.
Reviews Matthew Josephson's translation of Guillaume Apollinaire's THE POET ASSASSINATED.

127 "Three Gay Stories." *AM* 1 (March): 380-81.
Reviews James Branch Cabell's THE HIGH
PLACE, Aldous Huxley's ANTIC HAY, and Carl
Van Vechten's THE BLIND BOW-BOY.

128 "The Little Red Schoolhouse." *AM* 1 (April):
504-05.
Review of Upton Sinclair's THE GOSLINGS: A
STUDY OF THE AMERICAN SCHOOLS leads the
critic to comment on public education.

129 "Edgar Lee Masters." *AM* 2 (June): 250-52.
Review of MIRAGE, "one of the most idiotic
and yet one of the most interesting
American novels that I have ever read"
(250).

130 "Rambles in Fiction." *AM* 2 (July): 380-82.
Includes commentary on Ruth Suckow's
COUNTRY PEOPLE and John DosPassos's
STREETS OF NIGHT, among others.

131 "Ring W. Lardner." *AM* 2 (July): 376-77.
Unfavorable review of HOW TO WRITE SHORT
STORIES (WITH SAMPLES).

132 "Joseph Conrad." *NATION* 119 (20 August):
179.
Readers come away from Conrad not with
answers but with questions, for he is
always interested in approaching the
mysteries of life with a kind of
scientific "aloofness." This is not the
same essay as [30].

133 "The State of the Country." *AM* 3 (September):
123-25.
Review of Irving Babbitt's DEMOCRACY AND
LEADERSHIP.

134 "Tusitala." *AM* 3 (November): 378-80.
Reviews books by and about Robert Louis
Stevenson.

135 "Cabell." *AM* 3 (December): 509-10.
Review of James Branch Cabell's STRAWS AND
PRAYER-BOOKS: DIZAIN DES DIVERSIONS.

Magazine Articles

136 "Mark Twain on Himself." *AM* 3 (December): 507-08.
  Confesses disappointment in the humorist's autobiography (introduced by Albert Bigelow Paine).

1925

137 "What is Style?" *AM* 4 (March): 381-82.
  A review of W.C. Brownell's THE GENIUS OF STYLE leads to brief remarks on the subject and on those HLM considers stylists.

138 "ARROWSMITH." *AM* 4 (April): 507-09.
  Favors Sinclair Lewis's novel.

139 "New Fiction." *AM* 5 (July): 382-83.
  Reviews F. Scott Fitzgerald's THE GREAT GATSBY and Ellen Glasgow's BARREN GROUND, among others.

140 "Fiction Good and Bad." *AM* 6 (November): 379-81.
  Includes commentary on Joseph Conrad's SUSPENSE, Sherwood Anderson's DARK LAUGHTER, and Willa Cather's THE PROFESSOR'S HOUSE, among others.

141 "The English Novel." *AM* 6 (December): 509-10.
  H.G. Wells's CHRISTINA ALBERTA'S FATHER gets a lashing.

142 "My Dear Walpole." *BOOKMAN* 62 (December): 438-39.
  HLM answers his polite critic across the ocean. See [819].

1926

143 "Katzenjammer." *AM* 7 (January): 125-26.
  Walter Lippmann's THE PHANTOM PUBLIC is one of two books on democracy reviewed.

144 "Dreiser in 840 Pages." *AM* 7 (March): 379-81.
  Mixed praise and criticism for AN AMERICAN TRAGEDY.

145 "The Mystery of Poe." *NATION* 122 (17 March): 289-90.
Review of Joseph Wood Krutch's study leads to remarks on the poet.

146 "Fiction Good and Bad." *AM* 7 (April): 506-09.
Includes reviews of John DosPassos's MANHATTAN TRANSFER and Ruth Suckow's THE ODYSSEY OF A NICE GIRL.

147 "Books of Verse." *AM* 8 (June): 251-54.
Comments on recent works by Countee Cullen, Vachel Lindsay, Edgar Lee Masters, Conrad Aiken, and Stephen Vincent Benét, among several others.

148 "A Humorist Shows His Teeth." *AM* 8 (June): 254-55.
On Ring Lardner's THE LOVE NEST, AND OTHER STORIES.

149 "Sandburg's LINCOLN." *AM* 8 (July): 381-82.
Reviews the poet's biography of the president.

150 "Fiction." *AM* 8 (August): 509-10.
Includes remarks on COUNT BRUGA, by Ben Hecht, and THE SILVER STALLION: A COMEDY OF REDEMPTION, by James Branch Cabell.

151 "Wells Redivivus." *AM* 9 (December): 506-08.
On THE WORLD OF WILLIAM CLISSOLD: A NOVEL AT A NEW ANGLE, by H.G. Wells.

1927

152 "Literary Confidences." *AM* 10 (March): 382-83.
Includes remarks on Sherwood Anderson's TAR: A MIDWEST CHILDHOOD.

153 "The Low-Down on Hollywood." *PHOTOPLAY* 32 (April): 36-37, 118-20.

154 "Man of God: American Style." *AM* 10 (April): 506-08.
On Sinclair Lewis's ELMER GANTRY.

Magazine Articles

155 "Kulture in the Republic." *AM* 12 (October): 250-52.

156 "Testament." *THE AMERICAN REVIEW OF REVIEWS* 76 (October): 413-16.
Albert Shaw introduces "Mencken and His Aims" (412); then HLM explains what he believes, "at bottom and immovably" (413). Followed by a list of aphorisms entitled "As Mencken Sees It," 417-18.

157 "A Comedy of Fig-Leaves." *AM* 12 (December): 510.
On James Branch Cabell's SOMETHING ABOUT EVE.

158 "The Desert Epic." *AM* 12 (December): 508-10.
Includes praise for Willa Cather's DEATH COMES FOR THE ARCHBISHOP.

1928

159 "Inside Stuff." *AM* 13 (February): 253-54.
On Upton Sinclair's MONEY WRITES!

160 "Two Enterprising Ladies." *AM* 13 (April): 506-08.
Reviews the autobiographies of dancer Isadora Duncan and evangelist Aimée Semple McPherson.

161 "Fiction." *AM* 14 (May): 127.
Brief remarks on Thornton Wilder's THE BRIDGE OF SAN LUIS REY, Ruth Suckow's THE BONNEY FAMILY, and Ernest Hemingway's MEN WITHOUT WOMEN.

162 "The Rights of a Columnist: A Symposium on the Case of Heywood Broun Versus the New York WORLD." With others. *NATION* 126 (30 May): 607-09.
HLM defends the right of the columnist to free speech, but he advises the exercise of prudence in some instances.

163 "Babbitt Redivivus." *AM* 14 (June): 253-54.
On THE MAN WHO KNEW COOLIDGE, by Sinclair Lewis.

164 "Two Gay Rebels." *AM* 14 (June): 251-53.
New editions of the works of Samuel Butler and James Branch Cabell elicit opinions from HLM.

165 "What Is All This Talk About Utopia?" *NATION* 126 (13 June): 662-63.
On living in "the Maryland Free State" (662).

166 "Adolescence." *AM* 15 (November): 379-80.
Reviews Margaret Mead's COMING OF AGE IN SAMOA.

1929

167 "Escape and Return." *AM* 16 (April): 506-08.
On DODSWORTH, by Sinclair Lewis.

168 "The Story of a Saint." *AM* 16 (April): 508-09.
Comments on James Branch Cabell's THE WHITE ROBE.

169 "American Worthies." *AM* 17 (June): 255.
On E.W. Howe's autobiography, PLAIN PEOPLE.

170 "Experiments by Old Hands." *AM* 17 (June): 253-54.
Includes notice of Sherwood Anderson's HELLO TOWNS!

171 "Im Westen Nichts Neues." *AM* 17 (August): 510.
Review of ALL QUIET ON THE WESTERN FRONT, by Erich Maria Remarque.

172 "The Ambrose Bierce Mystery." *AM* 18 (September): 124-26.

173 "The New Humanism." *AM* 18 (September): 123-24.
These remarks on literary criticism were occasioned by the publication of T.S. Eliot's FOR LANCELOT ANDREWES.

174 "Two Southern Novels." *AM* 18 (October): 251-53.
Ellen Glasgow's THEY STOOPED TO FOLLY and Ward Greene's CORA POTTS.

Magazine Articles

175 "Stuart P. Sherman." *AM* 18 (December): 507-09.
Review of the rival critic's LIFE AND LETTERS, edited by Jacob Zeitlin and Homer Woodbridge.

1930

176 "American Worthies." *AM* 19 (January): 122-25.
Mentions books by Robert Penn Warren, Allen Tate, and Calvin Coolidge, among several others.

177 "Fiction by Adept Hands." *AM* 19 (January): 126-27.
On Ruth Suckow's CORA, James Branch Cabell's THE WAY OF ECBEN, and Ernest Hemingway's A FAREWELL TO ARMS.

178 "Bierce Emerges From the Shadows." *AM* 19 (February): 251-52.

179 "Ladies, Mainly Sad." *AM* 19 (February): 254-55.
Reviews Theodore Dreiser's A GALLERY OF WOMEN.

180 "On Breaking Into Type." *THE COLOPHON: A BOOK COLLECTOR'S QUARTERLY* 1 (February): n.p.
HLM tells the story behind the publication of his first book, a collection of poetry [1]. Reprinted in BREAKING INTO PRINT, compiled by Elmer Adler (New York: Simon and Schuster, 1937); and in CARROUSEL FOR BIBLIOPHILES, edited by William Targ (New York: Philip C. Duschnes, 1947) with altered title, "On Getting Into Print."

181 "The Life of the Poor." *AM* 19 (March): 381-82.
Reviews JEWS WITHOUT MONEY by Michael Gold.

182 "Smut-Snufflers." *AM* 20 (June): 253-54.
Ostensible review of D.H. Lawrence's PORNOGRAPHY AND OBSCENITY, as well as of several other books on censorship, but chiefly sets forth HLM's own views and experiences.

183 "Schwärmerei." *AM* 20 (July): 379-81.
 On the autobiography of Margaret Anderson (editor of the *LR*), MY THIRTY YEARS' WAR.

184 "What I Believe: Living Philosophies XII." *FORUM* 84 (September): 133-39.
 "Belief is faith in something that is known; faith is belief in something that is not known. In my own credo there are few articles of faith; in fact, I have been quite unable, in ten days and nights of prayer and self-examination, to discover a single one" (133). Reprinted in [389].

1931

185 "Uprising in the Confederacy." *AM* 22 (March): 379-81.
 Reviews I'LL TAKE MY STAND, by Twelve Southerners; i.e., Donald Davidson, John Gould Fletcher, Lyle H. Lanier, Andrew Nelson Lytle, Herman Clarence Nixon, Frank Lawrence Owsley, John Crowe Ransom, Allen Tate, John Donald Wade, Robert Penn Warren, Henry Blue Kline, and Stark Young.

186 "Footprints on the Sands of Time." *AM* 23 (July): 382-83.
 Includes remarks on Dreiser's DAWN.

187 "The Worst American State." With Charles Angoff. *AM* 24 (September): 1-16.
 Part I of a series of articles comparing a variety of statistics gathered on each of the states. Part II appears in October 1931, 175-88; Part III appears in November 1931, 355-71.

1932

188 "Harris on Shaw." *AM* 25 (February): 253-55.
 Review of Frank Harris's BERNARD SHAW invites a comparison of the two men.

189 "The Spanish Idea of a Good Time." *AM* 27 (December): 506-07.

Review of Ernest Hemingway's DEATH IN THE AFTERNOON.

1933

190   "A Lady of Vision." *AM* 28 (March): 382-83.
On Sinclair Lewis's ANN VICKERS.

191   "Shall We Abolish School 'Frills'? Yes." *ROTARIAN* 42 (May): 16-17, 48.
This and the following article, in which John Dewey takes the opposite stand, contributed to a debate that waged over the subject through several issues of *SCHOOL MANAGEMENT*, June through August 1933.

192   "Pongo Americanus." *AM* 29 (June): 254-55.
Review of Ring Lardner's LOSE WITH A SMILE; includes opinions on "the hallmarks of a competent writer of fiction" (254).

193   "A Southern Skeptic." *AM* 29 (August): 504-06.
THE OLD DOMINION EDITION OF THE WORKS OF ELLEN GLASGOW occasions commentary on the novelist.

194   "Hitlerismus." *AM* 30 (December): 506-10.
Discussion of the rise to power of Adolf Hitler, with the prediction that "we are probably in for another world war" (510).

195   "Ten Years." *AM* 30 (December): 385-87.
The magazine's co-founder explains his reasons for leaving the publication in the hands of a new editor, Henry Hazlitt.

1934

196   "Memoirs of an Editor." *VANITY FAIR* 41 (February): 16, 54.

197   "America's Hostility to Art." *VANITY FAIR* 42 (April): 21-22.

198   "Schoolhouses in the Red." *LIBERTY* 11 (16 June): 26-28.
Compares the contemporary scene in public

education and economics to that of his youth.

199 "What to Do with Criminals." *LIBERTY* 11 (28 July): 7-10.
Takes a firm stance on law enforcement and judicial penalties.

200 "Notes on the New Deal." *CURRENT HISTORY* 40 (August): 521-27.

201 "Was Europe a Success?" With Others. *NATION* 139 (3 October): 373-75.
A symposium of views presented in answer to a previous series of articles on the topic by Joseph Wood Krutch.

202 "Illuminators of the Abyss." *SATURDAY REVIEW OF LITERATURE* 11 (6 October): 155-56.
Of proletarian writing, "the worst of it is the fiction" (155).

203 "Why Nobody Loves a Politician." *LIBERTY* 11 (27 October): 16-17.
The politician is typically an untalented man of undistinguished background whose chief concern is the protection of his own job.

204 "Why Not an American Monarchy?" *VANITY FAIR* 43 (November): 21-22.

205 "A Year of Legal Liquor." *NATION* 139 (12 December): 666-67.
On the repeal of Prohibition. In the same periodical Oswald Garrison Villard responded with "A Reply to H.L. Mencken" 140 (9 January 1935): 35, and HLM came back with "Mr. Mencken Has the Last (to Date) Word," 140 (16 January 1935): 72-73.

1935

206 "The Red Bugaboo." *LIBERTY* 12 (26 January): 13-17.
Subtitled, "Presenting the Credo of One Who Thinks the Moscow Menace Considerably Exaggerated."

Magazine Articles

207 "The South Astir." *VIRGINIA QUARTERLY REVIEW* 11 (January): 47-60.
Sketches background for the contemporary "Agrarian" movement and critiques the thought of its "brethren," particularly Donald Davidson.

208 "The Future of English." *HARPER'S* 170 (April): 541-48.

209 "The Advance of Nomenclatural Eugenics in the Republic." *NEW YORKER* 11 (11 May): 44-52.
On the tendency of foreign immigrants to the U.S. to Americanize their names; the first in a series entitled "Onward and Upward with the Arts." Subsequent articles: "The Advance of Onomatalogy, The Art and Science of Naming Babies," 11 (25 May 1935): 32-40; "The Advance of Honorifics," 11 (17 August 1935): 30-37; "Report on the Progress of Euphemism" 11 (17 August 1935): 31-34; "The Advance of Municipal Onomastics" 11 (8 February 1936): 54-57; and "The Dizzy Rise (and Ensuing Bust) of Simplified Spelling" 12 (7 March 1936): 37-44.

1936

210 "Three Years of Dr. Roosevelt." *AM* 37 (March): 257-65.

211 "Ordeal of a Philosopher." *NEW YORKER* 12 (11 April): 21-24.
First of several autobiographical articles published in the *NY* which later comprised HAPPY DAYS [15], NEWSPAPER DAYS [16], and HEATHEN DAYS [18].

212 "The New Deal Mentality." *AM* 38 (May): 1-11.

213 "The Reds and Civil Rights." *AM* 38 (July): 284-89.

214 "The Case for Dr. [Alfred M.] Landon." *AM* 39 (October): 129-34.
HLM favored the overthrow of Roosevelt and

his New Deal in the 1936 presidential election.

215 "The Dole for Bogus Farmers." AM 39 (December): 400-08.

216 "Peace on Earth--Why We Have Wars." LIBERTY 13 (26 December): 24-25.
" ... because so many people enjoy [war]" (24).

1937

217 "The American Future." AM 40 (February): 129-36.
... and how communism, socialism, and capitalism fit into the picture.

218 "A Constitution for the New Deal." AM (June): 129-36.

219 "Utopia by Sterilization." AM 41 (August): 399-408.

1938

220 "The Triumph of the Have-Not." AM 43 (January): 16-22.
More criticism for Roosevelt's New Deal.

221 "The American Civil Liberties Union." AM 45 (October): 182-90.
Followed by "A Letter From the ACLU," 190-93; the same issue includes a letter to HLM from Harold L. Varney, 238-40, and a final word from HLM, 240.

1939

222 "Bringing Roosevelt Up to Date." AM 46 (March): 257-64.

223 "Thoughts on Current Discontents." AM 46 (April): 447-48.
List of aphorisms, chiefly on government.

224 "Thoughts on Current Discontents." AM 47 (June): 215.
More aphorisms on government and politics.

1940

225 "Bizarre Nomenclature, Mostly Feminine." *READER'S DIGEST* 36 (April): 71-72.
The first in a triumvirate of "Notes on the American Language." Subsequent articles include "War Slang," 36 (May 1940): 39, and "Scrambled Parts of Speech," 36 (June 1940): 99-100.

226 "British Speech Invaded." *SATURDAY REVIEW OF LITERATURE* 22 (1 June): 10.
Begins a series of articles on American language. Subsequent articles include "Our Borrowed Vocabulary" 22 (29 June 1940): 13; "Vocabulary Glorification" 22 (3 August 1940): 11; and "Some Southern Given Names" 22 (14 September 1940): 11.

1942

227 "'O.K.,' 1840." *AMERICAN SPEECH* 17 (April): 126-27.
A note on the possible origin of the term.

1943

228 "An Evening on the House." *ESQUIRE* 20 (December): 63, 233-34, 236, 238-39.
HLM reminiscing on the footloose days of Baltimore 1901; reprinted in *ESQUIRE's* 40th anniversary issue, October 1973, and in THE ARMCHAIR *ESQUIRE*, edited by Arnold Gingrich and L. Rust Hills (New York: Putnam, 1958).

1944

229 "War Words in England." *AMERICAN SPEECH* 19 (February): 3-15.

230 "Designations for Colored Folk." *AMERICAN SPEECH* 19 (October): 161-74.

231 "American Profanity." *AMERICAN SPEECH* 19 (December): 241-49.

1945

232 "Tale of a Traveller." *NEW YORKER* 21
(20 October): 52-66.
Recalls a Baltimore street cleaner of his youth named Jock.

233 "*AMERICAN SPEECH*, 1925-1945: The Founders Look Back." With Others. *AMERICAN SPEECH* 20 (December): 241-46.
Co-founders HLM, Louise Pound, Kemp Malone, and Arthur G. Kennedy reminisce.

1946

234 "The Current Suffixes." *AMERICAN SPEECH* 21 (February): 67-69.

235 "Bulletin on 'Hon.'" *AMERICAN SPEECH* 21 (April): 81-85.
On the use of the title of respect "Honorable."

236 "Verbs New and Old." *AMERICAN SPEECH* 21 (December): 303-05.

1947

237 "Names for Americans." *AMERICAN SPEECH* 22 (December): 241-56.

1948

238 "Love Story." *NEW YORKER* 23 (17 January): 23-26.
Story of Charlie and Irene of Baltimore.

239 "American Street Names." *AMERICAN SPEECH* 23 (April): 81-88.

240 "That Was New York: The Life of an Artist." *NEW YORKER* 24 (17 April): 64-71.
On the late Theodore Dreiser.

241 "The Podunk Mystery." *NEW YORKER* 24 (25 September): 71-77.
First in a series of "Postcripts to the American Language." Subsequent articles

Magazine Articles 43

> include "Hell and Its Outskirts" 24 (23 October 1948): 52-57; "The Vocabulary of the Drinking Chamber" 24 (6 November 1948): 62-67; "Department of Amplification" 24 (4 December 1948): 87; "Video Verbiage" 24 (11 December 1948): 102-05; "Scented Words" 25 (2 April 1949): 76-82; and "The Life and Times of O.K." 25 (1 October 1949): 56-61.

1949

242 "Some Opprobrious Nicknames." *AMERICAN SPEECH* 24 (February): 25-30.

1970

243 "Minority Report: Second Series." *MENCKENIANA* 33 (Spring): 1-4.
> The Sage in a rare moment of quiet introspection. Previously unpublished piece selected from the manuscript HLM consulted when compiling MINORITY REPORT [416].

1972

244 "Minority Report." *MENCKENIANA* 42 (Summer): 1-3.
> More material from that which HLM eventually left out of his book by the same name [416]; this essay is on the search for literary sources.

A v. Newspaper Articles

The following is a sampling of HLM's newspaper work, arranged strictly in chronological order. This list is highly selective, intended to indicate the wide range of subjects HLM covered in his forty-odd years as a journalist. Every newspaper title is from Baltimore, except where noted otherwise; Baltimore newspapers are cited only by their titles.

HLM was associated as a reporter or an editor with the following papers: morning and Sunday editions of the *HERALD* (1899-1906), the *EVENING NEWS* (June 1906), the *SUNPAPERS* (1906-1917), the New York *EVENING MAIL* (1917-1918), and again the *SUNPAPERS* (1920-1941, 1948). He also contributed articles to the Chicago *SUNDAY TRIBUNE* (1924-1928), the New York *AMERICAN* (1934-1935), the Associated Press, and a handful of other newspapers. For more information, consult THE MENCKEN BIBLIOGRAPHY [459]. Numerous articles have been collected in [415, 417, 422, 423, 424]; these are largely omitted here.

1899

245 "Team Stolen." *MORNING HERALD* (24 February): 4.
    This item of two sentences (occupying seven lines) on the theft of a horse and buggy is one of the two newspaper "stories" HLM first published; it is reprinted in THE VINTAGE MENCKEN [414]. The other immediately follows (one sentence, five lines), noting that a cineograph exhibition of war scenes was held in Hampden. Neither item is signed; HLM was writing for the *HERALD* as a volunteer without pay, trying to earn the good graces of the city editor and an official job as a reporter.

1904

246 "Theodore Roosevelt Named for President; Charles W. Fairbanks for Vice-President; Republicans Roused from Their Lethargy of First Session and Pandemonium Reigned When the Presidential Nomination Was Made." *MORNING HERALD* (24 June): 1.

One of a series of dispatches from the
Chicago Republican National Convention.

247 "William J. Bryan, Once Powerful, Goes Down to
Defeat Before the Forces that Will Nominate
Chief Judge Parker; Amid Cheers of His Friends
in the Galleries the Eloquent Nebraskan is
Vanquished by Votes of His Well Organized
Opponents." *MORNING HERALD* (8 July): 1.
One of a series of dispatches from the St.
Louis Democratic National Convention.

1910

248 "Good Old Baltimore." *EVENING SUN*
8 April): 6.
Defends the city against its detractors.

249 "William Shakespeare." *EVENING SUN*
(23 April): 6.
On the occasion of the playwright's
birthday, HLM comments on his characters,
language, and on the approaches of
scholars to his works.

250 "The Literary Life." *EVENING SUN* (6 May): 6.
On the difficulties faced by new poets and
novelists of getting their books into
print.

251 "A Negro State?" *EVENING SUN* (7 May): 6.
Reviews William Archer's THROUGH AFRO-
AMERICA, summarizing the complexities
involved in American race relations.

252 "On Jurisprudence." *EVENING SUN* (6 June): 6.

253 "Theodore Roosevelt: A Study of the Man."
EVENING SUN (17 June): 7.

254 "Notes on Morals." *EVENING SUN* (7 July): 6.
On puritanism and the stage.

255 "On Cigarettes." *EVENING SUN* (25 July): 6.
Blasts conventional notions about women
and smoking.

256 "The American." *EVENING SUN* (15 August): 6.
"Moral fervor marks him," he likes to see

people practice religion though he himself sees no need to do so; he is not superstitious but skeptical, and yet ...

257 "The Two Englishes." *EVENING SUN* (10 October): 6.
Asserts that the same English word can mean one thing in this country but another across the ocean; refers to recent comments by Brander Matthews.

258 "On Hanging." *EVENING SUN* (25 November): 6.
Realistic picture at how inefficiently and brutally such executions are carried off in the U.S. Comments that the American attitude "toward capital punishment is exactly like our attitude to many other outworn and preposterous things--we approve it officially and oppose it actually."

1911

259 "The Child-Actor." *EVENING SUN* (16 March): 6.
" ... that bumptious little beast."

260 "On Free Speech." *EVENING SUN* (25 March): 6.
The average American has much more in theory than he does in fact. Still, it is important to hear anyone and everyone out, for if we do not, "we may conceivably miss something very well worth hearing."

1913

261 "The Free Lance." *EVENING SUN* (5 June): 6.
On giving black men the right to vote yet not white women: both notions are grounded on the unsound theory that voting has anything to do with physical criteria, such as skin color and gender. "The Free Lance" column ran daily, with a few exceptions, from 8 May 1911 through 23 October 1915.

1914

262 "Schools Don't Attempt to Teach the Language Americans Speak." *EVENING SUN* (20 December): 2.

1915

263 "Notes for Proposed Treatise Upon the Origin and Nature of Puritanism." *EVENING SUN* (25 October): 6.

264 "Are the Germans Immoral? Of Course!" *EVENING SUN* (11 November): 12.
   The German has no patience with Anglo-Saxon ethics, no interest "in the moral theories of old women in pantaloons."

1916

265 "The Traffic in Babies in Baltimore." *EVENING SUN* (11 January): 6.
   On infant mortality and other issues of women and their children.

266 "In Defense of College Women." *EVENING SUN* (25 January): 8.
   Overturns some common misconceptions about both women and college.

267 "Doctor Seraphicus et Ecstaticus." *EVENING SUN* (14 March): 6.
   Evangelist Billy Sunday "merely does with extraordinary agility and gusto what many another sweating gentleman of God has done before him." Reprinted in [422].

1917

268 "O Fruehling, Wie Bist Du So Schoen!" *EVENING SUN* (12 April): 8.
   In praise of Robert Schumann's Symphony No. 1 in B Flat. Reprinted in [419].

269 "Germany United ... Germans to Go on Fighting." *SUN* (28 January): 1.
   The first of a series of dispatches written between January and March for the *SUN* and *ES* during HLM's stay in

Newspaper Articles

270 "Berlin at Time of Break." *SUN* (10 March): 1.
First in a series of dispatches (through 22 March 1917) from Germany called "The Diary of a Retreat," detailing disintegrating U.S.-German relations shortly before war was declared.

271 "San Cristóbal De La Habana." *EVENING SUN* 14 March): 6.
Attempting to return to the U.S. from Germany in early March 1917, HLM was delayed by a visit to Cuba to cover a revolution for the *SUNPAPERS*. The New York *WORLD* also published some of these articles, written throughout March.

272 "George Ade, American." New York *EVENING MAIL* (7 July): book page.
"The donkeys who write textbooks of American literature piously leave him out...."

273 "SISTER CARRIE's History." New York *EVENING MAIL* (4 August): book page.
Background on Dreiser's controversial novel.

274 "Bold Seer of West Strips American Life of Hypocrisy." New York *EVENING MAIL* (2 October): book page.
Praise for novelist E.W. Howe.

275 "Civilized Chicago." New York *EVENING MAIL* (23 October): 10.
Credits the city for its association with the best of American writers and other artists; New York pales by comparison.

276 "Mark Twain's Americanism." New York *EVENING MAIL* (1 November): 9.
Reprinted in [422].

277 "Virtuosi of Virtue." New York *EVENING MAIL* (20 November): 6.
On vice crusaders.

1918

278 "The Forgotten Man." New York *EVENING MAIL* (10 January): 8.
    Prohibitionists disregard the very man they claim to help--"the normal, decent, self-respecting citizen."

279 "The Secret of Life." New York *EVENING MAIL* (4 February): 8.
    On the progress of the biological sciences.

280 "The Intelligence of Women." New York *EVENING MAIL* (20 February): 13.
    Where it originates, how it has evolved, in what respects it is superior to that of men.

281 "How to Get a Husband." New York *EVENING MAIL* (31 May): 13.

282 "The Puritan Complex." New York *EVENING MAIL* (19 June): 7.
    A "psychoanalysis" thereof.

1920

283 "A Carnival of Buncombe." *EVENING SUN* (9 February): 8.
    On politics, this article is the first of a series of editorials that came to be known as the "Monday Articles," although their appearance was not firmly restricted to that day of the week. This one and several others are reprinted in [415].

284 "Henry Mencken Sees Death of Liberalism." *EVENING SUN* (11 June): 1-2.
    For every national political convention held between 1920 and 1948, excepting only those of 1944, HLM wrote dispatches and editorials for the *SUNPAPERS*, some of which were part of the "Monday Articles" series. This dispatch concerns the Republican convention held in Chicago, which nominated Harding and Coolidge.

Newspaper Articles

285 "Einstein." *EVENING SUN* (24 June): 19.
On America's penchant for foreign fads or "rages," of which HLM thinks the scientist one.

286 "Dull Day at San Francisco is Brightened for Mencken by Eloquent Widow Lady." *EVENING SUN* (2 July): 2.
Refers to one of the more interesting speakers at the Democratic National Convention, which nominated James M. Cox and Franklin D. Roosevelt.

1921

287 "Southern Letters." *EVENING SUN* (21 March): 10.
Comments on hopeful signs suggested by the rise of the periodicals *AW*, the *DD*, and the *REVIEWER*.

288 "A Great Moral Sport." *EVENING SUN* (25 April): 10.
Capital punishment is often justified on the grounds that it deters criminals, but the truth is it is practiced because so many Americans find it entertaining.

289 "On Censorships." *EVENING SUN* (7 June): 15.

290 "Mencken Explains Storm Over Case of Communists." *EVENING SUN* (20 October): 1.
Background on the Sacco and Vanzetti trial and re-trial.

1922

291 "The National Letters." *EVENING SUN* (23 January): 10.
Discusses the current "loosening of the Puritan grip" in American literature.

292 "For Better, For Worse." *EVENING SUN* (17 July): 10.
Finds most American marriages successful.

1923

293 "Democratic Reflections." *EVENING SUN*
(12 February): 12.
"Democracy, in essence, is simply a pastiche of all the delusions and follies that happen to be raging at the moment."

294 "Educational Rolling Mills." *EVENING SUN*
(16 April): 17.
On overcrowding in American colleges and universities.

295 "Max Ways as H.L. Mencken Knew Him." *EVENING SUN* (5 June): 21.
Obituary written in fond memory of the former editor of the Baltimore *HERALD* and HLM's first newspaper chief. Reprinted in [423].

296 "Below the Potomac." *EVENING SUN*
(18 June): 17.
On Southern labor and politics.

297 "Liberalism As A Falseface." *EVENING SUN*
(20 August): 10.
Many of those who claim to be liberals are nothing of the sort, for "Liberalism, when it is real, has no place in American politics."

1924

298 "On Journalism." *EVENING SUN*
(18 February): 15.
Affirms that advertising and wealthy owners of newspapers are not the great threats to journalism they are often made out to be.

299 "On Getting a Living." *EVENING SUN*
(12 May): 17.
Advocates that only students from families of sound economic means be allowed to enter the professions, so that these fields will be less burdened by dollar chasers.

300 "Vice-Presidential Battle Thrills Mencken After Dull Business of Naming 'Cal.'" *EVENING SUN* (13 June): 1-2.
Dispatch from the Republican National Convention held in Cleveland.

301 "Conventions Have Become Ill Managed and Inefficient Carnivals, Thinks Mencken." *EVENING SUN* (28 June): 1-2.
One of several dispatches from the Democratic National Convention held in New York.

302 "The Young Writer." Chicago *SUNDAY TRIBUNE* (9 November): part 5, pages 1-2.
Advice from a magazine editor and literary critic.

1925

303 "The Golden Age." *EVENING SUN* (9 February): 15.
On American business and the "Babbits" who conduct it.

304 "Scott Fitzgerald and His Work." Chicago *SUNDAY TRIBUNE* (3 May): part 9, pages 1, 3.

305 "The Tennessee Circus." *EVENING SUN* (15 June): 17.
On the Scopes trial, evolutionary theory in education, and the "Ku Klux Klergy."

306 "Homo Neandertalensis." *EVENING SUN* (29 June): 17.
The Scopes trial inspires remarks on the erroneous assumption "that human progress affects everyone."

307 "Mencken Finds Daytonians Full of Sickening Doubts About Value of Publicity." *EVENING SUN* (9 July): 1.
One of a series of articles covering the trial of teacher John Thomas Scopes for having taught evolutionary theory in a Tennessee public school. HLM sided with the defense, led by Clarence Darrow; William Jennings Bryan led the Creationist prosecution.

308 "Happy Days." *EVENING SUN*
(17 August): 13.
On "the incomparable gift for clowning that lies in the whole American people."

1926

309 "As H.L.M. Sees It: A Noose Or Poison For Beaten Presidential Candidates." *EVENING SUN* (10 April): op ed.
Those who are unsuccessful in their bid for the office are "soreheads [whose presence] upon the public stage constitutes a public nuisance." Although written chiefly for the Chicago *ST*, several of the "As H.L.M. Sees It" articles appeared first in the Baltimore *ES* on the previous Saturday, usually on the page opposite the editorial page; on at least two occasions, including this one, the *ES* printed articles which the *ST* did not use. For further background, see Adler's MENCKEN BIBLIOGRAPHY [459]: 98, 108.

310 "Babbitt Starts a Counter Offensive." Chicago *SUNDAY TRIBUNE* (18 April): part 8, page 1.
Having attacked the "Babbitts"--here, middle-class idealists, preachers of the gospel of Service--HLM finds he at least goaded them into being articulate.

311 "The Pulitzer Prizes." *EVENING SUN* (10 May): 19.
More often than not the committee fails to reward the finest work being produced each year.

312 "The Escape from Zion." *EVENING SUN* (20 September): 19.
Reviews Herbert Asbury's UP FROM METHODISM, an excerpt of which, published in the *AM*, initiated the "Hatrack" case.

313 "Good Life, Good Death, Says Mencken: Sterling Last of Free Artists." San Francisco *CHRONICLE* (18 November): 3.

Written on the occasion of the poet's suicide.

1927

314 "The Dark American." Chicago *SUNDAY TRIBUNE* (25 September): part 7, page 1.
Black America has not yet given us the artists it has the potential to develop.

315 "Meditation at Vespers." *EVENING SUN* (12 December): 21.
The Sage admits to thriving on confrontations, some of the best of which have been with clergymen.

1928

316 "Note for Eugenists." *EVENING SUN* (16 April): 17.
On "the failure of the Revolutionary aristocracy to produce a progeny competent to hold its position," with particular attention given the Daughters of the American Revolution.

317 "The Show Begins." *EVENING SUN* (4 June): 19.
Looking ahead to the national political conventions, particularly to the problem of supplying plenty of "booze" for the politicians, Prohibition notwithstanding.

318 "This, Says Mencken, Was the 'Most Low-Down' Convention Ever Held." *EVENING SUN* (16 June): 1.
The Kansas City Republican National Convention, which nominated Herbert Hoover and Charles W. Curtis.

319 "Honest Candidate Comes Out of Convention That Met Truth, Says Mencken." *EVENING SUN* (30 June): 1.
Albert E. Smith and Joseph T. Robinson were the Democratic nominees in Houston.

320 "Turning Worms." *EVENING SUN* (1 October): 17.
On the excesses of the Southern clergy and the Ku Klux Klan.

321 "Analysis Fails Mencken, Pondering Smith's Sway of Crowds: Just Has 'It.'" *EVENING SUN* (17 October): 1, 5.
    HLM wrote this and a number of other dispatches while covering the Al Smith presidential campaign tour.

322 "Gaudy Times." *EVENING SUN* (10 December): 21.
    The efforts of the reformers "to make the United States a completely moral nation" ought to prove "pleasant alike to saints and sinners."

323 "The War Upon Intelligence." *EVENING SUN* (31 December): 8.
    ... is being largely waged by American public education.

1929

324 "Doctor Illuminatus et Sublimis." *EVENING SUN* (18 March): 21.
    Methodist Bishop James Cannon, Jr., "is the first Pope the United States has ever had...."

325 "Bach at Bethlehem." *EVENING SUN* (20 May): 19.
    On the Bach Choir Festival at Bethlehem, Pennsylvania.

326 "The Trend of American Ethics." *EVENING SUN* (14 October): 25.
    All Congressmen are "yokels at heart" who bring to the daily practice of governing "the manners and ideals of the village Coca-Cola counter." They are "perfect revival fodder."

1930

327 "Christian Science Technique." *EVENING SUN* (3 March): 19.
    Concerning the efforts of Christian Scientists to supress a recent biography of Mary Baker Eddy.

328 "Purifying the Movies." *EVENING SUN* (14 April): 21.
    A censorship bill before the House

represents a "new masterpiece of wowserism." See also editorial page of the *ES* (27 May), where Canon William S. Chase responds to HLM's attack with a Letter to the Editor.

329 "Mencken Spanks Lewis for Nobel Prize Speech." *EVENING SUN* (31 December): 1, 3.
Associated Press interview, in which HLM laments the contents of Sinclair Lewis's acceptance speech and remarks that the contemporary outlook is good for young American writers.

1931

330 "Famine." *EVENING SUN* (19 January): 17.
Objecting to Federal relief of the hungry in Arkansas, this article drew fire from the state's legislature and other Arkansas statesmen.

331 "Believe It If You Can." *EVENING SUN* (10 August): 17.
Al Capone and the "mysteries" surrounding his case.

332 "The Eastern Shore Kultur." *EVENING SUN* (7 December): 25.
Vehemently condemns the recent lynching in Salisbury of a black man; a number of responses ensued in the *SUNPAPERS*.

333 "Blind Leaders of the Blind." *EVENING SUN* (28 December): 17.
The Communist movement in the U.S.

1932

334 "A Third of a Century." *EVENING SUN* (11 January): 17.
Now middle aged, HLM looks back on his early years in journalism.

335 "The Suffering Ether." *EVENING SUN* (22 February 1932): 15.
The content of radio music programs is "mainly bilge."

336 "Mencken Sees More Whoops Than Votes for Repeal Plank." *EVENING SUN* (13 June): 1, 6.
From the Republican National Convention held in Chicago, this and all other dispatches covering the summer's conventions were reprinted in MAKING A PRESIDENT [412].

337 "The Paramount Issue." *EVENING SUN* (25 July): 15.
... to HLM the summer Hoover and Roosevelt won the Republican and Democratic nominations was the repeal of Prohibition, not the Great Depression.

1934

338 "Notes on the Holy Land." *EVENING SUN* (2 April): 15.
Admiring words for Jerusalem from Baltimore's most famous infidel; followed by "Erez Israel" (9 April 1934: 17). Together these articles form the pamphlet EREZ ISRAEL [25].

339 "New Deal Psychology." *EVENING SUN* (21 May): 17.

340 "You-All: Confederate Trade Mark's Mysterious Origin." New York *AMERICAN* (16 July): 15.
One of the earliest in a series of weekly articles written for the *AMERICAN* between 1934 and 1936.

341 "Plague." *EVENING SUN* (13 August): 15.
The problem of syphilis in Baltimore.

342 "Forty Acres and a Mule." *EVENING SUN* (10 September): 17.
Upton Sinclair's socialism in California.

343 "$105,000,000,000." *EVENING SUN* (24 December 1934): 8.
Thanks to Roosevelt and his Brain Trust, taxes will be going up and interest rates on bank deposits down.

Newspaper Articles

1935

344 "To Whom It May Concern: Mr. Mencken Replies."
New York *AMERICAN* (11 January): 25.
In response to G.K. Chesterton's remarks concerning TREATISE ON RIGHT AND WRONG [13] given on the same page in "'Sensible Men': A Dissenting Note on H.L. Mencken's Democracy," HLM here says he stands by his professed opinions: "The worst of all mankind's botches is the botch of government."

345 "Huey." *EVENING SUN* (21 January): 15.
Credits Huey P. Long's "plan for bringing in the More Abundant Life" to Louisiana with more sense than the schemes of the Brain Trust or of Upton Sinclair's "Cow-State Utopians."

346 "The Curse of Mankind." *EVENING SUN* (4 November): 19.
... is government.

1936

347 "The Man of Science." New York *AMERICAN* (13 January): 15.
... is not the one who knows the most but rather he who seeks to know truth objectively, dispassionately.

348 "Pensions for Assassins." *EVENING SUN* (18 May 1936): 15.
Without capital punishment, taxpayers bear the burden of supporting criminals for the rest of their lives. Followed on 22 May by a Letter to the Editor from the Reverend Joseph J. Ayd, S.J.

349 "Mencken Finds Confidence in Convention City Almost Cornered by Landon Bloc." *EVENING SUN* (8 June): 1.
Dispatch from Cleveland, where the Republicans nominated Alfred M. Landon and Frank Knox. Between July and October HLM covered the Landon campaign tour, submitting dispatches for the *SUN*.

350 "Presentation of Platform Marked by Convention's Poky Pace, Says Mencken." *SUN* (26 June): 1.
One of several dispatches covering the Philadelphia Democratic National Convention, which nominated incumbent Roosevelt. In 1936 HLM also covered the Townsend and Coughlin conventions, both held in Cleveland.

351 "On Radical Professors." *EVENING SUN* (20 July): 13.
Parents are too often overzealous in their desire to protect their children from a variety of ideas, subversive or ridiculous or otherwise.

352 "The Radio Priest." *EVENING SUN* (24 August): 17.
Discusses Father Charles E. Coughlin's radio version of the economic stance taken in the encyclical of 15 May 1931, issued by Pope Pius XI.

353 "The Public Prints." *EVENING SUN* (14 December): 21.
Concerning the role newspapers play in political events and issues, with emphasis on Roosevelt's recent landslide victory. Reprinted in [423].

1937

354 "Juggernaut." *EVENING SUN* (22 March): 17.
"The right to drive [a car] should not be a right at all, but a privilege, and getting it should be made difficult." Irresponsible users of automobiles are the source of many traffic problems and accidents.

355 "A Proposed New Constitution for Maryland." *SUN* (12 April): 11-12.
HLM's plan "gets rid of the clumsy bicameral Legislature ... rearranges the counties on a more rational and economic basis, and ... attempts a complete reorganization of the executive and judicial departments. It also attempts to break

down ... the present nefarious party system, with its inevitable corruption."

356 "The University of Maryland: A Brief Outline of Its History." *SUN* (17 May): 11.
First in a series of articles on the university that ran through 5 June 1937.

357 "The Art of Swearing." *EVENING SUN* (24 May): 17.

358 "The Johns Hopkins Hospital: The Dispensary." *SUN* (6 July): 11.
First in a series of articles on the hospital running through 28 July 1937.

359 "Semper Fidelis." *EVENING SUN* (26 July): 15.
Uncomplimentary obituary for Joe Robinson, Senator from Arkansas.

360 "Labor Rows." *EVENING SUN* (27 December): 17.
The American Federation of Labor, the Congress of Industrial Organizations, and assembly-line troubles, particularly in the automobile industry.

1938

361 "The Drums Begin to Roll." *EVENING SUN* (24 January): 13.
With the New Deal in ill health, it begins to appear likely that Roosevelt will take a greater interest in European and Japanese discontent; here as elsewhere HLM asserts that most people "invariably enjoy wars" though they profess otherwise.

362 "Object Lesson." *EVENING SUN* (10 February): 23.
Presents six columns of dots (over 1,000,000 of them) and one column of explanation: the dots represent the number of current Federal employees supported by taxpayers.

363 With Philip M. Wagner. "Five Years of the New Deal." *EVENING SUN* (4 March): 27.
A full page detailing the nation's woes as a result of Roosevelt's administrations.

1939

364 "The Great Scramble." *SUN* (6 June): 13.
Criticizes Roosevelt's New Deal for having failed to handle immigration properly; suggests that our own "surplus" of "inferior"--i.e. chronically unemployed-- men be sent elsewhere, perhaps Russia.

1940

365 "On Academic Freedom." *SUN* (28 April): 8.
The debate over whether Bertrand Russell should be relieved of his position in the philosophy department of City College (New York) leads to comments on American public education addressed to the American Civil Liberties Union.

366 "Shadow of Roosevelt Heavy Over Chicago." *SUN* (13 July): 1.
... as the Democrat seeks a third term in office.

367 "Willkie Says New Deal is Wrecking Land." *SUN* (10 October): 1.
Having covered the Republican convention which nominated Wendell L. Willkie and Charles L. McNary, HLM then went on their campaign tour.

1941

368 "Below the Rio Grande." *SUN* (19 January): 10.
Roosevelt and his "New Dealers" should pay closer attention to the current governmental scene in Latin American countries, for there are valuable lessons to be learned.

1948

369 "Mencken Counts 'Em: Decibels Hit Ceiling in Keynote-Night Din." *SUN* (22 June): 1.
On the Republican convention, where Thomas E. Dewey and Earl Warren won the nomination. In early July HLM wrote dispatches from the Democratic convention at which Harry S. Truman and Alben W. Barkley were

nominated, and later that month he covered that of the Progressive Party (Henry A. Wallace and Glen H. Taylor). All three conventions were held in Philadelphia.

370 "Equal Rights in Parks: Mencken Calls Tennis Order Silly, Nefarious." *SUN* (9 November): 14. In his last editorial for the *SUNPAPERS*, HLM defends the right of blacks and whites to engage in sports in the same parks.

A vi.   Contributions

This list focuses on material HLM contributed to other works during his lifetime; subsequent essay and article reprintings, of which there have been hundreds, have been excluded. Although HLM's epigrams are often cited in dictionaries of quotations and the like, all such contributions are here omitted. HLM is the author unless otherwise noted.

1909

371 Ibsen, Henrik. A DOLL'S HOUSE. Newly translated from the definitive Dano-Norwegian text. Edited, with introduction (v-xxiv) and notes by HLM. Boston: Luce.

372 Ibsen, Henrik. LITTLE EYOLF. Newly translated from the definitive Dano-Norwegian text. Edited with introduction (v-xxi) and notes by HLM. Boston: Luce.

1910

373 Nietzsche, Freidrich. THE GIST OF NIETZSCHE. Arranged by HLM. Boston: Luce.
    A collection of "conclusions," as HLM calls them, of the best of the philosopher's thought. Reprinted: Folcroft, PA: Folcroft, Press, 1970, 1973; Belfast, ME: Bern Porter, 1973; Norwood, PA: Norwood Editions, 1977.

1913

374 Brieux, Eugène. *BLANCHETTE* AND *THE ESCAPE*: TWO PLAYS BY BRIEUX. With Preface (i-xxxvi) by HLM. Translated from the French by Frederick Eisemann. Boston: Luce.

1918

375 Ibsen, Henrik. THE MASTER BUILDER, PILLARS OF SOCIETY, HEDDA GABLER. Introduction (v-xii) by HLM. New York: Boni and Liveright.

1919

376 Howe, E.W. VENTURES IN COMMON SENSE. Edited with introduction (7-29) by HLM. New York: Knopf.
Praise for Howe's straightforward personality and prose sets up a contrasting sketch of the generally suspicious and therefore suspect American character. Volume II of the six-volume "Free Lance" Series.

1920

377 Baroja, Pío. YOUTH AND EGOLATRY. Edited with introduction (11-20) by HLM. Translated from the Spanish by Jacob S. Fassett, Jr. and Frances L. Phillips. New York: Knopf.
Considers the novelist "a product of the intellectual reign of terror that went on in Spain after the catastrophe of 1898" (11). Volume I of the "Free Lance" Series.

378 Muir, Edwin. WE MODERNS: ENIGMAS AND GUESSES. Edited with introduction (7-21) by HLM. New York: Knopf.
Praises the author's Nietzschean brand of iconoclasm. Volume IV of the "Free Lance" Series.

379 "Willa Cather." In THE BORZOI 1920: BEING A SORT OF RECORD OF FIVE YEARS' PUBLISHING, 28-31. Foreword by Alfred A. Knopf. Introduction by Maxim Gorky. New York: Knopf.
HLM praises Midwestern fiction in general and Cather's in particular, even to the point of offering a rare retraction of earlier critical remarks. Includes some remarks first made in reviews for the *SS*.

1921

380 Cabell, James Branch. THE LINE OF LOVE: DIZAIN DES MARIAGES. Introduction (vii-xiii) by HLM. New York: Robert M. McBride.

381 THE NIETZSCHE-WAGNER CORRESPONDENCE. Introduction (xi-xvii) by HLM. Edited by Elizabeth

Contributions

Foerster-Nietzsche. Translated by Caroline V. Kerr. New York: Liveright. Reprint. 1949.
HLM does not believe that the philosopher and the musician influenced one another's work permanently.

382 Wood, James N. DEMOCRACY AND THE WILL TO POWER. Introduction (7-17) by HLM. New York: Knopf.
Appraises the author's penetrating analysis of the essential traits of democracy. Volume V of the "Free Lance" Series.

1922

383 "Politics." In CIVILIZATION IN THE UNITED STATES, 21-34. Edited by Harold E. Stearns. New York: Harcourt; London: Cape.
The trouble with the U.S. Congress lies in the constitutional articles requiring that members be inhabitants of the states they represent, which leads to parochialism, and in the two-party system, which keeps every politician insecure about his job and therefore unwilling to speak and act with complete integrity.

1925

384 "Memorandum." In THE BORZOI 1925: BEING A SORT OF RECORD OF TEN YEARS OF PUBLISHING, 138-41. New York: Knopf.
Chiefly personal profile of friend and publisher Alfred A. Knopf.

1926

385 "Americanism." In ENCYCLOPAEDIA BRITANNICA, 104-05. 13th edition. Vol. 29. London and New York: Encyclopaedia Britannica.
HLM explains the term here and in the fourteenth edition of 1929, where it appears somewhat revised. Revised article was reprinted in subsequent editions until 1957.

1929

386 Huneker, James. ESSAYS BY JAMES HUNEKER. Selected with an introduction (ix-xxiii) by HLM. New York: Charles Scribner's Sons. Personal and professional remarks for one of the men HLM admired most. Reissued: New York: AMS Press, 1976.

387 "Havelock Ellis: The Most Admirable Englishman of His Time." In HAVELOCK ELLIS: IN APPRECIATION, 55-60. Edited by Joseph Ishill. Berkeley Heights, NJ: Oriole Press. Two short articles in which HLM professes admiration for the English psychologist's skepticism and "genuine culture" (57); the first is reprinted from the EP (24 September 1921), the second from BCR (February 1926).

1931

388 Cooper, James Fenimore. THE AMERICAN DEMOCRAT. Introduction (xi-xx) by HLM. New York: Knopf. The same introduction reprinted in subsequent editions: Knopf, 1956; Indianapolis: Liberty Classics, 1981.

389 "What I Believe." In LIVING PHILOSOPHIES, 179-93. With others. New York: Simon. Reprinted from FORUM, September 1930 [184]; the same appears in the 1939 edition edited by Clifton Fadiman (I BELIEVE: THE PERSONAL PHILOSOPHIES OF CERTAIN EMINENT MEN AND WOMEN OF OUR TIME, New York: Simon).

1935

390 Ibsen, Henrik. ELEVEN PLAYS. Introduction (vii-xiv) by HLM. New York: Modern Library. Reprints "Ibsen: Journeyman Dramatist" [108].

1936

391 Haardt, Sara Powell. SOUTHERN ALBUM. Edited, with a preface (vii-xxiii) by HLM. Garden City, NY: Doubleday.

HLM brought together this collection of
his wife's fiction a year after her death.

1937

392 Mencke, Johann Burkhard. THE CHARLANTRY OF
THE LEARNED (DE CHARLATANERIA ERUDITORUM) With
notes and introduction (3-45) by HLM. Translated from the German [sic] by Francis E. Litz.
New York and London: Knopf.
Title page incorrectly calls the Latin
original German. Lengthy preface by HLM
gives geneological, biographical, and
scholastic background leading up to this
eighteenth-century attack on fake learning
by HLM's ancestor.

1940

393 "Competent Man." In ALFRED A. KNOPF: QUARTER
CENTURY, 17-21. Norwood, MA: The Plimpton
Press.
Since competence was highly valued by HLM,
this is sound praise indeed for the
publisher. Reprinted in ALFRED A. KNOPF
AT 60 (New York: Privately printed, 1952).

1942

394 Mencken, August, ed. BY THE NECK: A BOOK OF
HANGINGS. Foreword (v-vii) by HLM. New York:
Hastings House.
HLM's brother edited this "selection from
contemporary accounts."

1944

395 STYLEBOOK: THE *SUNPAPERS* OF BALTIMORE.
Baltimore: A.S. Abell.
HLM is credited with most of the writing
and revisions in this manual, which has
been used by several other papers besides
the *SUNPAPERS*.

1946

396 Dreiser, Theodore. AN AMERICAN TRAGEDY.
Introduction (ix-xvi) by HLM. Memorial

edition. Cleveland: World Publishing. Reprint. 1948.

1948

397 "The American Language." In LITERARY HISTORY OF THE UNITED STATES, vol. 2: 663-75. Edited by Robert E. Spiller. New York: Macmillan.
The same article is reprinted in the one-volume revision of this work, 1953.

1949

398 "The Birth of New Verbs." In PHILOLOGICA: THE MALONE ANNIVERSARY STUDIES, 313-19. Edited by Thomas A. Kirby and Henry Bosley Woolf. Baltimore: Johns Hopkins Press.
HLM illustrates with characteristic liveliness the various ways Americans have expanded the body of English verbs.

B. ANTHOLOGIES, COLLECTIONS, SELECTIONS

This section lists anthologies, collections, and selections of HLM's articles and essays, including collections he edited himself. Cross-references within brackets [ ] indicate items which are annotated elsewhere in this volume.

1916

399 A BOOK OF BURLESQUES (OPUS 12). New York: John Lane.
    HLM's brief headnote indicates that these pieces "are chiefly reprinted, though with many changes, from the *SS*, the *BOHEMIAN*, and the Baltimore *ES*."

    Second and third editions: New York: Knopf, 1920; Fourth edition 1921, which was printed in England by Cape, 1923; Fifth edition by Knopf, 1924. The second edition of 1920 was reprinted in New York: Reprint House International, 1970, and in St. Clair Shores, MI: Scholarly Press, 1971. Edition of 1916 available from University Microfilms (Ann Arbor, MI). Contains:
      "Death: A Philosophical Discussion"
      "From the Programme of a Concert"
      "The Wedding: A Stage Direction"
      "The Visionary"
      "The Artist: A Drama without Words" [20]
      "Seeing the World"
      "From the Memoirs of the Devil"
      "Litanies for the Overlooked"
      "Asepsis: A Deduction in Scherzo Form"
      "Tales of the Moral and Pathological"
      "Epitalamium"
      "Portraits of Americans"
      "Panoramas of People"
      "The New Soule"
      "A Genealogical Chart of the Uplift"

400 A LITTLE BOOK IN C MAJOR (OPUS 11). New York: John Lane.
    Short collection of original epigrams.

Reprinted by University Microfilms (Ann Arbor, MI) in 1979.

1917

401 A BOOK OF PREFACES (OPUS 13). New York: Knopf. Second (revised) edition, 1918. Third edition, 1920 (except for new preface, same as second edition). Fourth printing, 1922 (London: Jonathan Cape) also has a new preface; this version used for subsequent printings. In 1928 Knopf brought it out as a Borzoi Pocket Book. Edition of 1928 reprinted: New York: Octagon Press, 1977; Ann Arbor, MI: University Microfilms, no date.
Contains:
"Joseph Conrad" [30]
"Theodore Dreiser" [34]
"James Huneker" [29]
"Puritanism as a Literary Force" [33]

1918

402 DAMN! A BOOK OF CALUMNY. New York: Philip Goodman. Second and third editions were actually reprintings of the first. Fourth edition includes a few textual changes and a preface; Knopf reissued this in 1918, omitting the first word of the original.

1919

403 PREJUDICES: FIRST SERIES. New York: Knopf. Reissued 1923 and 1924 by Knopf. English edition: London: Cape, 1921. Edition of 1919 reprinted: New York: Octagon Books, 1977; Ann Arbor, MI: University Microfilms, no date.
Contains:
"Criticism of Criticism of Criticism" [39]
"The Late Mr. Wells"
"Arnold Bennett"
"The Dean" [40]
"Professor Veblen" [45]
"The New Poetry Movement" [43]
"The Heir of Mark Twain"

"Hermann Sudermann"
"George Ade"
"The Butte Bashkirteseff" [38]
"Six Members of the Institute" [46]
"The Genealogy of Etiquette" [41]
"The American Magazine" [35]
"The Ulster Polonius" [48]
"An Unheeded Law-Giver" [49]
"The Blushful Mystery" [37]
"George Jean Nathan" [42]
"Portrait of an Immortal Soul" [44]
"Jack London"
"Among the Avatars" [36]
"Three American Immortals" [47]

1920

404 PREJUDICES: SECOND SERIES. New York: Knopf.
English edition: London (Cape), 1921.
Reprinted: New York: Octagon Books, 1977;
Ann Arbor, MI: University Microfilms, no date.
Contains:
"The National Letters" [52]
"Roosevelt: An Autopsy" [53]
"The Sahara of the Bozart" [31]
"The Divine Afflatus" [50]
"Scientific Examination of a Popular Virtue"
"Exeunt Omnes" [51]
"The Allied Arts"
"The Cult of Hope"
"The Dry Millennium"
"Appendix on a Tender Theme"

1922

405 PREJUDICES: THIRD SERIES. New York: Knopf.
English edition: London (Cape), 1923.
Edition of 1922 reprinted by Octagon Books (New York), 1977.
Contains:
"On Being an American" [61]
"Huneker: A Memory" [58]
"Footnote on Criticism" [57]
"Das Kapital" [54]
"Ad Imaginem Dei Creavit Illum"
"Star-Spangled Men" [62]
"Five Men At Random" [56]

"The Nature of Liberty"
"The Novel" [60]
"The Forward-Looker"
"Memorial Service" [59]
"Education"
"Types of Men" [63]
"The Dismal Science" [55]
"Matters of State"
"Reflections on the Drama"
"Advice to Young Men"
"Suite Americaine"

1924

406 PREJUDICES: FOURTH SERIES. New York: Knopf.
English edition: London (Cape), 1925.
Edition of 1924 reprinted by Octagon Books
(New York), 1977.
Contains:
"The American Tradition" [65]
"The Husbandman" [68]
"High and Ghostly Matters" [67]
"Justice Under Democracy"
"Reflections on Human Monogamy" [73]
"The Politician" [72]
"From a Critic's Notebook" [66]
"Totentanz" [74]
"Meditations in the Methodist
Desert" [69]
"Essay in Constructive Criticism"
"On the Nature of Man" [71]
"Bugaboo"
"On Government" [70]
"Toward a Realistic Aesthetic" [75]
"Contributions to the Study of Vulgar
Psychology"
"The American Novel" [64]
"People and Things"

1925

407 AMERICANA 1925. Edited by HLM. New York:
Knopf; London: Hopkinson.
Collects hundreds of excerpts taken from
various U.S. newspapers, handbills, adver-
tisements, and other similar sources
regularly reprinted in AM's "Americana"

Collections

section throughout 1925. Reprinted by the *AM* in 1926.

1926

408 AMERICANA 1926. Edited by HLM. New York: Knopf; London: Hopkinson.
Similar to the collection of 1925, with the exception of "an Appendix from Foreign Parts ... [and] notes for the use of foreign readers" (vii).

409 PREJUDICES: FIFTH SERIES. New York: Knopf.
English edition: London (Cape), 1927.
Reprinted by Octagon Books (New York), 1977.
Contains:
"Four Moral Causes" [79]
"Four Makers of Tales" [78]
"In Memoriam: W.J.B." [82]
"The Hills of Zion" [81]
"Beethoven"
"Rondo on an Ancient Theme" [85]
"Protestantism in the Republic"
"From the Files of a Book Reviewer"
"The Fringes of Lovely Letters" [80]
"Essay in Pedagogy" [77]
"On Living in Baltimore" [84]
"The Last New Englander"
"*THE NATION*" [83]
"Officers and Gentlemen"
"Golden Age"
"Edgar Saltus"
"Miscellaneous Notes"
"Catechism" [76]

1927

410 PREJUDICES: SIXTH SERIES. New York: Knopf.
English edition: London (Cape), 1928.
Edition of 1927 reprinted: New York: Octagon Books, 1977; Ann Arbor, MI: University Microfilms, no date.
Contains:
"Journalism in America" [95]
"From the Memoirs of a Subject of the United States"
"The Human Mind" [91]
"Clarion Call to Poets" [88]

"Souvenirs of a Book Reviewer" [98]
"Five Little Excursions" [90]
"Hymn to the Truth" [92]
"The Pedagogy of Sex" [97]
"Metropolis" [96]
"Dives into Quackery" [89]
"Life Under Bureaucracy"
"In the Rolling Mills" [93]
"Ambrose Bierce" [86]
"The Executive Secretary"
"Invitation to the Dance" [94]
"Aubade"
"Appendix from Moronia" [87]

1928

411 MENCKENIANA: A SCHIMPFLEXIKON: EXPURGATED EDITION. New York: Knopf.
Collection of anti-HLM invective, of which there was never an "unexpurgated" edition. Reprinted: New York: Octagon Books, 1977; Ann Arbor, MI: University Microfilms, no date.

1932

412 MAKING A PRESIDENT: A FOOTNOTE TO THE SAGA OF DEMOCRACY. New York: Knopf.
Compilation of material on the two national political conventions of 1932, taken from the Baltimore *ES*. See [336].

1949

413 A MENCKEN CHRESTOMATHY. New York: Knopf.
Draws from the six PREJUDICES books [403, 404, 405, 406, 409, 410], A BOOK OF BURLESQUES [399], DAMN! A BOOK OF CALUMNY [402], IN DEFENSE OF WOMEN [6], MAKING A PRESIDENT [412], NOTES ON DEMOCRACY [11], and TREATISE ON RIGHT AND WRONG [13] to form a collection of over 200 of the author's own favorites from his out-of-print works. Some essays are slightly revised. Reprinted: Franklin Center, PA: Franklin Library, 1980; New York: Random House, 1982 (paperback).

1955

414 THE VINTAGE MENCKEN. Gathered by Alistair Cooke. New York: Knopf.
  Brief but valuable introduction, sketching HLM's life, times, and career. Reprints many of HLM's best pieces, including portions of the DAYS autobiographies [15, 16, 18], so as to distinguish this collection from the CHRESTOMATHY [413] by featuring a biographical dimension. Most of the other items were originally printed during the first two decades of the century.
  Contains:
  "Introduction to the Universe"
  "The Baltimore of the Eighties"
  "Adventures of a Y.M.C.A. Lad"
  "Text for Newspaper Days"
  "First Appearance in Print" [245]
  "Recollection of Notable Cops"
  "Theodore Dreiser" [34]
  "Gore in the Caribbees"
  "Pater Patriae"
  "Quid Est Veritas?"
  "The Art Eternal"
  "The Skeptic"
  "The Incomparable Buzz-Saw"
  "A Blind Spot"
  "Abraham Lincoln" [56]
  "[Henry Cabot] Lodge"
  "Cavia Cobaya"
  "The National Letters" [52]
  "Star-Spangled Men" [62]
  "The Archangel Woodrow"
  "The Libertine"
  "The Lure of Beauty"
  "The Good Man"
  "The Anglo-Saxon" [65]
  "Holy Writ"
  "Masters of Tone"
  "The Noble Experiment"
  "The Artist"
  "Chiropractic"
  "The Hills of Zion" [81]
  "In Memoriam: W.J.B." [82]
  "The Author at Work"
  "Valentino" [87]
  "A Glance Ahead"

"The Libido for the Ugly" [90]
"Travail"
"A Good Man Gone Wrong"
"The Comedian"
"Mr. Justice Holmes"
"The Calamity of Appomattox"
"The New Architechture"
"The Nomination of Franklin Delano Roosevelt"
"A Good Man in a Bad Trade"
"Coolidge"
"The Wallace Paranoia"
"Mencken's Last Stand" [370]
"Sententiae"
"Exeunt Omnes" [51]
"Epitaph"

1956

415 A CARNIVAL OF BUNCOMBE: H.L. MENCKEN AT HIS BEST ... ON POLITICS. Edited by Malcolm Moos. Baltimore: Johns Hopkins Press.
Introduction is a general overview of Mencken's love-hate relationship with American politics--and vice versa. Also gives biographical sketch with emphasis on his convention work. Selections are from the "Monday Articles." Issued in paperback with Foreword by Joseph Epstein, Chicago and London: University of Chicago Press, 1984.
Contains:
"Normalcy"
"The Carnival of Buncombe" [283]
"The Clowns in the Ring"
"Bayard Vs. Lionheart"
"Campaign Notes"
"The Last Round"
"In Praise of Gamaliel"
"The Last Gasp"
"Optimistic Note"
"Gamalielese"
"Gamalielese Again"
"Who's Loony Now?"
"Making Ready for 1924"
"Next Year's Struggle"
"Calvinism"
"Calvinism (Secular)"
"The Impending Plebiscite"

Collections

"The Clowns March In"
"Post-Mortem"
"Breathing Space"
"Labor in Politics"
"The New Woodrow"
"Meditations on the Campaign"
"Notes on the Struggle"
"The Coolidge Buncombe"
"Mr. Davis' Campaign"
"The Voter's Dilemma"
"Autopsy"
"Twilight"
"Cal as Literatus"
"The Coolidge Mystery"
"Onward, Christian Soldiers:
   Hoover and Al"
"Al Smith and His Chances"
"The Struggle Ahead"
"Al"
"The Impending Combat"
"Real Issues at Last"
"Civil War in the Confederacy"
"Al and the Pastors"
"The Hoover Manifesto"
"Onward, Christian Soldiers!"
"The Campaign Opens"
"The Show Begins"
"Der Wille Zur Macht"
"Prophetical Musings"
"Al in the Free State"
"The Eve of Armageddon"
"Autopsy"
"The Men Who Rule Us"
"Roosevelt Minor"
"Looking Ahead"
"Little Red Riding Hood"
"The Hoover Bust"
"Hoover in 1932"
"Imperial Purple"
"The Men Who Rule Us"
"The Impending Carnage"
"Where Are We At?"
"The Hoover Bust"
"Pre-Mortem"
"A Time to Be Wary"
"The Tune Changes"
"Vive le Roi!"
"Roosevelt"
"The Burden of Omnipotence--

　　　　　Roosevelt and Alf"
　　　"1936"
　　　"The Show Begins"
　　　"The More Abundant Dialectic"
　　　"The Combat Joins"
　　　"Burying the Dead Horse"
　　　"After the New Deal"
　　　"Sham Battle"
　　　"The Choice Tomorrow"
　　　"Coroner's Inquest"

416　MINORITY REPORT: H.L. MENCKEN'S NOTEBOOKS. New York: Knopf.
　　　Over four hundred miscellaneous notes previously unpublished, compiled after HLM's debilitating stroke with the help of his secretary. Other material from the manuscript was published later in *MENCKENIANA* [243, 244].

　　　　　　　　　1958

417　THE BATHTUB HOAX AND OTHER BLASTS AND BRAVOS FROM THE CHICAGO *TRIBUNE*. Edited with introduction and notes by Robert McHugh. New York: Knopf. Reprint. New York: Octagon Books, 1977.
　　　Contains:
　　　"A Neglected Anniversary
　　　　(The Bathtub Hoax)" [32]
　　　"Melancholy Reflections"
　　　"Hymn to the Truth" [92]
　　　"The Believing Mind"
　　　"The Bill of Rights"
　　　"The Comstockian Imbecility"
　　　"The Anatomy of Wowserism"
　　　"Padlocks"
　　　"The Battle of Ideas"
　　　"The Birth Control Hullabaloo"
　　　"Equality Before the Law"
　　　"Essay on Constructive Criticism"
　　　"Hints for Novelists"
　　　"Yet More Hints for Novelists"
　　　"Poe's Start in Life"
　　　"The Case of Dreiser"
　　　"H.L. Mencken on Mark Twain"
　　　"Robert Louis Stevenson"
　　　"Beethoven, Obituary March 26, 1827"
　　　"The Music of the American Negro"

Collections

    "On Realism"
    "View of Literary Gents"
    "The Avalanche of Books"
    "Fundamentalism: Divine and Secular"
    "The Rev. Clergy"
    "Cousin Jocko"
    "Jacquarie"
    "Man as a Mammal"
    "Havelock Ellis"
    "On Eugenics"
    "Human Monogamy"
    "Another Long-Awaited Book"
    "Holy Writ"
    "The United States Senate"
    "The National Conventions"
    "Notes on Government"
    "Blackmail Made Easy"
    "A Long-Felt Want"
    "Vive le Roi!"
    "The Pedagogue's Utopia"
    "On Going to College"
    "The Language We Speak"
    "Babel"
    "The Emperor of Dictionaries"
    "The American Scene"
    "On Connubial Bliss"
    "Dreams of Peace"
    "On Human Progress"
    "The South Rebels Again"
    "The Sad Case of Tennessee"
    "The Movies"
    "The Telephone Nuisance"
    "Victualry as a Fine Art"
    "On Controversy"

418 PREJUDICES: A SELECTION. Compiled by James T. Farrell, with introduction. New York: Vintage.
    Contains:
        "Criticism of Criticism of Criticism" [39]
        "George Ade"
        "The Genealogy of Etiquette" [41]
        "The Ulster Polonius" [48]
        "George Jean Nathan" [42]
        "Three American Immortals" [47]
        "Roosevelt: An Autopsy" [53]
        "The Sahara of the Bozart" [31]
        "The Cerebral Mime (The Allied Arts)"
        "The Cult of Hope"

"On Being An American" [61]
"Huneker: A Memory" [58]
"The Nature of Liberty"
"Memorial Service" [59]
"The King (Types of Men)" [63]
"The Dismal Science" [55]
"Patriotism (Advice to Young Men)"
"Virtue (Suite Américaine)"
"The Husbandman" [68]
"The Politician" [72]
"On Government" [70]
"The Capital of a Great Republic
 (People and Things)"
"Bilder Aus Schöner Zeit (People and
 Things)"
"Conrad (Four Makers of Tales)" [78]
"Lardner (Four Makers of Tales)" [78]
"Heretics (The Files of a Book
 Reviewer)"
"On Living in Baltimore" [84]
"The Champion (Miscellaneous Notes)"
"Definition (Miscellaneous Notes)"
"Journalism in America" [95]
"On Controversy (The Human Mind)" [91]
"The Emperor of Wowsers (Souvenirs of
 a Book Reviewer)" [98]
"Hymn to the Truth" [92]
"Chiropractic (Dives into
 Quackery)" [89]
"The Executive Secretary"

1961

419 H.L. MENCKEN ON MUSIC. Selected by Louis
Cheslock. New York: Knopf.
Includes Cheslock's remarks on HLM as an
amateur musician and a history of the
Saturday Night Club. Besides a sampling
of HLM's passing comments on or allusions
to music, also contains:
"The Three B's"
   Bach at Bethelehem (May 1923)
   Bach at Bethelehem (May 1928)
   Bach at Bethelehem (May 1929)
   Two Days of Bach
   (Interlude)
   Beethoven
   Old Ludwig and his Ways
   Beethoveniana

Collections

    (Interlude)
    Brahms
"More of the Masters"
    Schubert
    Schubert
    Wagner (Symbiosis and the Artist)
    Wagner (The Eternal Farce)
    Franz Joseph Haydn
    Johann Strauss
    Schumann (O, Fruehling, Wie Bist Du
        So Schoen!) [268]
    Mendelssohn
    Dvorák (An American Symphony)
"Operas and Operettas"
    Opera
    Grand Opera in English
    The Tower Duet in IL TROVATORE
    THE MIKADO
    The Passing of Gilbert
    PINAFORE at 33
"Band Music"
    Italian Bands
    Wind Music
"Tempo di Valse"
"Wedding Music"
    New Wedding March Needed
    Enter the Chruch Organist
"Catholic Church Music"
"National Music"
    English Songs
    Russian Music
"Popular Songs of the Plain People"
    A Plea for the Old Songs
    The Folk-Song
    American Folk-Song
    The Music of the American Negro
"Music and Other Vices"
    Virtuous Vandalism
    Music After the War
"More Review"
    Ernest Newman and Others
    The Poet and the Scientist
"Occupational Hazard"
    Music as a Trade
    The Reward of the Artist
"Little Concert-Halls"
"'Light' Motifs"
    On Tenors
    Mysteries of the Tone-Art

Masters of Tone
"Morals and Music"
Music and Sin
The Music-Lover
"The End of a Happy Life"

1965

420 THE AMERICAN SCENE: A READER. Selected and Edited, with introduction and commentary, by Huntington Cairns. New York: Vintage. Reprinted. 1982. Includes many of the most famous HLM essays as well as a handful of interesting letters and miscellaneous, rarely anthologized pieces.
Contains:
"On Being an American" [61]
"The Husbandman" [68]
"The National Letters" [52]
"Theodore Dreiser" [34]
"The Sahara of the Bozart" [31]
"Criticism of Criticism of Criticism" [39]
"Footnote on Criticism" [57]
"The Poet and His Art"
"Professor Veblen" [45]
"The Politician" [72]
"Imperial Purple"
"In Memoriam: W.J.B." [82]
"Last Words"
"Journalism in America" [95]
"The Hills of Zion" [81]
"The Spell of Journalism"
"The American Language"
"Hell and Its Outskirts"
"The Vocabulary of the Drinking Chamber"
"The Nature and Origin of Religion"
"The Nature and Origin of Morality"
"James Fenimore Cooper"
"Mark Twain"
"James Gibbons Huneker" [386]
"Ambrose Bierce" [86]
"Ludwig von Beethoven"
"Recollections of Notable Cops"
"A Girl from Red Lion, PA"
"Beaters of Breasts"
"Christmas Story" [27]

Collections

"The Divine Afflatus" [50]
"Star-Spangled Men" [62]
"Death: A Philosophical Discussion"
"The Libertine"
"Random Notes"
"Gnomes"
"The Shrine of Mnemosyne"
"Three American Immortals" [47]

1968

421 H.L. MENCKEN'S *SMART SET* CRITICISM. Selected and edited by William H. Nolte. Ithaca, NY: Cornell University Press.
Chooses from among HLM's *SS* reviews of over two thousand books, with an eye toward who and what from the period is still of particular interest. Contains:
"Diagnosis of Our Cultural Malaise"
"Our Literary Centers"
"William Lyon Phelps and Others"
"The Professor Doctors"
"Paul Elmer More"
"Private Reflections"
"Professor Pattee and Professor Sherman"
"The Novelist as Messiah"
"A Definition"
"O. Henry"
"The Raw Material of Fiction"
"Point of View"
"On Playgoers--And on Hauptmann, Synge, and Shaw"
"Getting Rid of the Actor"
"Chesterton's Picture of Shaw"
"Shaw as Platitudinarian"
"Strindberg--A Final Estimate"
"The Greatest Stylist of Modern Times"
"Lizette Woodworth Reese"
"Ezra Pound"
"The Troubadours A-Twitter"
"Holy Writ"
"Huneker in Motley"
"An Apostle of Rhythm"
"A First-Rate Music Critic"
"Hall Caine and John D. Rockefeller"
"George Moore"
"Henry Ford"

"In the Altogether"
"The Style of Woodrow"
Vox Populi
"The Taste for Romance"
"The New Thought, Dreams, and Christian Science"
"ZULEIKA DOBSON"
"Havelock Ellis"
"Osculation Anatomized"
"The Advent of Psychoanalysis"
"The Anatomy of Ochlocracy"
"The Way to Happiness"
"To Drink or Not to Drink"
"A Novel Thus Begins"
"The Story of a Resourceful Wife"
"A Non-Cure for the World's Ills"
"A Faded Charmer"
"Earnest Messages"
"Brief Dismissals"
"Mush for the Multitude"
"Lachrymose Love"
"Mark Twain"
 Popularity Index
 Twain and Howells
 Our One Authentic Giant
 Final Estimate
"Friedrich Nietzsche"
 The Prophet of the Superman
 Transvaluation of Morals
"James Gibbons Huneker"
 Importer of Foreign Flavors
 Huneker's Confessions
"Oscar Wilde"
 A Note on Oscar Wilde
 The Accounting of a Tartuffe
 Portrait of a Tragic Comedian
"H.G. Wells"
 H.G. Wells *Redivivus*
"Joseph Conrad"
 Probing the Russian Psyche
 Conrad's Self-Portrait
 VICTORY
 A Good Book on Conrad
 Conrad Revisited
"Theodore Dreiser"
 A Modern Tragedy
 The Creed of a Novelist
 De Profundis
"Anatole France"

Collections

        A Gamey Old Gaul
     "Willa Cather"
        Her First Novel
        Willa Cather vs. William Allen White
     YOUTH AND THE BRIGHT MEDUSA
     "James Branch Cabell"
        A Refined Scoffer
     "Sherwood Anderson"
        Something New under the Sun
        The Two Andersons
        Muddleheaded Art
     "Sinclair Lewis"
        The Story of an American Family
        Portrait of an American Citizen
     "F. Scott Fitzgerald"
        Two Years Too Late
        A Step Forward
     "A Book for the Gourmet"
     "The Nature of Vice"
     "Novels to Reread"
     "A Review of Reviewers"
     "An Autobiographical Note"
     "The Incomparable Billy"
     "The Irish Renaissance"
     "Taking Stock"
     "The Negro as Author"
     "Scherzo for the Bassoon"
     "Fifteen Years" [121]

              1973

422 THE YOUNG MENCKEN: THE BEST OF HIS WORK.
     Collected by Carl Bode. New York: Dial Press.
        Brings together much that is not easily
        available elsewhere as well as much that
        is, pieces that HLM wrote between the ages
        of 16 and 37.
     Contains:
        "Ode to the Pennant on the Centerfield
           Pole"--first published piece (a
           poem), appeared summer 1896 in
           the Baltimore *AMERICAN*
        "Y.M.C.A. Star Course"
        "Academy of Sciences"
        "Sewer Sleuths Rescued Her Boa"
        "The Flight of the Victor"
        "How J. Atticus Pluto Became an
           Expert Handholder and Subsequently
           Hit the Cobbles"

"The Tin-Clads," from VENTURES INTO VERSE [1]
"A Rondeau of Statesmanship"
"The Song of the Slapstick"
"The Ballad of Ships in Harbor"
"Charles J. Bonaparte, A Useful Citizen"
"Senator Fairbanks Will Accept the Second Place on the Ticket"
"A Jewish African State"
"By Way of Introduction," from GEORGE BERNARD SHAW: HIS PLAYS [2]
"Grossvater Wilhelm"
"Education," from THE PHILOSOPHY OF FRIEDRICH NIETZSCHE [3]
"Sauerkrat Redivivus"
"The Good, the Bad and the Best Sellers"
"Afterwards"
"Mencken's Reply to LaMonte's Sixth Letter," from MEN VERSUS THE MAN [4]
"The Common Negro"
"The Two Englishes"
"The Expurgators"
"The Dramatic Critic"
"Der Rosenkavalier"
"Round One!"
"The Varieties"
"The Meredith of Tomorrow"
"Up the Valley"
"On Dreams"
"A Symphony"
"On Bartenders"
"On Alcohol"
The Free Lance, 9 May
The Free Lance, 13 May
The Free Lance, 5 March
"The Bards in Battle Royal"
The Free Lance, 15 March
"Pertinent and Impertinent"
"The Beeriad"
"Good Old Baltimore"
"The American" [103]
"The American: His Morals"
"The American: His Language"
"The American: His Ideas of Beauty"
"The American: His Freedom"
"The American: His New Puritanism"
The Free Lance, 8 July

Collections 89

"Song"
"The Barbarous Bradley"
"The Mailed Fist and Its Prophet" [106]
"The Old Trails"
"Litany for Magazine Editors"
"The Flapper"
"The Wedding: A Stage Direction"
"Invocation"
The Free Lance, 9 June
The Free Lance, 16 July
The Free Lance, 23 October
"Mobilizing the Mountebanks"
"Eine Kleine Sinfonie in F Dur"
"Doctor Seraphicus et Ecstaticus" [267]
"James Huneker"
"Answers to Correspondents"
"Joseph Conrad"
"Epigrams," from A LITTLE BOOK
  IN C MAJOR [400]
"For Americanos," from A BOOK OF
  BURLESQUES [399]
"If You Have Tears to Shed--!"
"The Dreiser Bugaboo" [107]
"Mark Twain's Americanism" [276]
"The Sahara of the Bozart" [31]

1975

423 A GANG OF PECKSNIFFS: AND OTHER COMMENTS ON
NEWSPAPER PUBLISHERS, EDITORS AND REPORTERS.
Selected by Theo Lippman, Jr. New Rochelle,
NY: Arlington House.
    Thorough introduction to HLM as a
    newspaperman. Contains excerpts from
    Donald H. Kirkley's interview with HLM, as
    well as:
    "Newspaper Morals"
    "On Journalism"
    "A Gang of Pecksniffs"
    "Max Ways as H.L. Mencken
      Knew Him" [295]
    "Watterson's Editorials Reveal 'Vacuity
      of Journalism'"
    "The Newspaper Man"
    "The Reporter at Work"
    "Memoirs of an Editor"
    "A Wholesaler in Journalism"
    "Learning How to Blush"
    "More Tips for Novelists"

"Notes on Journalism"
"Adams as an Editor"
"Journalism in America" [95]
"The Case of Hearst"
"Georgia Twilight"
"Twenty Years"
"Journalism in the United States"
"Tainted News"
"Twenty-five Years"
"Speech to the Associated Press"
"The Public Prints [353]
"Speech to the American Society of
 Newspaper Editors"
"A Note on News"
"The Newspaper Guild"
"Memo to Paul Patterson"
"On False News"
"Speech to the National Conference of
 Editorial Writers"

1976

424 MENCKEN'S LAST CAMPAIGN: H.L. MENCKEN ON THE 1948 ELECTION. Edited with introduction by Joseph C. Goulden. Washington, DC: New Republic Book Company.
Reprints HLM's SUNPAPERS coverage of the 1948 presidential conventions.

1980

425 A CHOICE OF DAYS: ESSAYS FROM "HAPPY DAYS," "NEWSPAPER DAYS," AND "HEATHEN DAYS." Selected with an introduction by Edward L. Galligan. New York: Knopf.
Selects twenty chapters from HLM's three-volume autobiography [15, 16, 18], just as HLM set twenty as the maximum number of essays in each of his DAYS volumes.
Contains:
"Introduction to the Universe"
"The Caves of Learning"
"The Baltimore of the Eighties"
"The Head of the House"
"The Training of a Gangster"
"Larval Stage of a Bookworm"
"Strange Scenes and Far Places"
"Allegro Con Brio"
"Drill for a Rookie"

Collections

"The Days of the Giants"
"Recollections of Notable Cops"
"A Girl from Red Lion, PA"
"The Synthesis of News"
"Fire Alarm"
"Adventures of a YMCA Lad"
"The Tone Art"
"Gore in the Caribbees"
"Romantic Intermezzo"
"The Noble Experiment"
"Vanishing Act"

C.   LETTERS

This list includes books and articles which collect or contain a portion of HLM's correspondence. Other items in this volume which quote, excerpt, or reprint individual letters include [4, 420, 463, 483, 491, 518, 573, 705, 760, 935, 952, 985, 990, 995, 1097, 1121, 1137, 1239, 1245, 1281, 1304]. See also MAN OF LETTERS: A CENSUS OF THE CORRESPONDENCE OF H.L. MENCKEN [463].

1929

426   Newman, Frances. FRANCES NEWMAN'S LETTERS. Edited by Hansell Baugh, with a prefatory note by James Branch Cabell. New York: Liveright.
    Includes four from HLM.

1958

427   Durham, Frank. "Mencken as Missionary." *AMERICAN LITERATURE* 29 (January): 478-83.
    The texts of letters written to Henry Sydnor Harrison in 1916 concerning Dreiser's THE GENIUS.

1959

428   Dreiser, Theodore. LETTERS OF THEODORE DREISER: A SELECTION. Edited by Robert H. Elias. 3 vols. Philadelphia: University of Pennsylvania Press.
    Contains several from HLM; see index.

1960

429   Sinclair, Upton. MY LIFETIME IN LETTERS. Columbia: University of Missouri Press.
    Over a hundred letters passed between the two men; twenty-seven from HLM are included here.

1961

430 LETTERS OF H.L. MENCKEN. Selected and annotated by Guy J. Forgue with a personal note by Hamilton Owens. New York: Knopf. Because the total number of HLM's available letters remains incomplete, Forgue confines himself to those of literary and personal interest--though even these limiting criteria have resulted in an extensive, valuable collection. Selections date from 1900 to 1956. Paperback edition: Boston: Northeastern University Press, 1981; includes a Foreword by Daniel Aaron.

1962

431 Cabell, James Branch. BETWEEN FRIENDS: LETTERS OF JAMES BRANCH CABELL AND OTHERS. Edited by Padraic Colum and Margaret Freeman Cabell; introduction by Carl Van Vechten. New York: Harcourt.

1963

432 Fitzgerald, F. Scott. THE LETTERS OF F. SCOTT FITZGERALD. Edited by Andrew Turnbull. New York: Scribner.
    HLM is mentioned in several letters between the novelist and others, and is the addressee in a half dozen more. See index.

1968

433 Castagna, Edwin. "Mellow Mencken: Some of H.L.M.'s Friendly Correspondence." *MANUSCRIPTS* 20 (Summer): 3-12.
    Includes letters between HLM and Upton Sinclair, Gerald W. Johnson, Blanche Knopf, Dr. Howard Kelly, Dr. Hugh H. Young, William Manchester, and M.A.H. Dente.

434 "Manchester's Mencken." *MENCKENIANA* 26 (Summer): 1-8.
    Reprints the texts of letters that passed between HLM and the biographer as he wrote

his master's thesis, which he later expanded into a book [490].

1972

435 "Letters to Jack Conroy." *NEW LETTERS: A MAGAZINE OF FINE WRITING* 39: 16-28.
Three from HLM.

1976

436 THE NEW MENCKEN LETTERS. Edited by Carl Bode. New York: Dial Press. Reprint. 1977.
During HLM's last years his secretary Rosalind Lohrfinck worked at collecting and transcribing his vast correspondence. One large group of letters was donated to the New York Public Library, "with the stipulation that they stay sealed for a quarter of a century after his death, in other words until January 1971" (11). Thus Bode had access to these and others which Forgue had not enjoyed. All these letters were previously unpublished, except where some of them had been excerpted, and they date from 1905 to 1955.

1977

437 Faulkner, William. SELECTED LETTERS OF WILLIAM FAULKNER. Edited by Joseph Blotner. New York: Random House.
Three to HLM. See index.

1979

438 Lindsay, Vachel. LETTERS OF VACHEL LINDSAY. Edited by Marc Chenetier. New York: Burt Franklin.
Four from the poet to HLM.

439 Morton, Bruce. "Twelve New H.L. Mencken Letters." *MANUSCRIPTS* 31 (Summer): 170-80.
These are from HLM to Charles Lowe Swift, a former editor of the Baltimore *EH*.

1980

440 Fitzgerald, F. Scott. THE CORRESPONDENCE OF F. SCOTT FITZGERALD. Edited by Matthew J. Bruccoli and Margaret Duggan, with assistance from Susan Walker. New York: Random House.
Reprints texts of a number of letters to and from HLM, as well as the texts of several inscriptions included in each other's books.

1982

441 LETTERS FROM BALTIMORE: THE MENCKEN-CLEATOR CORRESPONDENCE. Edited by P.E. Cleator, with a Foreword by Carl Bode. London and Toronto: Associated University Presses.
Collects the letters that passed between HLM and British writer Cleator.

1986

442 DREISER-MENCKEN LETTERS: THE CORRESPONDENCE OF THEODORE DREISER AND H.L. MENCKEN, 1907-1945. Edited by Thomas P. Riggio. 2 vols. Philadelphia: University of Pennsylvania Press.
Reprints over a thousand items from the known body of correspondence; annotates in an appendix those letters not reprinted.

443 "ICH KUSS DIE HAND": THE LETTERS OF H.L. MENCKEN TO GRETCHEN HOOD. Edited by Peter W. Dowell. University: University of Alabama Press.
Contains over 130 letters HLM sent his friend the opera singer.

1987

444 MENCKEN AND SARA: A LIFE IN LETTERS, THE PRIVATE CORRESPONDENCE OF H.L. MENCKEN AND SARA HAARDT. Edited by Marion Elizabeth Rodgers. New York: McGraw-Hill.
Illuminates a rarely seen side of HLM; offers a thorough introduction, with biographical sketch of Sara.

Part 2

Secondary Bibliography

D. BIBLIOGRAPHIES

Besides the following works, many selected bibliographies appear in full-length studies of HLM and occasionally within magazine or journal articles; these have not been mentioned here. See Sections E, F, G, H, and J.

1920

445 Henderson, F.C. [pseud]. BIBLIOGRAPHY. In H.L. MENCKEN: FANFARE, 21-32. New York: Knopf.
    The first HLM bibliography was compiled by the Sage himself working incognito and is here printed with [769] and [778].

1923

446 Moss, David, comp. "H.L. (Henry Lewis [sic]) Mencken." No. 31 of AMERICAN FIRST EDITIONS: A SERIES OF BIBLIOGRAPHICAL CHECKLISTS. Edited by Merle Johnson and Frederick M. Hopkins. PUBLISHER'S WEEKLY 103 (28 April): 1327-28.

1924

447 Frey, Carroll. A BIBLIOGRAPHY OF THE WRITINGS OF H.L. MENCKEN. With a Foreword by HLM. Philadelphia: The Centaur Bookshop.
    Reprinted: Folcroft Library Editions (Folcroft, PA), 1976; Norwood Editions (Norwood, PA), 1977; R. West (Philadelphia), 1978.

1927

448 Kennedy, Arthur Garfield. A BIBLIOGRAPHY OF WRITINGS ON THE ENGLISH LANGUAGE FROM THE BEGINNING OF PRINTING TO THE END OF 1922. Cambridge, MA: Harvard University Press; New Haven, CT: Yale University Press.
    See nos. 11583, 11617, 11627, and 11637, which pertain to THE AMERICAN LANGUAGE [7] and to several articles HLM wrote on the subject.

1929

449 Manly, John Matthews, and Edith Rickert, eds. CONTEMPORARY AMERICAN LITERATURE: BIBLIOGRAPHIES AND STUDY OUTLINES, 236-39. Introduction and revision by Fred B. Millett. New York: Harcourt.
Includes primary and secondary citations.

1939

450 Burke, William Jeremiah. THE LITERATURE OF SLANG. New York: New York Public Library.
Highlights HLM's work in philology and reviews of THE AMERICAN LANGUAGE [7]. See index.

1940

451 Millett, Fred B. CONTEMPORARY AMERICAN AUTHORS: A CRITICAL SURVEY AND 219 BIO-BIBLIOGRAPHIES, 480-86. New York: Harcourt.
Updates Manly and Rickert [449].

1942

452 Blanck, Jacob Nathaniel. MERLE JOHNSON'S AMERICAN FIRST EDITIONS, 358-61. 4th ed., rev. and enl. New York: Bowker.

1947

453 West, Herbert Faulkner. THE MIND ON THE WING: A BOOK FOR READERS AND COLLECTORS, 177-203. New York: Coward-McCann.
A checklist of items in the HLM collection at Dartmouth Library.

1950

454 Swan, Bradford F. "Making a Mencken Collection." YALE UNIVERSITY GAZETTE 24: 101-113.
On the Yale collection donated by the author.

Bibliographies

1954

455 Leary, Lewis G. ARTICLES ON AMERICAN LITERATURE, 1900-1950, 211-13. Durham, NC: Duke University Press.

1957

456 Porter, Bernard H. H.L. MENCKEN: A BIBLIOGRAPHY. Pasadena, CA: Geddis Press. Reprinted in *TCL* 4 (October 1958): 100-07.

1960

457 Modern Language Association of America. American Literature Group. Committee on Manuscript Holdings. AMERICAN LITERARY MANUSCRIPTS: A CHECKLIST OF HOLDINGS IN ACADEMIC, HISTORICAL, AND PUBLIC LIBRARIES IN THE UNITED STATES, 252-53. Austin: University of Texas Press.

458 Reference Department, University of Pennsylvania Library. INDEX TO ARTICLES ON AMERICAN LITERATURE, 1951-1959, 245-46. Boston: G.K. Hall.
Updates Leary [455].

1961

459 Adler, Betty. HLM: THE MENCKEN BIBLIOGRAPHY. Baltimore: Johns Hopkins University Press.
The most complete list to date of HLM's works, accompanied by a selective list of secondary materials. Kept up to date by the journal *MENCKENIANA* [460], which Adler founded. See also the two Supplements to THE MENCKEN BIBLIOGRAPHY [465, 473].

1962

460 *MENCKENIANA: A QUARTERLY REVIEW*. Baltimore: Enoch Pratt Free Library, since 1962.
Includes articles on Mencken and abstracts of articles published elsewhere as they appear. Nearly every issue contains a "Bibliographic Checklist" of new and

reprinted material. Keeps Adler and the two Supplements [459, 465, 473] up to date.

1965

461 Adler, Betty, comp. A CENSUS OF "VENTURES INTO VERSE" BY HENRY LOUIS MENCKEN. Baltimore: Enoch Pratt Free Library.
This pamphlet attempts to record the whereabouts and ownership of all known, extant copies of HLM's first book, a collection of poetry which has become a rarity among his works [1]. Revised and enlarged edition of this census (1972) includes the essay "Analysis" by John S. Van E. Kohn.

1967

462 ------. A DESCRIPTIVE LIST OF H.L. MENCKEN COLLECTIONS IN THE U.S. Baltimore: Enoch Pratt Free Library.

1969

463 ------. MAN OF LETTERS: A CENSUS OF THE CORRESPONDENCE OF H.L. MENCKEN. Baltimore: Enoch Pratt Free Library.
A guide to the locations of letters to and from HLM known to date, with information on restrictions. A special section concerns correspondence relating to THE AMERICAN LANGUAGE [7].

464 Nolte, William H. THE MERRILL CHECKLIST OF H.L. MENCKEN. Columbus, OH: Merrill Publishing.

1971

465 Adler, Betty, comp. HLM: THE MENCKEN BIBLIOGRAPHY, A TEN-YEAR SUPPLEMENT, 1962-1971. Baltimore: Enoch Pratt Free Library.
Updates her earlier work [459], making no changes in format or criteria for inclusion; primary and secondary. See also [473].

466 Boude, Katherine S., comp. THE MENCKEN COLLECTION, JULIA ROGERS LIBRARY, GOUCHER COLLEGE. Baltimore: Friends of the Goucher College Library.

467 Duke, Maurice. "*THE REVIEWER*: A Bibliographical Guide to a Little Magazine." *RESOURCES FOR AMERICAN LITERATURE STUDIES* 13 (Spring): 58-97.
  Includes primary and secondary HLM citations.

1972

468 Johnson, Richard C., and G. Thomas Tanselle. "Addenda to Bibliographies of Sherwood Anderson, the Brownings, Carlyle, Stephen Crane, Epictetus, Irving, James, Kipling, Leacock, London, Machen, Markham, and Mencken: Haldeman-Julius Little Blue Books." *PAPERS OF THE BIBLIOGRAPHICAL SOCIETY OF AMERICA* 66 (First Quarter): 66.

1975

469 Pizer, Donald, Richard W. Dowell, and Frederick E. Rusch. THEODORE DREISER: A PRIMARY AND SECONDARY BIBLIOGRAPHY. Boston: G.K. Hall.
  Includes many HLM items on the novelist. See index.

1976

470 West, James L.W., III. "The Mencken-Fitzgerald Papers: An Annotated Checklist." *PRINCETON UNIVERSITY LIBRARY CHRONICLE* 38 (Autumn): 21-45.
  "This checklist locates and describes all known and currently available primary materials which have bearing on the Mencken-Fitzgerald relationship" (21-22).

1983

471 Johanson, Donald. "Collecting Mencken." *MENCKENIANA* 8 (Winter): 1-5.
  Gives a cross-sectional view of what primary and secondary materials are worth reading and collecting.

1984

472 "Articles, Fiction, Poetry, and Reviews About the West Selected from THE AMERICAN MERCURY, 1924-31." MENCKENIANA 89 (Spring): 11-14.
That over a hundred items are listed here is indicative of HLM's interest in the region.

1986

473 Fitzpatrick, Vincent. HLM: THE MENCKEN BIBLIOGRAPHY, A SECOND TEN-YEAR SUPPLEMENT, 1972-1981. Baltimore: Enoch Pratt Free Library.
Updates Adler's bibliography and ten-year Supplement [459, 465].

E. BIOGRAPHIES, REMINISCENCES, MEMOIRS

See also [15, 16, 18, 19, 425, 689] and essays by Knopf and Manchester in [578].

1924

474 Boyd, Ernest. "H.L. Mencken." In PORTRAITS: REAL AND IMAGINARY, 165-67. New York: George H. Doran.

1925

475 ------. H.L. MENCKEN. New York: Robert M. McBride.
Although not very thorough, this is a lively, personal account from a long-time friend; includes a generous sampling of HLM's own remarks.

476 Goldberg, Isaac. THE MAN MENCKEN: A BIOGRAPHICAL AND CRITICAL SURVEY. New York: Simon and Schuster.
Expands on a booklet entitled H.L. MENCKEN, published as no. 611 in the Little Blue Books series (Gerard, KA: Haldeman-Julius, 1924).

477 Hergesheimer, Joseph. "Mr. Henry L. Mencken." In THE BORZOI 1925: BEING A SORT OF RECORD OF TEN YEARS OF PUBLISHING, 102-06. New York: Knopf.
The novelist and friend recalls the public and private HLM.

1931

478 Clark, Emily. "H.L. Mencken." In INNOCENCE ABROAD, 109-26. New York: Knopf.
Describes several meetings and talks with HLM and his advice for the journal she edited, the Richmond *REVIEWER*.

479 Smith, S. Stephenson. THE CRAFT OF THE CRITIC, 33-37. New York: Thomas Y. Crowell.
Recalls a conversation held with the Sage in Berlin. See index for other references.

1932

480 Nathan, George Jean. THE INTIMATE NOTEBOOKS OF GEORGE JEAN NATHAN, 94-121. New York: Knopf.
> Personal reflections on his rewarding friendship and professional association with HLM. Reprinted in Charles Angoff's THE WORLD OF GEORGE JEAN NATHAN (New York: Knopf, 1952).

1935

481 Stearns, Harold. THE STREET I KNOW, 193-204. New York: Lee Furman.
> Background on HLM's role in the author's compilation of CIVILIZATION IN THE UNITED STATES, to which HLM contributed the essay "Politics" [383].

1937

482 Wright, Richard. BLACK BOY: A RECORD OF CHILDHOOD AND YOUTH. New York: Harper and Brothers. Reprint. 1945.
> Chapter Thirteen chiefly concerns HLM as the writer whose work showed the young novelist that it was possible to approach America critically yet openly.

1939

483 Untermeyer, Louis. "The Bad Boy of Baltimore." In FROM ANOTHER WORLD: THE AUTOBIOGRAPHY OF LOUIS UNTERMEYER, 184-205. New York: Harcourt, Brace.
> Recalls their friendship and prints excerpts from several letters. See index for other references.

1943

484 Smith, H. Allen. LIFE IN A PUTTY KNIFE FACTORY, 170-77. Garden City, NY: Doubleday, Doran and Company.
> Recollections by an interviewer of HLM.

485 Tully, Jim. "H.L. Mencken." In A DOZEN AND ONE, 229-42. Hollywood, CA: Murray and Gee.

Reminiscences by a friend and writer whom HLM encouraged.

486 Wilson, Edmund, ed. THE SHOCK OF RECOGNITION: THE DEVELOPMENT OF LITERATURE IN THE UNITED STATES RECORDED BY THE MEN WHO MADE IT. New York: Doubleday, Doran and Company.
Profile of HLM (1155-59) heads a selection of his essays.

1948

487 Patterson, Grove. I LIKE PEOPLE: THE AUTO-BIOGRAPHY OF GROVE PATTERSON, 276-78. New York: Random House. Reprint. 1954.
A brief reminisce by a fellow newspaperman and editor of the Toledo *BLADE*.

1950

488 Kemler, Edgar. THE IRREVERENT MR. MENCKEN. Boston: Little, Brown.
Emphasis is on Mencken the iconoclast. Reissued in paperback, 1963.

489 Knopf, Alfred A. "Reminiscences of Hergesheimer, Van Vechten, and Mencken." *YALE UNIVERSITY LIBRARY GAZETTE* 24 (April): 145-64.
HLM "has probably influenced me more than any one else ... " (157). Address delivered 22 February 1950 at Sterling Memorial Library.

490 Manchester, William. DISTURBER OF THE PEACE: THE LIFE OF H.L. MENCKEN. Introduction by Gerald W. Johnson. New York: Harper and Brothers.
The author's M.A. thesis (Missouri) forms the basis of this biography. Issued by Andrew Melrose (London) in 1952 with new title, THE SAGE OF BALTIMORE: THE LIFE AND RIOTOUS TIMES OF H.L. MENCKEN. First edition reissued in paperback by Collier Books (New York), 1962; second edition with new introduction by the author published by University of Massachusetts Press (Amherst), 1986.

491 Van Vechten, Carl. "Random Notes on Mr. Mencken of Baltimore." *YALE UNIVERSITY LIBRARY GAZETTE* 24 (April): 165-71.
    Includes excerpts from HLM's letters to the author.

1951

492 Dreiser, Helen. MY LIFE WITH DREISER, 114-18. Cleveland and New York: World Publishing.
    Recalls a visit to 1524 Hollins Street.

1954

493 Hecht, Ben. A CHILD OF THE CENTURY. New York: Simon.
    Fond memories of HLM's words and deeds of bravery, of his unflagging intellectual energy, and of his help and influence during Hecht's early writing career. See index.

494 Stone, Edward. "Baltimore's Friendly Dragon." *GEORGIA REVIEW* 9 (Fall): 347-53.
    The author recalls HLM's assistance while writing his M.A. thesis on the Sage's debt to Nietzsche, and a subsequent personal meeting.

1956

495 Angoff, Charles. H.L. MENCKEN: A PORTRAIT FROM MEMORY. New York: Thomas Yoseloff.
    Although the author admits his own subjective role, this work should be read critically, for Angoff's word on HLM is generally discredited by other HLM associates and scholars.

496 Cooke, Alistair. "The Last Happy Days of H.L. Mencken." *ATLANTIC MONTHLY* 197 (May): 33-38.
    Recollections of the 1948 presidential conventions, the last ones HLM covered for the Baltimore *SUNPAPERS*.

497 Farrell, James T. "Personal Memories of H.L. Mencken." *NEW LEADER* 39 (13 February): 7.

498 McHugh, Robert P. "The Last Days of Mencken." *AMERICAN MERCURY* 83 (July): 17-20.
    Recalls an interview with HLM slyly obtained.

499 O'Hara, John. "Appointment with O'Hara." *COLLIERS* 137 (13 April): 6, 8.
    Remembers meeting HLM, and wonders at the American capacity for tolerance, since none of HLM's many enemies ever shot him or even put a pie in his face. Also compares the satirist to Will Rogers.

1957

500 Nathan, George Jean. "The Happiest Days of H.L. Mencken." *ESQUIRE* 48 (25 October): 146-50.
    Reviews high moments of their friendship. Partially reprinted as "The Wit: H.L. Mencken" in *ESQUIRE'S WORLD OF HUMOR* (New York: Esquire; Harper and Pow, 1964).

1958

501 Durr, Robert Allen. "The Last Days of H.L. Mencken." *YALE REVIEW* 48 (Autumn): 58-77.
    A personal glimpse into HLM's daily life by one who saw him often in his last year.

502 Smith, H. Allen. "The Most Unforgettable Character I've Met." *READER'S DIGEST* 73 (December): 93-97.
    Quotes HLM on government and women; recalls their meetings and states that "many people believe that Henry L. Mencken was a gross and evil man, satanical and anti-social. Yet the plain truth is that he was a good man, one of the most polite and thoughtful gentlemen who ever wore shoe leather" (94).

1959

503 Knopf, Alfred A. "For Henry With Love." *ATLANTIC MONTHLY* 203 (May): 50-54.
    A personal memoir by HLM's friend and publisher.

504 Thurber, James. "Mencken and Nathan and Ross."
In THE YEARS WITH ROSS, 70-85. Boston and
Toronto: Little, Brown.
   Begins with a recollection of a dinner
party that included HLM, George Jean
Nathan, and Harold Ross, then moves on
to a discussion of Ross as editor of the
NY.

1960

505 Walt, James. "Morning, Noon, and Night."
MICHIGAN ALUMNUS QUARTERLY REVIEW 66
(27 February): 138-45.
   This and a subsequent essay in the same
periodical, "Shadows at Noon: Mencken in
the Twenties" (21 May 1960): 220-29, are
announced as excerpts from a biography in
progress, but the book has yet to be published.

1961

506 Gingrich, Arnold. "How to Become the Second-Best Authority on Almost Anything." *ESQUIRE* 55 (April): 6.
   Memories of an evening spent with HLM and Theodore Dreiser.

1962

507 DeKruif, Paul. THE SWEEPING WIND: A MEMOIR.
New York: Harcourt, Brace.
   The doctor-turned-writer mentions HLM
fondly and often. See pages 7, 8, 29, 37,
46-47, 53, 64, 66, 76, 84, 85, 88, 91,
125-26, 130, 133, 135-36, 141, 157, 159,
203, 238.

508 Krutch, Joseph Wood. MORE LIVES THAN ONE. New
York: William Sloane.
   Recollections of HLM, Nathan, the *SS*,
and the Scopes trial; also of HLM's
comments on writing in general, the
author's in particular. See index for
references.

Biographies

509 Nathan, Adele Gutman. "Mencken and the Little Theatre Movement." In two parts. *MENCKENIANA* 3 and 4 (Fall, Winter): 9-11, 4-6.
    The story behind the first Baltimore performance of THE ARTIST [20].

510 Sinclair, Mary Craig. SOUTHERN BELLE. Memorial Edition. Phoenix: Sinclair Press.
    The wife of Socialist writer Upton Sinclair recalls one of HLM's visits to them as well as the two men's disagreements concerning Prohibition. See index.

511 Sinclair, Upton. THE AUTOBIOGRAPHY OF UPTON SINCLAIR. New York: Harcourt, Brace, and World.
    Recalls moments of friendship and debate (chiefly over Prohibition) with HLM. See index.

1963

512 Angoff, Charles. "Mencken: Prejudices and Prophecies." *SATURDAY REVIEW* 46 (10 August): 44-45.
    Recalls HLM's opinions of various periodicals of the day, particularly *RD*, *TIME*, the *NY*, *PT*, and the *NATION*. His comments that HLM disparaged *RD* are soundly refuted by Henry J. Freyliger, Alfred A. Knopf, and DeWitt Wallace in the "Letters to the Editor" section of *SR* 46 (12 October 1963): 48-49. Angoff's essay is reprinted in his TONE OF THE TWENTIES AND OTHER ESSAYS (New York: A.S. Barnes, 1966).

513 Babcock, C. Morton. "H.L. Mencken's 'Circus Days.'" *MENCKENIANA* 7 (Fall): 9-11.
    On HLM's clowning personality.

514 Sheean, Vincent. DOROTHY AND RED. Boston: Houghton Mifflin.
    On journalist Dorothy Thompson, her husband Sinclair Lewis, and their acquaintance with HLM. See index.

515 Smith, H. Allen. A SHORT HISTORY OF FINGERS
     (AND OTHER STATE PAPERS). Boston and Toronto:
     Little, Brown.
        See "A Friend in Baltimore" (76-93) and
     "A Wink at a Homely Girl" (94-100).

516 Wagner, Philip M. "Mencken Remembered."
     AMERICAN SCHOLAR 32 (Spring): 256-74.
        By Baltimore SUN editor and junior friend
     to the Sage.

                        1964

517 Angoff, Charles. "H.L. Mencken: A Postscript."
     SOUTH ATLANTIC QUARTERLY 63 (Spring): 227-39.
        Biographical anecdotes, particularly
     regarding HLM's relationship with his
     publisher Alfred A. Knopf, wife Sara
     Haardt, and friends George Jean Nathan and
     Philip Goodman. Reader beware, for Angoff
     is known to have stretched the truth in
     much that he wrote about HLM. Reprinted
     in SAQ 76 (August 1977): 466-78 and in
     Angoff's TONE OF THE TWENTIES AND OTHER
     ESSAYS (New York: A.S. Barnes, 1966).

518 Hecht, Ben. "About Mencken." In LETTERS FROM
     BOHEMIA, 68-83. Garden City, NY: Doubleday.
        Recalls meetings with HLM and his en-
     couragement for the young writer, re-
     printing a sampling of their correspond-
     ence.

519 Krutch, Joseph Wood. "This Was Mencken: An
     Appreciation." In IF YOU DON'T MIND MY SAYING
     SO ... ESSAYS ON MAN AND NATURE, 149-54. With
     a Foreword by John K. Hutchens. New York:
     William Sloane.
        Praise for HLM's prose; first published in
     the NATION 182 (11 February 1956): 109-10.
     Reprinted in [582].

520 Owens, Hamilton. "The SUNPAPERS' History."
     MENCKENIANA 12 (Winter): 3-4.
        HLM served as general editor of Gerald W.
     Johnson's history of the newspaper written
     in celebration of its centennial [14].

Biographies

> The following pages reprint several letters that passed between HLM and Johnson during the project.

1965

521 Dolmetsch, Carl R. "Mencken in Virginia." *MENCKENIANA* 13 (Spring): 6-9.
On HLM's relationship to his second favorite state and some of its literati.

522 Mayfield, Sara. "Days of Grace." *MENCKENIANA* 15 (Fall): 8-11.
On her early acquaintance with HLM and Sara Haardt.

523 Pouder, G.H. "Mencken and Cabell." *MENCKENIANA* 15 (Fall): 1-5.

524 Swanberg, W.A. "Mencken and Dreiser." *MENCKENIANA* 15 (Fall): 6-8.

1966

525 Oppenheimer, George. THE VIEW FROM THE SIXTIES. New York: David McKay.
Memories of the HLM of the twenties by a Knopf editor. See index.

526 West, Herbert Faulkner. THE IMPECUNIOUS AMATEUR LOOKS BACK: THE AUTOBIOGRAPHY OF A BOOKMAN. Hanover, NH: Westholm.
Memories of HLM's wit, of the two men's friendship, and of the creation of the Dartmouth College collection of Menckeniana. See index for references.

1967

527 Owens, Hamilton. "Address on Opening of the Mencken Room, April 17, 1956." *MENCKENIANA* 23 (Fall): 4-9.

1968

528 Johns, Bud. THE OMBIBULOUS MR. MENCKEN: A DRINKING BIOGRAPHY. San Francisco: Synergistic Press.

A brief, fun whirl through information and pictures concerning HLM's recreational drinking.

529 Mayfield, Sara. THE CONSTANT CIRCLE: H.L. MENCKEN AND HIS FRIENDS. New York: Delacorte Press.
A portrait of HLM and his intimates by one among that number during his middle years and beyond.

1969

530 Anderson, Charles R. "Mencken's Last Blast: A Reminiscence." *MENCKENIANA* 31 (Fall): 4-7.
On one of HLM's last lectures.

531 Anderson, Sherwood. SHERWOOD ANDERSON'S MEMOIRS: A CRITICAL EDITION. Edited by Ray Louis White. Chapel Hill: University of North Carolina Press.
Anderson recalls HLM's reaction to WINESBURG, OHIO, among other moments. See index for references.

532 Bode, Carl. MENCKEN. Carbondale and Edwardsville: Southern Illinois University Press.
Probably the best biography available to date. Reissued in paperback, Baltimore and London: Johns Hopkins University Press, 1986.

533 Cheslock, Louis. "A Little Light Music." *MENCKENIANA* 31 (Fall): 7-10.
On the Saturday Night Club.

534 Fishbein, Morris. "Henry Mencken and the *AMERICAN MERCURY*." In MORRIS FISHBEIN, M.D.: AN AUTOBIOGRAPHY, 118-23. Garden City, NY: Doubleday.
Recalls writing several medical articles and a short story for the magazine. See index for other references.

1970

535 Dorsey, John. "The Writer Never Gives Up." Baltimore *SUNDAY SUN MAGAZINE* (29 March): 4, 6-7.
> Maryland novelist James M. Cain recalls HLM and Sara Haardt.

536 Dunlap, Richard L. "The Sage at Dusk: An Account of H.L. Mencken's Last Interview." *MENCKENIANA* 35 (Fall): 7-10.

537 Shaw, Bynum. "Scopes Reviews the Monkey Trial." *ESQUIRE* 74 (November): 86, 88, 90, 94.
> Now retired, the man who tested a Tennessee anti-evolutionism statute recalls the trial's most famous and outspoken journalist, HLM.

1971

538 Gingrich, Arnold. NOTHING BUT PEOPLE: THE EARLY DAYS AT *ESQUIRE*, A PERSONAL HISTORY, 1928-1958. New York: Crown.
> Glances backward to friendships with HLM and George Jean Nathan and to skirmishes with the forces of censorship in the "Hatrack" and other incidents. See index.

539 Mayfield, Sara. EXILES FROM PARADISE: ZELDA AND SCOTT FITZGERALD. New York: Delacorte Press.
> Refers often to the pair's association with HLM, Sara Haardt, the *SS*, and the *AM*. See index.

540 Stenerson, Douglas C. H.L. MENCKEN: ICONOCLAST FROM BALTIMORE. Chicago: University of Chicago Press.
> Analyzes HLM's temperament and his relationship to his times.

1972

541 Butcher, Fanny. "H.L. Mencken." In MANY LIVES --ONE LOVE, 399-410. New York: Harper and Row.

Recollections of friend "Heinie" from the Chicago *TRIBUNE's* literary editor. See index for other references.

542   Saroyan, William. "Hollins Street, Baltimore, 1940." In PLACES WHERE I'VE DONE TIME, 152-54. New York: Praeger.
Briefly recalls a visit to HLM.

1973

543   Smith, H. Allen. "Mencken: A Memorandum." In LOW MAN RIDES AGAIN, 246-51. Garden City, NY: Doubleday.
Recounts a 1941 visit to HLM in Baltimore.

1974

544   Cheslock, Louis. "Some Personal Memories of H.L.M." *MENCKENIANA* 49 (Spring): 3-11.
Lecture delivered 15 September 1973 at EPFL by the friend with whom HLM most shared his love of music.

545   Dolmetsch, Carl. "Mencken, Henry Louis." In ENCYCLOPEDIA OF AMERICAN BIOGRAPHY, 752-53. Edited by John A. Garraty and Jerome L. Sternstein. New York: Harper and Row.

546   Keuhl, Linda. "Talk With Mr. Knopf." *NEW YORK TIMES BOOK REVIEW* (24 February): 2-3, 12, 14, 16, 18, 20.
The paragraphs in which the publisher recalls HLM are reprinted in *MENCKENIANA* 50 (Summer 1974): 6.

547   Wagner, Philip. "H.L. Mencken." In AMERICAN WRITERS: A COLLECTION OF LITERARY BIOGRAPHIES, 99-121. Edited by Leonard Unger. Vol. III. New York: Charles Scribner's Sons.

1975

548   Manchester, William. "The Last Years of H.L. Mencken." *ATLANTIC MONTHLY* 236 (October): 82-90.

549 Strode, Hudson. THE ELEVENTH HOUSE: MEMOIRS. New York and London: Harcourt, Brace, Jovanovich.
    The playwright recalls his admiration for and meetings with HLM. See index.

550 Wilson, Edmund. THE TWENTIES: FROM NOTEBOOKS AND DIARIES OF THE PERIOD. Edited with introduction by Leon Edel. New York: Farrar, Straus, and Giroux.
    Fellow journalist and literary critic recalls HLM and his influence on the era.

1976

551 Farrell, James T. "A Chance Meeting with Mencken and [Edgar Lee] Masters." In JAMES T. FARRELL: LITERARY ESSAYS, 1954-1974, 79-83. Collected and edited by Jack Alan Robbins. Port Washington, NY, and London: Kennikat Press.

1977

552 Abhau, W.C. "Cousin Harry." MENCKENIANA 63 (Fall): 2-4.

553 Bowden, Henry Warner. "Mencken, Henry Louis." In DICTIONARY OF AMERICAN RELIGIOUS BIOGRAPHY, 302-04. Westport, CT: Greenwood Press.
    This thumbnail biographical sketch mentions the Scopes trial, during which HLM battled the forces of fundamentalism.

554 Cooke, Alistair. "H.L. Mencken: The Public and the Private Face." In SIX MEN, 83-117. New York: Knopf.

555 Sabo, William J. "An Interview with Rear Admiral William C. Abhau, U.S.N. (Ret.), Cousin of H.L. Mencken." MENCKENIANA 62 (Summer): 7-12.
    Recollections from one of the family.

1980

556 Dolmetsch, Carl. "'HLM' and 'GJN': The Editorial Partnership Re-examined." MENCKENIANA 75 (Fall): 29-39.

Makes use of information gleaned from the HLM correspondence opened in 1971 by the New York Public Library to correct ideas set forth by previous biographies. See Knopf's response [1105].

557   Fitzpatrick, Vincent, and Frederick N. Rasmussen. "American Letters' Unsettled Debt: Mencken and Printing." MENCKENIANA 75 (Fall): 21-29.
HLM as devotee of the printing press, beginning with a gift from his father in 1888.

558   Sandler, Gilbert. "The Mount Washington Days of H.L. Mencken." MENCKENIANA 74 (Summer): 1-6.
Background on HLM's boyhood summers.

1982

559   Miles, Elton. "H.L. Mencken." In DICTIONARY OF LITERARY BIOGRAPHY. Vol. 11, part 2: AMERICAN HUMORISTS: 1800-1950, 323-31. Edited by Stanley Trachtenberg. Detroit, MI: Gale Research Company.

1983

560   Haugen, Einar. "The Three Faces of Mencken." MENCKENIANA 86 (Summer): 1-6.
Recalls HLM as linguist, writer, and conversationalist.

561   Thaler, David S. "H.L. Mencken and the Baltimore Polytechnic Institute." MENCKENIANA 87 (Fall): 10-13.
Sketch of HLM's schooldays.

1984

562   McElveen, J. James. "H.L. Mencken." In DICTIONARY OF LITERARY BIOGRAPHY. Vol. 29, AMERICAN NEWSPAPER JOURNALISTS, 1926-1950, 223-40. Edited by Perry J. Ashley. Detroit, MI: Gale Research Company.

F. BOOKS AND PAMPHLETS

1920

563 H.L. MENCKEN: FANFARE. New York: Knopf.
Pamphlet containing Burton Rascoe, "Fanfare" [769], Vincent O'Sullivan, "The American Critic" [778], and F.C. Henderson (HLM), "Bibliography" [445].

1925

564 Van Roosbroeck, Gustave L. THE REINCARNATION OF H.L. MENCKEN. New York: The Institute of French Studies, Columbia University.
This pamphlet associates HLM with an eighteenth-century tradition of skepticism in which even his ancestor Johann Burckhardt Mencke participated.

1926

565 Logan, J.D. A LITERARY CHAMELEON: A NEW ESTIMATE OF MR. H.L. MENCKEN. Milwaukeee, WI: Privately printed.
On the critic's "mental colorization," the continual flux of his mind (15).

566 Salisbury, William. THE BALTIMORE PHENOMENON. New Rochelle, NY: Independent Publishing.
Reprint of criticisms first published as "Mencken, the Foe of Beauty," AP 1 (July): 34-49.

1927

567 Harrison, Joseph B. A SHORT VIEW OF MENCKENISM IN MENCKENESE. Seattle: University of Washington Bookstore.

1929

568 Schmidt, W.E.F. MENCKEN, MONKEYS, AND MEN. Des Moines, IA: Pearl Publishing.
Part 2 focuses on the critic's favorite words and phrases.

1931

569 Daly, Joseph A. MENCKEN AND EINSTEIN LOOK AT RELIGION. New York: The Paulist Press. The first section of this pamphlet is on HLM; suggests that his criticism of religion results from over-intellectualizing what cannot be comprehended by the mind.

1962

570 Singleton, M.K. H.L. MENCKEN AND THE *AMERICAN MERCURY* ADVENTURE. Durham, NC: Duke University Press. Thorough, valuable history of the magazine's early years--its conception, birth, management, contents, contributors, and reception.

1966

571 Nolte, William H. H.L. MENCKEN: LITERARY CRITIC. Middletown, CT: Wesleyan University Press. Summary and analysis of HLM's literary criticism, especially as seen in cultural and historical contexts. Issued in paperback in 1967 by the University of Washington Press.

1967

572 Forgue, Guy Jean. H.L. MENCKEN: L'HOMME, L'OEUVRE, L'INFLUENCE. Paris: Minard Lettres Modernes. On the man, his work, and his influence. In French.

1969

573 Nolte, William H. THE MERRILL GUIDE TO H.L. MENCKEN: AN ESSAY. Columbus, OH: Merrill Publishing.

Books and Pamphlets

1974

574 Hobson, Fred C., Jr. SERPENT IN EDEN: H.L. MENCKEN AND THE SOUTH. Chapel Hill: University of North Carolina Press.
> On HLM's curious relationship with the American South. Considers the ways in which his notorious "Sahara of the Bozart" [31] contributed to the flowering of the Southern renascence.

1977

575 Williams, W.H.A. H.L. MENCKEN. Boston: G.K. Hall.
> Compresses the most important biographical and critical information into a small, useful volume. Part of Twayne's United States Authors Series.

1978

576 Douglas, George H. H.L. MENCKEN: CRITIC OF AMERICAN LIFE. Hamden, CT: Archon Books.
> Assesses HLM's attitude toward America, especially as it compares with that of others before and since him.

577 Fecher, Charles A. MENCKEN: A STUDY OF HIS THOUGHT. New York: Knopf.
> On HLM the philosopher, literary critic, political analyst, and prose stylist.

1980

578 Dorsey, John, ed. ON MENCKEN. New York: Knopf.
> Combines essays from prominent HLM associates and scholars with several reprinted essays and letters by HLM. Published on the occasion of HLM's birthday centennial. Contains:
> William Manchester, "Mencken in Person"
> Huntington Cairns, "Mencken of Baltimore"
> Alistair Cooke, "Mencken and the English Language"

Charles A. Fecher, "The Comfortable
   Bourgeois: The Thought of H.L.
   Mencken"
Malcolm Moos, "Mencken, Politics, and
   Politicians"
William H. Nolte, "The Literary Critic"
Carl Bode, "Mencken in His Letters"
Alfred A. Knopf, "H.L. Mencken:
   A Memoir"

579 Wingate, P.J., ed. H.L. MENCKEN'S UN-NEGLECTED ANNIVERSARY. Hockessin, DE: Holly Press.
Reprints HLM's "A Neglected Anniversary" [32], "Melancholy Reflections," "Hymn to the Truth" [92], and W.P. Jerome's "A Baltimore Episcopalian" [1029]. Other chapters by the editor are on HLM's love of hoaxes and on the many writers who continue to take his "history" of the bathtub as truth.

1984

580 Martin, Edward A. H.L. MENCKEN AND THE DEBUNKERS. Athens: University of Georgia Press.
Analyzes the satire practiced by HLM and other American humorists, such as Don Marquis and Sinclair Lewis, during this century's first three decades.

581 Scruggs, Charles. THE SAGE IN HARLEM: H.L. MENCKEN AND THE BLACK WRITERS OF THE 1920'S. Baltimore: Johns Hopkins University Press.
Separates HLM's real attitudes toward blacks from the legendary ones; examines his contributions to the development of the Harlem Renaissance.

1987

582 Stenerson, Douglas C., ed. CRITICAL ESSAYS ON H.L. MENCKEN. Boston: G.K. Hall.
Reprints a number of essays on HLM and includes two new ones written for this collection (see Hobson and Scruggs, below).
Contains:

George Jean Nathan, "On H.L. Mencken" [583]
Elizabeth Shepley Sergeant, "H.L. Mencken" [599]
Gerald W. Johnson, "Henry L. Mencken" [901]
"An Interpretation of Shaw" Reviews GEORGE BERNARD SHAW: HIS PLAYS [2]
"An Account of Nietzsche" Reviews THE PHILOSOPHY OF FRIEDRICH NIETZSCHE [3]
Burton Rascoe, "Fanfare" [769]
Randolph Bourne, "H.L. Mencken" [768]
Stuart P. Sherman, "Beautifying American Literature" [770]
James Weldon Johnson, "American Genius and Its Locale" [771]
Francis Hackett, "The Living Speech" [775]
Ernest A. Boyd, "American Literature or Colonial?" [781]
Percy H. Boynton, "American Literature and the Tart Set" [782]
Hunter T. Stagg, "PREJUDICES: SECOND SERIES," a review [404]
Edmund Wilson, "H.L. Mencken" [798]
Walter Lippmann, "H.L. Mencken" [823]
George S. Schuyler, "Views and Reviews"
Irving Babbitt, "The Critic and American Life" [835]
I.J. Semper, "H.L. Mencken: Doctor Rhetoricus" [629]
Reinhold Niebuhr, "TREATISE ON THE GODS," a review [12]
"Mr. Mencken Leaves the *MERCURY*" [853]
J.B. Dudek, "A Philological Romance" Reviews THE AMERICAN LANGUAGE, 4th edition [7]
Louis Kronenberger, "H.L. Mencken" [670]
Hamilton Owens, "HAPPY DAYS," a review [867]
Hamilton Owens, "NEWSPAPER DAYS," a review [867]
Harold Whitehall, "Linguistic Patriot"
Van Wyck Brooks, "Mencken in Baltimore" [662]

Joseph Wood Krutch, "This Was Mencken: An Appreciation" [519]
Edward A. Martin, "H.L. Mencken's Poetry" [929]
Douglas C. Stenerson, "The 'Forgotten Man' of H.L. Mencken" [947]
M.K. Singleton, "Rhetoric and Vision in Mencken's Satire: The 'Medieval' Mob" [691]
Raven I. McDavid, Jr. "The Impact of Mencken on American Linguistics" [943]
Carl Dolmetsch, "Mencken as a Magazine Editor" [953]
Vincent Fitzpatrick, "Private Voices of Public Men: The Mencken-Dreiser Inscriptions," a revised version of [1102]
Hobson, Fred. "'This Hellawful South': Mencken and the Late Confederacy"
Scruggs, Charles. "H.L. Mencken and James Weldon Johnson: Two Men Who Helped Shape a Renaissance"

G. CHAPTERS AND SECTIONS OF BOOKS

1920

583 Nathan, George Jean. "On H.L. Mencken." In THE BORZOI 1920: BEING A SORT OF RECORD OF FIVE YEARS' PUBLISHING, 34-36. New York: Knopf.
Reveals the key to their long friendship: "mutual approval" (34). Reprinted in [582].

1922

584 Pattee, Fred Lewis. "A Critic in C Major." In SIDE-LIGHTS ON AMERICAN LITERATURE, 56-97. New York: Century.
Credits HLM with energy and flair as a journalist, but denies that he is a first-rate literary critic.

585 Sherman, Stuart P. "Mr. Mencken, the Jeune Fille, and the New Spirit in Letters." In AMERICANS, 1-12. New York: Charles Scribner's Sons.
HLM "has no heart" (9); the modern young reader "has no soul" (3); and the new spirit in letters is distinctly less satisfying aesthetically than the old one.

586 Untermeyer, Louis. HEAVENS. New York: Harcourt, Brace.
See especially pages 75-80, in which the author parodies HLM as he might react to afterlife in heavenly spheres.

1923

587 Harris, Frank. "H.L. Mencken, Critic." In CONTEMPORARY PORTRAITS: FOURTH SERIES, 143-54. New York: Brentano's.

588 Scheffaner, Herman George. DAS LAND GOTTES: DAS GESICHT DES NEUEN AMERIKA. Hannover: Paul Steegemann.

See especially the chapter entitled "Das Politische Leben" ("The Political Life"), in which pages 119-25 are devoted to HLM. In German.

1924

589 Boynton, Percy H. "The Younger Set and the Puritan Bogey." In SOME CONTEMPORARY AMERICANS: THE PERSONAL EQUATION IN LITERATURE, 231-41. Chicago: University of Chicago Press.
> HLM as the "high priest" (234) of the young American iconoclasts.

590 Farrar, John, ed. "H.L. Mencken." In THE LITERARY SPOTLIGHT, 108-15. With portrait caricatures by William Gropper. New York: George H. Doran.
> Personal profile of HLM written anonymously by Burton Rascoe and reprinted in his BEFORE I FORGET [644].

591 Van Doren, Carl. "Smartness and Light: H.L. Mencken." In MANY MINDS, 120-35. New York: Knopf.
> Discusses HLM as one whose chief gift is his ability to tap "a strong vein of discontent with democracy" already alive in the nation (123).

1925

592 Calverton, V.F. "The Vandeville Critic, H.L. Mencken." In THE NEWER SPRIT: A SOCIOLOGICAL CRITICISM OF LITERATURE, 165-79. New York: Boni and Liveright.
> Accuses HLM of superficiality.

593 Spies, Heinrich. KULTUR UND SPRACHE IM NEUEN ENGLAND. Leipzig: Teubner.
> In his German-language study of culture and speech in New England, the translator of the German edition of THE AMERICAN LANGUAGE [7] draws often upon HLM's work. See index.

1926

594 Goldberg, Isaac. THE THEATRE OF GEORGE JEAN NATHAN. New York: Simon and Schuster.
References to HLM abound, as do references to the *SS* and the *AM;* includes some scenarios the two men considered for plays once they completed their HELIOGABALUS [10]. See index.

595 Michaud, Régis. PANORAMA DE LA LITTERATURE AMERICAINE CONTEMPORAINE. Paris: Simon Kra.
See pages 232-34, which sketch HLM's role as a leader of rebellious American intellectuals. In French.

596 Sherman, Stuart P. "H.L. Mencken as Liberator." In CRITICAL WOODCUTS, 235-43. With illustrations by Bertrand Zadig. New York and London: Charles Scribner's Sons.
Favorable comparison between HLM and Heinrich Heine soon gives way to an attack of the former on a number of counts.

597 Strachey, J. St. Loe. AMERICAN SOUNDINGS, 193-202. New York: D. Appleton.
Discusses HLM's brand of satire, especially as manifested in the *AM*'s "Americana" department [118].

1927

598 Elgström, Anna Lenah, and Gustaf Collijn. "En Intervju om Amerikansk Litteratur." In U.S.A.: LIV OCH TEATER, 114-26. Stockholm: Albert Bonniers.
On HLM's hometown of Baltimore and his favorite literary figures. In Swedish.

599 Sergeant, Elizabeth Shepley. "H.L. Mencken: He Must and Will Be Titan." In FIRE UNDER THE ANDES, 239-57. New York: Knopf. Reprint. Port Washington, NY: Kennikat Press, 1966.
Mixes personal reminiscence with commentary on HLM's ideas and how they influenced his era. First published in the *NATION* 124 (16 February 1927): 174-78. Reprinted in [582].

Chapters and Sections of Books

600 Sinclair, Upton. MONEY WRITES! New York: Albert and Charles Boni.
Chapter VIII, "Artificial Selection" (34-38), is on HLM as editor of the *AM* and therefore in a powerful position to say which writers shall succeed and which shall not. Chapter XXVI, "Boobus Americanus" (129-35), is on HLM as a personality more interested in amusing and shocking audiences than in telling them the facts.

601 Takagaki, Matsuo. AMERIKA BUNGAKU. Tokyo: Kenkyu-sha.
Includes a chapter on HLM in the context of American literature, and several other brief references; index and bibliography are in English, text in Japanese.

1928

602 Benchley, Robert. "Mr. Mencken Reviews Mr. Nathan and Vice Versa." In 20,000 LEAGUES UNDER THE SEA, OR DAVID COPPERFIELD, 95-97. With illustrations by Gluyas Williams. New York: Henry Holt.
Parodies HLM and Nathan; the "vice versa" is the following chapter, "Clinical Notes," 98-100.

603 Findahl, Theo. MANHATTAN BABYLON: EN BOK OM NEW YORK IDAG. Oslo: Gyldendal Norsk.
See pages 72-79 on the American man of letters. In Norwegian.

604 Hays, Arthur Garfield. "Freedom of the Press." In LET FREEDOM RING, 157-92. New York: Boni and Liveright.
The lawyer who defended HLM and the *AM* against the charges filed by the secretary of the Boston Watch and Ward Society, J. Frank Chase, in the "Hatrack" case here tells his side of the story.

605 More, Paul Elmer. THE DEMON OF THE ABSOLUTE. Volume 1 of THE NEW SHELBURNE ESSAYS. Princeton, NJ: Princeton University Press.
A portion of the title essay (2-11) discusses HLM as one among "the foes of

standards" (6) in literary criticism. Appeared in slightly different form in "The Modern Currents in American Literature," *FORUM* 79 (January 1928): 127-36.

606 Shaw, Charles Green. "H.L. Mencken." In THE LOW-DOWN, 51-61. New York: Holt.
Portrait of HLM's personality and lifestyle.

607 Williams, Michael. "A Prayer for Mr. Mencken." In CATHOLICISM AND THE MODERN MIND, 223-38. New York: Dial Press.
The editor of *COMMONWEAL* places HLM "on the side of the angels" (238).

1929

608 Canby, Henry Seidel. "H.L. Mencken." In AMERICAN ESTIMATES, 58-61. New York: Harcourt, Brace.
On HLM's attitude toward the American middle class and democracy as evidenced by his 1925 collection of AMERICANA [407].

609 DeCasseres, Benjamin. THE SUPERMAN IN AMERICA. Seattle: University of Washington Chapbooks.
See especially pages 15-18 for comments comparing HLM to such fellow advocates of the superior man as James Huneker and Friedrich Nietzsche.

610 DiRobilant, Irene. VITA AMERICANA (STATI UNITI DEL NORD-AMERICA). Torino, Italy: Fratelli Bocca.
On HLM and the *AM*; in Italian. See index.

611 Levinson, André. "L'Ironie de H.L. Mencken." In FIGURES AMERICAINES, 95-109. Paris: Victor Attinger.
On HLM the humorist. In French.

612 Rascoe, Burton. A BOOKMAN'S DAYBOOK. Edited by C. Hartley Grattan. New York: Horace Liveright.
Includes "A Psychograph of Mencken" (25-26), "How Mencken and Nathan Play" (81-84), "Pulling Mencken's Leg" (161-62),

"Mencken: Shirtsleeve Autocrat" (195-96), and "Mencken on Eating and Yodelers" (240-41), all reprinted from the New York *HT*.

613 Schmaulhausen, Samuel D. "H.L. Mencken: Idol of the Booboisie." In OUR CHANGING HUMAN NATURE, 214-30. New York: Macaulay.
   One of "Three Psychoanalytic Portraits," this one states in elaborate terms that HLM is no longer all he is often built up to be.

614 Wickham, Harvey. "The Meaning of Mencken." In THE IMPURITANS, 229-34. New York: Dial Press.
   Where HLM goes wrong in considering himself an "impuritan."

1930

615 Cabell, James Branch. "Dreams on Cosmogeny: A Note as to H.L. Mencken." In SOME OF US: AN ESSAY IN EPITAPHS, 105-18. New York: Robert M. McBride.
   HLM is a force in American letters to be reckoned with.

616 Chesterton, G.K. "The Sceptic as Critic." In THE THING: WHY I AM A CATHOLIC, 1-11. New York: Dodd, Mead.
   HLM deserves praise for the strength of his revolutionary spirit but criticism for being too devoid of faith in any set of standards.

617 DeCasseres, Benjamin. MENCKEN AND SHAW: THE ANATOMY OF AMERICA'S VOLTAIRE AND ENGLAND'S OTHER JOHN BULL. New York: Silas Newton.
   The first half is a series of loosely connected observations and opinions on HLM.

618 Pattee, Fred Lewis. "Mencken." In THE NEW AMERICAN LITERATURE, 1890-1930, 415-32. New York and London: Century.
   No-nonsense criticism for HLM the "literary Mussolini" (416).

619 Pearce, Eugene L. "The Counter-Blow." In STATESMEN AND GADFLIES, 85-98. New York: Privately printed.
     An "open letter" to HLM expressing vehement disapproval of his William Jennings Bryan obituary [82].

1931

620 Allen, Frederick Lewis. ONLY YESTERDAY: AN INFORMAL HISTORY OF THE NENETEEN-TWENTIES. New York and London: Harper Brothers.
     Coverage of HLM and the AM in pages 230-44 of the chapter entitled "The Revolt of the Highbrows."

621 Boynton, Percy Holmes. "Mr. Mencken Does His Bit." In THE CHALLENGE OF MODERN CRITICISM, 29-46. Chicago: Thomas S. Rockwell.
     Compares HLM to Edgar Allan Poe: both are "swashbucklers" (33), but the former is successful only because he came along at the right moment in American history.

622 Strunsky, Simeon. THE REDISCOVERY OF JONES, 60-66. Boston: Little, Brown.
     On HLM's views of the common man.

623 Woolf, Leonard. AFTER THE DELUGE: A STUDY OF COMMUNAL PSYCHOLOGY, 258-68. Vol. 1. New York: Harcourt, Brace.
     Criticizes HLM's misguided attack on democracy, chiefly set forth in NOTES ON DEMOCRACY [11].

1932

624 Brooks, Van Wyck. "Mencken and the Prophets." In SKETCHES IN CRITICISM, 26-33. New York: E.P. Dutton.
     Corrects a few of HLM's notions as to why American literature has failed to fulfill the prophecies of such nineteenth-century writers as Ralph Waldo Emerson and Walt Whitman.

625 Chesterton, G.K. "On Mr. Mencken and Fundamentalism." In ALL IS GRIST: A BOOK OF

ESSAYS, 49-53. New York: Dodd. 2nd ed.
London: Methuen, 1933. Reprint. 1967, 1971,
1977.

626 Dudley, Dorothy. DREISER AND THE LAND OF THE
FREE. New York: H. Smith. Reprint. New York:
Beechhurst Press, 1946.
> Includes a profile of HLM (260-66) and various other references pertaining to his relationship with the novelist.

627 Knox, Ronald. "Menckeniana." In BROADCAST
MINDS, 121-53. London: Sheed and Ward.
> Criticism from a clergyman for TREATISE ON THE GODS [12], partly because HLM did not from the beginning "make up his mind whether he was making an attack on religion or an attack on the clergy" (125).

628 Rogers, Cameron. "The Maverick Turned Bell
Mare." In OH SPLENDID APPETITE!, 85-97. New
York: John Day.
> Asserts that HLM's role as mover and shaker has very nearly been fulfilled and that he will soon pass into the background.

629 Semper, I.J. THE RETURN OF THE PRODIGAL AND
OTHER ESSAYS. New York: Edward O'Toole.
> See "H.L. Mencken and Catholicism" (63-85), on TREATISE ON THE GODS [12]; and "H.L. Mencken: Doctor Rhetoricus" (86-111), on HLM as a rhetorician. This last essay is reprinted in [582].

1933

630 Combs, George Hamilton. "H.L. Mencken, the
Celebrant of Cynicism." In THESE AMAZING
MODERNS, 31-52. St. Louis, MO: Bethany Press.
> Delivers a cool indictment of HLM as intolerant though intelligent, full of wit but not humor.

631 Hicks, Granville. THE GREAT TRADITION: AN
INTERPRETATION OF AMERICAN LITERATURE SINCE THE
CIVIL WAR. New York: Macmillan.

Compares HLM with other literary critics of this century's first two decades, pointing out several of his faults. See index.

1934

632 Crandall, Allen. ISAAC GOLDBERG: AN APPRECIATION. Sterling, CO: Privately printed.
Pages 53-58 give background on Goldberg's biography of HLM [476].

633 Partridge, Eric. SLANG TODAY AND YESTERDAY. London: Routledge, 1933. Reprint. New York: Macmillan.
See especially Part IV on American slang, which draws heavily on HLM's treatment of the subject in THE AMERICAN LANGUAGE [7]. See index for other references.

634 Rascoe, Burton, and Groff Conklin, eds. THE SMART SET ANTHOLOGY. New York: Reynal and Hitchcock.
See Rascoe's introduction, pages xiii-xliv.

1935

635 Forsythe, Robert [Kyle S. Crichton]. "In Defense of Mr. Mencken." In REDDER THAN THE ROSE, 1-12. New York: Covici Friede.
Satirizes HLM to the point of sarcasm.

636 Shafer, Robert. PAUL ELMER MORE AND AMERICAN CRITICISM, 114-19. New Haven: Yale University Press.
Contrasts the critic with HLM, much to the latter's disfavor. See index for other brief mentions.

637 Spotswood, Claire Myers. THE UNPREDICTABLE ADVENTURE: A COMEDY OF WOMAN'S INDEPENDENCE. Garden City, NY: Doubleday, Doran and Company.
Chapter 12 (332-54) opens with a parody of HLM.

638 Sullivan, Mark. OUR TIMES: THE UNITED STATES, 1900-1925. Vol. 6 of THE TWENTIES. New York and London: Charles Scribner's Sons.

See pages 413-21 in particular, which profile HLM as a national figure.

1936

639 Gillis, Adolph, and Roland Ketchum. "Henry Louis Mencken: Watchdog of Liberty." In OUR AMERICA: A SURVEY OF CONTEMPORARY AMERICA AS EXEMPLIFIED IN THE LIVES AND ACHIEVEMENTS OF TWENTY-FOUR MEN AND WOMEN DRAWN FROM REPRESENTATIVE FIELDS, 234-50. Boston: Little, Brown.
Profile emphasizing HLM's individualism.

640 Taylor, Walter Fuller. "Naturalism and the Cultural Battle: H.L. Mencken and Sinclair Lewis." In A HISTORY OF AMERICAN LETTERS, 380-90. With Bibliographies by Harry Hartwick. New York: American Book Company.
On HLM's ideas as "corollaries of scientific materialism" (381). See index for other references.

1937

641 Cleaton, Irene and Allen. BOOKS & BATTLES: AMERICAN LITERATURE, 1930-1930. Boston: Houghton Mifflin.
Devotes several short sections to the controversial HLM. See index.

642 Frank, Waldo. "Mr. Mencken, King of the Philistines." In IN THE AMERICAN JUNGLE (1925-1936), 135-39. New York: Farrar and Rinehart.
A debunking of the philosophical debunker.

643 Loggins, Vernon. "Iconoclasm: H.L. Mencken." In I HEAR AMERICA ... LITERATURE IN THE UNITED STATES SINCE 1900, 228-38. New York: Thomas Y. Crowell.
Despite his shortcomings, HLM as a disciple of George Bernard Shaw is an invaluable force of iconoclasm in early twentieth-century American letters. See index for other mentions.

644 Rascoe, Burton. "H.L. Mencken." In BEFORE I FORGET, 438-42. Garden City, NY: Doubleday.

Reprint of a personal portrait written anonymously for John Farrar's THE LITERARY SPOTLIGHT [590]. HLM also mentioned in connection with Rascoe's "Fanfare" [769] and with Stuart P. Sherman, 354-57.

1938

645 Forsythe, Robert [Kyle Samuel Crichton]. "Winken, Blinken and Nod." In READING FROM LEFT TO RIGHT, 74-80. Illustrated by William Gropper. New York: Covici Friede.
    HLM, Nathan, and Ernest Boyd as obsolete figures that refuse to go entirely away.

646 Kagan, Solomon R. LIFE AND LETTERS OF FIELDING H. GARRISON. Boston: The Medico-Historical Press.
    The doctor much admired the literary critic. See index.

647 Pegler, Westbrook. "Farewell to Mencken (1936)." In THE DISSENTING OPINIONS OF MISTER WESTBROOK PEGLER, 312-15. New York: Charles Scribner's Sons.
    On HLM's misplaced loyalties in the presidential campaigns of 1936. Reprinted from the New York WT.

1939

648 Smith, Bernard. FORCES IN AMERICAN CRITICISM: A STUDY IN THE HISTORY OF AMERICAN LITERARY THOUGHT. New York: Harcourt, Brace.
    See pages 304-13 of his chapter on "The War of Traditions" and the index for other references.

649 Van Doren, Carl and Mark. AMERICAN AND BRITISH LITERATURE SINCE 1890, 150-53. 1925. Rev. and enl. New York: Appleton-Century-Crofts. Reprint. 1953.
    Offers a brief look at HLM as a satirist.

1940

650 MacDougall, Curtis D. HOAXES. New York: Macmillan. Reprint. New York: Dover, 1958.

The "bathtub hoax" story [32] retold.
See index.

1941

651 Gold, Michael. "At King Mencken's Court." In
HOLLOW MEN, 11-25. New York: International
Publishers.
Blasts HLM and the *AM* for exhibiting
"intellectual fascism" (25).

1942

652 Footner, Hulbert. "The Sage of West Baltimore." In MARYLAND MAIN AND THE EASTERN
SHORE, 57-71. Illustrated by Louis Ruyl. New
York and London: D. Appleton-Century.
Portrait of HLM as a prominent personality
in the city.

653 Ralbag, J. Howard. "An Answer to H.L.
Mencken." In HOPE FOR HUMANITY. New York:
Victory Publishing.
A rabbi addresses the issues of religion
and atheism.

1946

654 Evans, Bergen. THE NATURAL HISTORY OF
NONSENSE, 258-62. New York: Knopf.
The story of HLM's "bathtub hoax" [32] as
a modern-day version of Swift's "Tale of a
Tub."

655 Holbrook, Stewart H. LOST MEN OF AMERICAN
HISTORY, 340-44. New York: Macmillan.
On HLM's denunciation of Prohibition
during Warren G. Harding's administration.

656 Van Gelder, Robert. "Mencken on Literature and
Politics." In WRITERS AND WRITING, 20-23. New
York: Charles Scribner's Sons.
Reprint of an interview first published in
the New York *TIMES*, 11 February 1940.

657 Wilson, Earl. "Mencken, Ickes, and God." In
PIKES PEEK OR BUST, 54-58. Garden City, NY:
Doubleday.
Professional envy for debunkers HLM,
Harold Ickes, and Westbrook Pegler.

1947

658 Geismar, Maxwell. "H.L. Mencken: On the Dock." In THE LAST OF THE PROVINCIALS: THE AMERICAN NOVEL, 1915-1925, 3-66. Boston: Houghton Mifflin.
    A tough assessment of HLM's thought and attitudes as an index to early twentieth-century America.

1948

659 Cunz, Dieter. THE MARYLAND GERMANS: A HISTORY. Princeton, NJ: Princeton University Press.
    Includes a brief sketch of HLM as one of German descent and German sympathies. See index.

660 Greene, Ward. "The Baltimore Nonpareil." In STAR REPORTERS AND 34 OF THEIR STORIES, 226-55. New York: Random House.
    Background on HLM's coverage of the 1925 Scopes trial, including excerpts from the Baltimore *ES*.

1952

661 Bewley, Marius. "Mencken and the American Language." In THE COMPLEX FATE: HAWTHORNE, HENRY JAMES AND SOME OTHER AMERICAN WRITERS, 193-210. London: Chatto.
    Argues that HLM's philological work is as limited as his literary criticism.

662 Brooks, Van Wyck. "Mencken in Baltimore." In THE CONFIDENT YEARS: 1885-1915, 455-74. New York: E.P. Dutton.
    Profiles HLM in the context of his city and the literature of turn-of-the-century America. Reprinted in [582].

663 Wilson, Edmund. "Mencken's Democratic Man." In THE SHORES OF LIGHT: A LITERARY CHRONICLE OF THE TWENTIES AND THIRTIES, 293-97. New York: Farrar, Straus, and Young.
    Reprint of a review of NOTES ON DEMOCRACY [11] first published in the *NR* 49 (15 December 1926): 110-11. Also appears in Wilsons's A LITERARY CHRONICLE, 1920-1950

(New York: Doubleday, 1952; reprinted 1956). See index for numerous other references to HLM, including those within the noted "All-Star Literary Vaudeville" essay.

664 Wish, Harvey. "The 'Lost Generation' and Henry L. Mencken." In SOCIETY AND THOUGHT IN MODERN AMERICA: A SOCIAL AND INTELLECTUAL HISTORY OF THE AMERICAN PEOPLE FROM 1865, 466-88. New York: Longmans.
American writers of the twenties and their ally HLM encouraged in one another a narcissism that prevented them from seeing their era as it was.

1954

665 Farrell, James T. "Dr. Mencken: Criticus Americanus." In REFLECTIONS AT FIFTY AND OTHER ESSAYS, 42-57. New York: Vanguard Press.
Gives credit and criticism to HLM where due, emphasizing his contribution as a literary critic and a lover of writing. First published in NWW no. 6 (Fall 1954): 64-76.

666 Williams, William Carlos. "An Incredible Neglect Redefined." In SELECTED ESSAYS OF WILLIAM CARLOS WILLIAMS, 170-74. New York: Random House. Reprint. 1969.
Reprint of a review of THE AMERICAN LANGUAGE [7], first published in the NAR 242 (Autumn 1936): 181-84. Also appears in his SELECTED WORKS (New York: Random House, 1954).

1955

667 Hoffman, Frederick J. THE TWENTIES: AMERICAN WRITING IN THE POSTWAR DECADE. Revised edition. New York: Viking.
A penetrating assessment of HLM and the niche he carved into the decade. See index.

668 Kronenberger, Louis. "H.L. Mencken." In THE REPUBLIC OF LETTERS: ESSAYS ON VARIOUS WRITERS, 236-43. New York: Knopf.

HLM played a necessary role, but he could sometimes abuse it. Reprint of "An Ill-Will Tour of the American Mind," first published in the *SRL* 32 (6 August 1949): 38, 40, 42.

1956

669 Sinclair, Upton. THE CUP OF FURY. Great Neck, NY: Channel Press.
An entire chapter and a handful of other references are devoted to the difference of opinion exercised between the author and HLM on the subject of alcohol; mentions also HLM's indirect connection with the suicide of poet and alcoholic George Sterling. See index.

1959

670 Kronenberger, Louis. "H.L. Mencken." In AFTER THE GENTEEL TRADITION: AMERICAN WRITERS SINCE 1910, 100-11. Edited by Malcolm Cowley. 1936. Reprint. Gloucester, MA: Peter Smith.
On HLM's "utter inadequacy" (104) as well as his widespread attraction for his generation. See index for several other references to HLM throughout the volume, as well as a thumbnail biographical sketch. First published in the *NR* 88 (7 October 1936): 243-45. Reprinted in [582].

671 Leary, Lewis. "H.L. Mencken: Changeless Critic in Changing Times." In THE YOUNG REBEL IN AMERICAN LITERATURE, 97-117. Edited by Carl Bode. London: Heinemann. Reprint. New York: Praeger, 1960.
Praises HLM for his "grit" and "resonance," but expresses the belief that his egoism was his downfall (115). Lecture delivered 1957 at London's American Embassy. Reprinted (with slight revisions and a new title, "H.L. Mencken and the Reluctant Human Race") in the author's SOUTHERN EXCURSIONS: ESSAYS ON MARK TWAIN AND OTHERS, 192-208 (Baton Rouge: Louisiana State University Press, 1971).

Chapters and Sections of Books

672 May, Henry F. THE END OF AMERICAN INNOCENCE: A STUDY OF THE FIRST YEARS OF OUR OWN TIME, 1912-1917. New York: Knopf.
Devotes several short sections to HLM as a man of his era. See index.

1960

673 Boorstin, Daniel J. AMERICA AND THE IMAGE OF EUROPE: REFLECTIONS ON AMERICAN THOUGHT. Cleveland and New York: World Publishing.
Briefly discusses HLM's comparisons of the U.S. with Europe. See index.

674 Partridge, Eric. "H.L. Mencken: An Appreciation, 1956." In A CHARM OF WORDS: ESSAYS AND PAPERS ON LANGUAGE, 68-71. New York: Macmillan.

1961

675 Aaron, Daniel. WRITERS ON THE LEFT: EPISODES IN AMERICAN LITERARY COMMUNISM. New York: Harcourt, Brace and World.
HLM "served a country he pretended to despise as a kind of reactionary liberator who cut through the undergrowth of provincialism and prejudice and cleared a path for finer minds. Finally, he outlived his usefulness" (109). See index for other references.

676 Schorer, Mark. SINCLAIR LEWIS: AN AMERICAN LIFE. New York, Toronto, and London: McGraw-Hill.
HLM figures prominently throughout; see index.

1962

677 Spiller, Robert E. "The Critical Rediscovery of America." In A TIME OF HARVEST: AMERICAN LITERATURE 1910-1960, 1-8. Edited by Spiller. New York: Hill and Wang.
Brief look at HLM's critical debates. See also Maxwell Geismar's chapter "Society and the Novel," pages 33-41, which mentions HLM briefly.

1963

678 Davidson, Donald. THE SPYGLASS: VIEWS AND REVIEWS, 1924-1930. Selected and edited by John Tyree Fain. Nashville: Vanderbilt University Press.
"... Mencken, the destroyer, necessary as he may be in his role as an occasional stimulant or a gadfly, is not to be trusted as a purveyor of ideas," though his humor is to be praised (130-31). Review of NOTES ON DEMOCRACY [11], first published 12 December 1926 in the Nashville TENNESSEAN. Also appears in THE SUPERFLOUS MEN: CONSERVATIVE CRITICS OF AMERICAN CULTURE, 1900-1945, edited by Robert M. Crunden (Austin and London: University of Texas Press, 1977).

679 Goldhurst, William. "H.L. Mencken." In F. SCOTT FITZGERALD AND HIS CONTEMPORARIES, 74-104. Cleveland and New York: World Publishing.
On what Fitzgerald learned early in his career from HLM.

680 Simon, John. "A Breath of Smoky Air." In ACID TEST, 227-79. New York: Stein and Day.
Praises the Caedmon recording of an interview with HLM conducted by Donald Howe Kirkley in 1948.

1964

681 Nelson, Frederic. "Ten Days That Shook Baltimore." In BACHELORS ARE PEOPLE, TOO, 146-54. Washington, DC: Public Affairs Press.
On HLM's marriage to Sara Haardt, and on President Franklin D. Roosevelt's rough treatment of the journalist in a speech to the Gridiron Club.

682 Sinclair, Andrew. ERA OF EXCESS: A SOCIAL HISTORY OF THE PROHIBITION MOVEMENT. New York: Harper Colophon Books.
First published as PROHIBITION: THE ERA OF EXCESS (Boston: Little, Brown, 1962); includes numerous references to HLM's opinions on the subject. See index.

683 Yates, Norris W. THE AMERICAN HUMORIST: CONSCIENCE OF THE TWENTIETH CENTURY, 142-64. Ames: Iowa State University Press. Reprint. New York: Citadel, 1965.
Analysis of HLM the poseur.

1965

684 Cargill, Oscar. "Mencken and the South." In TOWARD A PLURALISTIC CRITICISM, 131-40. Carbondale and Edwardsville: Southern Illinois University Press.
Reprint of an article first published in the GaR 6 (Winter 1952): 369-76.

685 Goodfellow, Donald M. "H.L. Mencken: Scourge of the Philistines." In SIX SATIRISTS, 85-100. No. 9 in the Carnegie Series in English. Pittsburgh, PA: Carnegie Institute of Technology.
Biographical and critical essay emphasizing HLM as the blaster of conventional mores and tastes.

686 Rosner, Joseph. "Everybody Vs. Mencken." In THE HATER'S HANDBOOK, 163-66. New York: Delacorte Press. Reprint. 1967.
Quotes several of HLM's antagonists; other references to HLM occur throughout.

687 Swanberg, W.A. DREISER. New York: Charles Scribner's Sons.
This biography is dedicated to "the memory of H.L. Mencken, who knew Dreiser at his best and worst, and fought for the best." See index for numerous references.

688 Wilson, Edmund. THE BIT BETWEEN MY TEETH: A LITERARY CHRONICLE OF 1950-1965. New York: Farrar, Straus and Giroux.
The author's review of the Kemler biography [488], "Mencken Through the Wrong End of the Telescope," first published in the NY 26 (6 May 1950): 102-06 and here reprinted, leads him to remark on the "dazzling ... phenomenon" (29) of the 1920s and on HLM's role in its spirit. Other references occur throughout the book; see index.

Chapters and Sections of Books

1966

689 Dolmetsch, Carl R. THE *SMART SET*: A HISTORY AND ANTHOLOGY. With an Introductory Reminiscence by S.N. Behrman. New York: Dial Press.
Anthology section reprints HLM's "Si Mutare Potest Aethiops Pellum Suam" and (with Nathan) "Répétition Générale" [109].

690 Loos, Anita. A GIRL LIKE I. New York: Viking.
Actress and author of GENTLEMEN PREFER BLONDES fondly recalls her friendship and romance with "Menck," who inspired the book, in the years before his marriage. See pages 21, 55, 131, 132, 137, 145, 146, 150, 163, 213-19, 220, 245, 254, 264-67.

691 Singleton, M.K. "Rhetoric and Vision in Mencken's Satire: The 'Medieval' Mob." In THE TWENTIES: POETRY AND PROSE, 20 CRITICAL ESSAYS, 74-77. Edited by Richard E. Langford and William E. Taylor. Deland, FL: Everett Edwards Press.
Surveys HLM's ideas and stylistic traits with particular emphasis on his use of medieval metaphors. Reprinted in [582].

1967

692 Cowley, Malcolm. THINK BACK ON US ... A CONTEMPORARY CHRONICLE OF THE 1930'S. Edited with introduction by Henry Dan Piper. Carbondale and Edwardsville: Southern Illinois University Press.
Reprints "Mencken: The Former Fugleman" from the *NR* 81 (21 November 1934): 50-51, which discusses HLM's attitude toward proletarian writers (70-74); and "The *SMART SET* Legend" from the *NR* 81 (16 January 1935): 281, a review of Rascoe and Conklin's SMART SET ANTHOLOGY [684] (248-50).

693 O'Connor, Richard. "Bierce and 'My Dear Mencken.'" In AMBROSE BIERCE: A BIOGRAPHY, 291-96. Boston and Toronto: Little, Brown.
Makes a claim for the two writers' similarity. See index for other references.

694 Rubin, Louis D., Jr. "H.L. Mencken and the National Letters." In THE CURIOUS DEATH OF THE NOVEL: ESSAYS IN AMERICAN LITERATURE, 101-19. Baton Rouge: Louisiana State University Press.
Predicts that HLM's role as "a maker and a finder" of good literature will prove more significant to the nation's history than his twenties-era role as "idol-shatterer" (100). See index for other references.

695 Ruland, Richard. THE REDISCOVERY OF AMERICAN LITERATURE: PREMISES OF CRITICAL TASTE, 1900-1940. Cambridge, MA: Harvard University Press. See "H.L. Mencken, Iconoclastic, Conservative: Literature and the Aristocracy of Efficiency" (97-136); and "Exemplum: The Sherman-Mencken Debate" (137-65). The first chapter analyzes HLM's literary, social, and political thought; the second concerns the two critics' different approaches to issues in contemporary fiction, particularly Dreiser's naturalism. See index for other references.

696 Sklar, Robert. F. SCOTT FITZGERALD: THE LAST LAOCOON. New York: Oxford University Press. HLM figures prominently throughout; see index.

1968

697 Buitenhuis, Peter. "A Hunter of Sacred Cows: The Value of H.L. Mencken." In FIVE AMERICAN MODERNS: MARY MCCARTHY, STEPHEN CRANE, J.D. SALINGER, EUGENE O'NEILL, H.L. MENCKEN, 77-96. Toronto: Roger Ascham Press.
Surveys HLM's career and attitudes, emphasizing the healthy role he played as chief American iconoclast. First published in WHR 14 (Winter 1960): 16-28.

698 Cooke, Alistair. "HLM: RIP." In TALK ABOUT AMERICA, 120-27. New York: Knopf.
Obituary first given as a BBC broadcast.

699 DeCamp, L. Sprague. THE GREAT MONKEY TRIAL. Garden City, NY: Doubleday.

Chapters and Sections of Books 145

On HLM as the most prominent of the journalists covering the Scopes trial of 1925. See index.

700 Hartshorne, Thomas L. THE DISTORTED IMAGE: CHANGING CONCEPTIONS OF THE AMERICAN CHARACTER SINCE TURNER. Cleveland: Case Western Reserve University.
See especially his chapter entitled "The American Character in the 1920's: Rebels and Critics" and the index for other references.

701 Mott, Frank Luther. A HISTORY OF AMERICAN MAGAZINES: 1905-1930. Vol. 5 of 5 vols. Cambridge, MA: Harvard University Press.
Thorough, engaging histories of the *AM* (3-26) and the *SS* (246-72).

702 Shapiro, Karl. TO ABOLISH CHILDREN AND OTHER ESSAYS. Chicago: Quadrangle Books.
See especially pages 233-36 of the essay entitled "A *Malebolge* of Fourteen Hundred Books," in which HLM is briefly compared with writer Norman Mailer for their use of shock techniques.

1969

703 Dolmetsch, Carl Richard. "The Writer in America: The Strange Case of 'S.S. Van Dine.'" In LITERATUR UND SPRACHE DER VEREINIGTEN STAATEN, 153-64. Edited by Hans Galinsky. Heidelberg: Carl Wirter.
Background on Willard Huntinton Wright's ("S.S. Van Dine") association with HLM, Nathan, the *SS*, and their collectively authored EUROPE AFTER 8:15 [5]. In English.

704 McDavid, Raven I., Jr. "H.L. Mencken: THE AMERICAN LANGUAGE" [7]. In LANDMARKS OF AMERICAN WRITING, 261-69. Edited by Hennig Cohen. New York: Basic Books.

705 Moers, Ellen. TWO DREISERS. New York: Viking.
Refers to HLM's part in the shaping of Dreiser's early literary career, with excerpts from letters. See index.

706 Ruland, Richard. "Recalling H.L. Mencken." In AMERICA AT RANDOM: FROM *THE NEW YORK TIMES'* OLDEST EDITORIAL FEATURE, "TOPICS OF THE TIMES," A CENTURY OF COMMENT ON AMERICA AND AMERICANS, 218-20. Edited by Herbert Mitgang. New York: Coward-McCann.
    First published in the *TIMES* (18 June 1966), this brief essay was written on the occasion of the tenth anniversary of HLM's death; quotes several writers on HLM, and laments the loss of his healthy spirit in American criticism.

1970

707 Downs, Robert B. "The Great Debunker." In BOOKS THAT CHANGED AMERICA, 197-206. New York: Macmillan.
    A good introduction to HLM, with a sampling of pithy remarks taken from the PREJUDICES books [403, 404, 405, 406, 409, 410].

708 Halper, Albert. "Mencken." In GOOD-BYE, UNION SQUARE: A WRITER'S MEMOIR OF THE THIRTIES, 121-25. Chicago: Quadrangle Books.
    A novelist recalls selling his first short story to a major magazine, in this case the *AM*; see index for other references.

709 Hensley, Donald M. BURTON RASCOE. New York: Twayne.
    See "Rascoe's Early Essential Mencken" (68-77), which forms part of Chapter 3; Rascoe was one of HLM's earliest defenders. Other references to HLM abound; see index.

1971

710 Churchill, Allen. "The Baltimore Anti-Christ." In THE LITERARY DECADE, 163-78. Englewood Cliffs, NJ: Prentice-Hall.
    Surveys the careers of HLM and Knopf, with particular attention to their *AM* enterprise. See index for numerous other references.

Chapters and Sections of Books

711 McCormick, John. THE MIDDLE DISTANCE: A COMPARATIVE HISTORY OF AMERICAN IMAGINATIVE LITERATURE: 1919-1932. New York: Free Press.
   Altogether a very critical portrait; see index.

712 Weaver, Mike. WILLIAM CARLOS WILLIAMS: THE AMERICAN BACKGROUND. Cambridge, Eng.: Cambridge University Press.
   Pages 79-81 sketch the poet's praises and criticisms for HLM's AMERICAN LANGUAGE [7].

1972

713 Aldridge, John W. THE DEVIL IN THE FIRE: RETRO-SPECTIVE ESSAYS ON AMERICAN LITERATURE AND CULTURE, 1951-1971. New York: Harper's Magazine Press.
   The attitudes of HLM and Sinclair Lewis are frequently associated, and HLM's "On Being an American" [61] is discussed. Some of this material appeared previously in *HM* and in Aldridge's IN THE COUNTRY OF THE YOUNG (New York: Harper's Magazine Press, 1969). See index.

714 Longstreet, Stephen. WE ALL WENT TO PARIS: AMERICANS IN THE CITY OF LIGHT, 1776-1971. New York: Macmillan.
   See "The Sea Trip of H.L. Mencken" (271-76) for descriptions of HLM's two journeys to the city.

715 Tebbel, John. A HISTORY OF BOOK PUBLISHING IN THE UNITED STATES. 4 vols. New York and London: R.R. Bowker, 1972-81.
   See indexes to volumes 2-4, which mention HLM often in the context of American publishing history.

1973

716 Farr, Finis. O'HARA: A BIOGRAPHY. Boston and Toronto: Little, Brown.
   Writer John O'Hara greatly admired HLM. See index for references.

717 Rubin, Louis D., Jr. "If Only Mencken Were Alive ...." In THE COMIC IMAGINATION IN AMERICAN LITERATURE, 217-30. Edited by Rubin. New Brunswick, NJ: Rutgers University Press.
A good introduction to HLM as journalist, critic, and humorist. See index for other references.

718 Weeks, Edward. MY GREEN AGE. Boston and Toronto: Little, Brown.
Once editor of the *AtlM*, the author writes of the rival *AM* and its editor; includes a brief retelling of the "Hatrack" episode. See index.

1974

719 Brustein, Robert. "H.L. Mencken (The New Mencken Letters)." In CRITICAL MOMENTS: REFLECTION ON THEATRE AND SOCIETY, 1973-1979, 25-29. New York: Random House.
Passing acknowledgment of Carl Bode's new volume of HLM letters [436] leads to comments on the personality behind them. Reprinted from the New York *TIMES*, 1976.

720 Spiller, Robert E., et al, eds. LITERARY HISTORY OF THE UNITED STATES. 4th ed. 2 vols. New York: Macmillan. See index.

721 Wagner, Philip. "H.L. Mencken." In MAKERS OF AMERICAN THOUGHT: AN INTRODUCTION TO SEVEN AMERICAN WRITERS, 85-119. Edited by Ralph Ross. Minneapolis: University of Minnesota Press.
Surveys the most important biographical and bibliographical information to be had; also describes and evaluates HLM's thought, prose style, and various facets of his personality. First published as no. 62 of the University of Minnesota Pamphlets on American Writers, 1966.

1975

722 Gerber, Philip. WILLA CATHER. Boston: Twayne.
An admiring HLM showed insight into the novelist's work on several occasions. See index.

Chapters and Sections of Books

723 Payne, Darwin. THE MAN OF ONLY YESTERDAY: FREDERICK LEWIS ALLEN. New York: Harper and Row.
As editor of *HM*, Allen sought contributions from HLM in the 1940's, although he had sharply criticized HLM in the 1920's. See index for references.

1976

724 Edmiston, Susan, and Linda D. Civino. LITERARY NEW YORK: A HISTORY AND GUIDE. Boston: Houghton Mifflin.
On HLM, George Jean Nathan, the *SS*, and the *AM* as they were associated with the city. See index.

725 Farrell, James T. JAMES T. FARRELL: LITERARY ESSAYS, 1954-1974, 122-23. Collected and edited by Jack Alan Robbins. Port Washington, NY, and London: Kennikat Press.
Reprints on pages 5-15 Farrell's introduction to PREJUDICES: A SELECTION [418] and on pages 122-23 a review of Forgue's edition of HLM's correspondence [430].

726 Pizer, Donald. THE NOVELS OF THEODORE DREISER: A CRITICAL STUDY. Minneapolis: University of Minnesota Press.
References to HLM abound. See index.

727 Wertheim, Arthur Frank. THE NEW YORK LITTLE RENAISSANCE: ICONOCLASM, MODERNISM, AND NATIONALISM IN AMERICAN CULTURE, 1908-1917. New York: New York University Press.
Gives much attention to HLM and his connections with writers and critics of the day. See index.

1977

728 Fenchak, Paul. "Slavic Studies in Maryland." In THE UKRAINIANS OF MARYLAND, 275-98. Edited by Fenchak, Stephen Basarab, and Wolodymyr Sushko. Baltimore: Ukrainian Education Association of Maryland.
On HLM's contribution to the subject.

729 Fetherling, Doug. THE FIVE LIVES OF BEN HECHT. Toronto: Lester and Orpen. Refers often to the friendship and professional association between the two writers. See index.

730 Forgue, Guy Jean. "H.L. Mencken et le sud." In SEMINAIRES 1976, 183-95. Edited by Jean Beranger, et al. Talence: Centre de Recherches sur l'Amerique anglophone. On HLM's relationship to the American South; in French.

731 Yardley, Jonathan. RING: A BIOGRAPHY OF RING LARDNER. New York: Random House. Frequently mentions HLM's various responses to the humorist's work and his peculiarly American language. See index.

1978

732 Bruccoli, Matthew J. SCOTT AND ERNEST: THE AUTHORITY OF FAILURE AND THE AUTHORITY OF SUCCESS, 56-58, 70, 122. New York: Random House.
Contains references to Fitzgerald's and Hemingway's associations with HLM and the *AM*.

733 Dabney, Virginius. ACROSS THE YEARS: MEMOIRS OF A VIRGINIAN. Garden City, NY: Doubleday. A fellow newspaperman writes of HLM's influence and professional assistance. See index.

734 Wagniere, Harriet Helms. "Behind the Scenes: Charles Angoff and the *AMERICAN MERCURY*." In THE OLD CENTURY AND THE NEW: ESSAYS IN HONOR OF CHARLES ANGOFF, 79-93. Edited by Alfred Rosa. Rutherford, NJ: Fairleigh Dickinson University Press; London: Associated University Presses.
Frequently cites Angoff's controversial HLM biography [495]. Other references to HLM recur throughout this collection of essays: 7, 8, 35, 36, 37, 40, 41, 70, 71, 73, 74, 75, 76, 77, and 78.

1979

735 Kraft, Stephanie. "H.L. Mencken and the Hollins Street House." In NO CASTLES ON MAIN STREET: AMERICAN AUTHORS AND THEIR HOMES, 14-22. Chicago: Rand McNally.

736 McDavid, Raven I., Jr. DIALECTS IN CULTURE: ESSAYS IN GENERAL DIALECTOLOGY. Edited by William A. Kretzschmar, Jr., et al. University, AL: University of Alabama Press.
   See "Mencken Revisited" [931], "American English" [930], "Review of H.L. Mencken 1945 (THE AMERICAN LANGUAGE: SUPPLEMENT I)" [877], and "Review of H.L. Mencken 1948 (THE AMERICAN LANGUAGE: SUPPLEMENT II)" [877].

1980

737 Gaffey, James P. FRANCIS CLEMENT KELLEY AND THE AMERICAN CATHOLIC DREAM. 2 vols. Bensenville, IL: Heritage Foundation.
   Numerous references to HLM as a friend of the bishop. See index to each volume.

738 Gayle, Addison. RICHARD WRIGHT: ORDEAL OF A NATIVE SON. Garden City, NY: Doubleday.
   Retells the story of the black novelist's discovery of HLM and A BOOK OF PREFACES [401], which so influenced him. See index.

739 Hakutani, Yoshinobu. YOUNG DREISER: A CRITICAL STUDY. Cranbury, NJ, and London: Associated University Presses.
   Several references to HLM; see index.

740 Way, Brian. F. SCOTT FITZGERALD AND THE ART OF SOCIAL FICTION. London: Edward Arnold.
   Gives due attention to HLM's influence on Fitzgerald's early work. See index for references.

1981

741 Betts, Glynne Robinson. "H.L. Mencken." In WRITERS IN RESIDENCE: AMERICAN AUTHORS AT HOME, 70-71. New York: Viking Press.
   Includes photographs and brief text.

742 Mariani, Paul. WILLIAM CARLOS WILLIAMS: A NEW WORLD NAKED. New York: McGraw-Hill, 1981.
   On the poet's admiration for THE AMERICAN LANGUAGE [7] but distaste for Menckenian cultural interpretations. See index.

743 Nelson, Randy F. THE ALMANAC OF AMERICAN LETTERS. Los Altos, CA: William Kaufmann.
   Retells the stories of the "Hatrack" case and the "bathtub hoax" [32]; also cites remarks by and about HLM, including a formal denunciation made by the Ku Klux Klan. See index.

744 Nelson, Raymond. VAN WYCK BROOKS: A WRITER'S LIFE. New York: E.P. Dutton.
   Quotes the critic's disparaging comments about HLM's "adolescent" writing (225). See index for other references.

745 Quine, W.V. "Mencken's AMERICAN LANGUAGE." In THEORIES AND THINGS, 203-08. Cambridge, MA and London: The Belknap Press of Harvard University Press.
   Remarks on the virtues and faults of HLM's study in linguistics [7] and the abridgement which came later. First appeared in the *NYRB* 1 (9 January 1964):7.

1982

746 Bryer, Jackson R., ed. THE SHORT STORIES OF F. SCOTT FITZGERALD: NEW APPROACHES IN CRITICISM. Madison: University of Wisconsin Press.
   Several of these essays allude to or discuss the HLM-Fitzgerald connection. See index.

747 Hoopes, Roy. CAIN. New York: Holt, Rinehart and Winston.

Mentions HLM often as a mixed influence in the life and work of the novelist and screenwriter. See index.

748 Kazin, Alfred. ON NATIVE GROUNDS: AN INTERPRETATION OF MODERN AMERICAN PROSE LITERATURE. 1942. Reprint, with a Preface to the Fortieth Anniversary Edition. New York: Harcourt, Brace, Jovanovich, 1982.
At the end of Chapter 7, considers HLM's place among the post-World War I generation of "esthetic newspapermen" (199). Other brief references to HLM occur throughout book. See index.

749 Riggio, Thomas P., James L.W. West, III, and Neda M. Westlake, eds. THEODORE DREISER: AMERICAN DIARIES, 1902-1926. Philadelphia: University of Pennsylvania Press.
Dreiser refers often to HLM; see index.

750 Serge, Ricard. "Mencken on Roosevelt: Autopsy of an Autopsy." In THE TWENTIES. 21-33. Preface by Barbara Smith Lemeunier. Aix-en-Provence: Université de Provence.
Takes issue with remarks on President Theodore Roosevelt made by HLM in his "Roosevelt: An Autopsy" [53]. In English.

1983

751 Hobson, Fred. TELL ABOUT THE SOUTH: THE SOUTHERN RAGE TO EXPLAIN. Baton Rouge and London: Louisiana State University Press.
On HLM's associations with or views of such Southerners as Walter Hines Page, Howard Odum, W.J. Cash, and Donald Davidson and his fellow "Agrarians." See index.

752 Inge, M. Thomas, and Edgar E. MacDonald, eds. JAMES BRANCH CABELL: CENTENNIAL ESSAYS. Baton Rouge and London: Louisiana State University Press.
Much mention of HLM; see index.

753 **Langer, Elinor.** JOSEPHINE HERBST. Boston and Toronto: Little, Brown.

On the writer's work on the SS staff and her publication of anonymous submissions to the magazine. See index.

754 LeVot, André. F. SCOTT FITZGERALD: A BIOGRAPHY. Translated by William Byron. Garden City, NY: Doubleday.
Gives background on Fitzgerald's early admiration for and later disenchantment with HLM; see index. The French original omits the novelist's first initial in the title (Paris: Julliard, 1979).

755 Muraire, Andre. "The New Deal Mentality." In A NEW DEAL READER, 21-35. Edited by Groupe de Recherche et d'Etudes Nord-Americaines. Aix-en-Provence: Université de Provence.
Analyzes HLM's "The New Deal Mentality" [212] and his attitude toward Franklin D. Roosevelt. In French.

756 Nolan, William F. HAMMETT: A LIFE AT THE EDGE. New York: Congdon and Weed.
Credits HLM and Nathan with "discovering" the detective novelist and publishing his work in the SS and in their pulp magazines, SAUCY STORIES and THE BLACK MASK. See index.

1984

757 Clayton, Bruce. FORGOTTEN PROPHET: THE LIFE OF RANDOLPH BOURNE. Baton Rouge and London: Louisiana State University Press.
On the two critics' different views of Dreiser, World War I, the artist's position in America, and other topics. See index.

758 "Henry Louis Mencken." In TWENTIETH-CENTURY LITERARY CRITICISM, 355-98. Vol. 13. Edited by Dennis Poupard and James E. Person, Jr. Detroit, MI: Gale Research Company.
Brief biographical sketch followed by comments from more than thirty Mencken contemporaries and scholars.

759 Mellow, James R. INVENTED LIVES: F. SCOTT AND ZELDA FITZGERALD. Boston: Houghton Mifflin.

Comments often on the novelist's ambivalent attitude toward HLM. See index.

760 Modlin, Charles E., ed. SHERWOOD ANDERSON: SELECTED LETTERS. Knoxville: University of Tennessee Press.
Prints three of the novelist's letters to HLM and other letters that refer to him. See index.

1985

761 Flora, Joseph M. "Fiction in the 1920s: Some New Voices." In THE HISTORY OF SOUTHERN LITERATURE, 279-90. Edited by Louis D. Rubin, Jr., et al. Baton Rouge and London: Louisiana State University Press.
HLM helped to pave the way for the Southern renascence through his literary and cultural criticism and through his promotion of such writers as Frances Newman, Julia Peterkin, DuBose Heyward, T.S. Stribling, and Evelyn Scott (but he overlooked, says the author, Elizabeth Madox Roberts). Further mention of HLM occurs in other essays in this collection; see index.

762 Griffin, Joseph. THE SMALL CANVAS: AN INTRODUCTION TO DREISER'S SHORT STORIES. Rutherford, Madison, and Teaneck, NJ: Fairleigh Dickinson University Press.
On HLM's approval of Dreiser's short fiction, partially indicated by his willingness to publish him in the *SS* and the *AM*. See index.

763 Kneebone, John T. SOUTHERN LIBERAL JOURNALISTS AND THE ISSUE OF RACE, 1920-1944. Chapel Hill and London: University of North Carolina Press.
On HLM's "Sahara" essay [31], his comments on the Scopes trial, and his encouragement of liberal journalism in the South. See index.

764 Munson, Gorham. THE AWAKENING TWENTIES: A MEMOIR-HISTORY OF A LITERARY PERIOD. Baton Rouge and London: Louisiana State University Press.

On HLM and Nathan's editorship of the *SS*, among other topics. See index.

765 Shivers, Frank R., Jr. MARYLAND WITS AND BALTIMORE BARDS: A LITERARY HISTORY WITH NOTES ON WASHINGTON WRITERS. Baltimore: Maclay. HLM appears often, especially in connection with his native city; see index.

766 Wingate, P.J. "The Sage of Baltimore." In BEFORE THE BRIDGE, 127-41. Centreville, MD: Tidewater Publishers. Recalls first hearing about HLM during the Scopes trial, then reading portions of IN DEFENSE OF WOMEN [6] and THE AMERICAN LANGUAGE [7].

1986

767 Wellek, René. A HISTORY OF MODERN CRITICISM: 1750-1950. Vol. 6: American Criticism, 1900-1950. New Haven, CT, and London: Yale University Press. In pages 3-10 of his chapter "Criticism Before the New Criticism," the author analyzes HLM's literary criticism and his impact on early twentieth-century American writing.

1987

767a Bulsterbaum, Allison. "H.L. Mencken." In ENCYCLOPEDIA OF AMERICAN HUMORISTS. Edited by Steven H. Gale. New York: Garland Publishing.

H. ARTICLES

The following is a selected, partially annotated list of magazine and newspaper articles on HLM. Some of the more important reviews of HLM's works are included, as are a few reviews of books on HLM. Other articles which were subsequently reprinted in books may be found in Section G, and those which mention HLM but do not focus on him are listed in Section I. Numbers preceding the parentheses in MENCKENIANA citations refer to issue, not volume.

1917

768 Bourne, Randolph. "H.L. Mencken." NEW REPUBLIC 13 (24 November): 102-03.
 Review of A BOOK OF PREFACES [401]; laments that HLM is a "moralist" despite the fact that he is also a "robust hater of uplift and puritanism" (102).
 Reprinted in [582].

769 Rascoe, Burton. "Fanfare." Chicago Sunday Tribune (11 November): part 8, page 7.
 Reviews A BOOK OF PREFACES [401] and other HLM writing to date. Reprinted as part of a pamphlet generally known as FANFARE [563]. Reprinted also in [582].

770 Sherman, Stuart P. "Beautifying American Literature." NATION 105 (19 November): 593-94.
 Biting review of A BOOK OF PREFACES [401] by one of HLM's heartiest antagonists.
 Reprinted in [582].

1918

771 Johnson, James Weldon. "American Genius and Its Locale." New York AGE (20 July): editorial page.
 Although the author praises HLM for his charm and his gift for discovering truth, he disagrees with him as to the reason the

South has produced little viable literature since the Civil War. Reprinted in [582].

772 "Three Views of H.L. Mencken." *THE LITTLE REVIEW* 4 (January): 10-14.
    Raoul Root, jh (Jane Heap), and *LITTLE REVIEW* editor Margaret Anderson comment on A BOOK OF PREFACES [401].

773 Untermeyer, Louis. "A Preface to ____." *LIBERATOR* 1 (May): 43-45.
    Reviews A BOOK OF PREFACES [401].

1919

774 Gilman, Lawrence. "The American Language." *NORTH AMERICAN REVIEW* 209 (May): 697-703.
    On HLM's book by the same name [7].

775 Hackett, Francis. "The Living Speech." *NEW REPUBLIC* 19 (31 May): 155-56.
    Reviews THE AMERICAN LANGUAGE [7]. Reprinted in [582].

776 Harris, Frank. "American Values: Howe and Mencken." *PEARSON'S MAGAZINE* 40 (January): 112-13.
    E.W. Howe of Kansas and HLM do not view businessmen in the same light; the editor of *PEARSON'S* sides with the latter in his belief that they do not form a superior class of people.

777 Matthews, Brander. "Developing the American from the English Language." *NEW YORK TIMES BOOK REVIEW* (30 March): 157, 164, 170.
    Lengthy review of THE AMERICAN LANGUAGE [7] with much reference to Mark Twain's remarks on the subject.

778 O'Sullivan, Vincent. "The American Critic." *NEW WITNESS* [London] (28 November): 30-32.
    Reprinted as part of the pamphlet *FANFARE* [563].

1920

779 Beard, Charles A. "On Puritans." *NEW REPUBLIC* 25 (1 December): 15-17.

Articles

The American historian offers some cordial corrections to HLM's judgments of the New England settlers.

780 Boyd, Ernest A. "A Modern Reactionary." *ATHENAEUM* No. 4698 (14 May): 637-38.
Hails PREJUDICES: FIRST SERIES [403], A BOOK OF BURLESQUES [399], and HELIOGABALUS [10] as evidence of HLM's rising significance in American letters.

781 ------. "American Literature or Colonial?" *FREEMAN* 1 (17 March): 13-15.
Takes HLM's side in the critical debate over the value of native American works. Reprinted in [582].

782 Boynton, Percy H. "American Literature and the Tart Set." *FREEMAN* 1 (7 April): 88-89.
Responds to Boyd's claim [781] that the upholders of "old-world standards" (88) stand to be improved by the attacks of such impressionist critics as HLM. Reprinted in [582].

783 Braley, Berton. "Three--Minus One." New York *SUN* (6 December): 16.
Famous poem with "Mencken / Nathan / And God" refrain, often parodied (see [800], for instance). This poem is itself a parody of Eugene Field's "Wynken, Blynken, and Nod."

784 Huxley, A.H. "American Criticism." *ATHENAEUM* No. 4679 (2 January): 10.
Reviews PREJUDICES: FIRST SERIES [403].

785 "Mr. Mencken and the Prophets." *FREEMAN* 2 (13 October): 103-04.
Ventures an explanation for the fact that, as HLM points out in "The National Letters" [52], American writers have failed to meet the challenge posed by the literary "prophets" of the nineteenth century.

786 Parkhurst, Winthrop. "Prejudices." *DIAL* 68 (February): 267-72.

Review of PREJUDICES: FIRST SERIES [403] leads to assessment of HLM as one of our best critics, despite his flaws.

787 "A Reviewer's Note-Book." *FREEMAN* 2 (24 November): 262-63.
Argues that, contrary to HLM's claims, the American writer needs less appreciation from his native audience, more nourishment for his endeavors to begin with. See Rascoe's answer [796].

788 Wilson, Edmund. "Some Reviews of Job." *DIAL* 68 (April): 469-72.
Parodies HLM, James Huneker, and the *NATION*.

1921

789 Boyd, Ernest A. "Mencken, or Virtue Rewarded." *FREEMAN* 2 (2 February): 491-92.
On HLM's career thus far and the reasons for his popularity, despite his unconventional notions.

790 Fitzgerald, F. Scott. "The Baltimore Anti-Christ." *BOOKMAN* 53 (March): 79-81.
Mixed review of PREJUDICES: SECOND SERIES [404].

791 Harris, Frank. "H.L. Mencken: Critic." *PEARSON'S MAGAZINE* 46 (May): 405-08.
Admiration for HLM's literary insight, with particular attention to the first two PREJUDICES volumes [403, 404].

792 "Have We No Critics?" *NEW REPUBLIC* 28 (12 October): 174-75.
On Conrad Aiken's response to HLM's criticism of Henry James.

793 Krutch, J.W. "Antichrist and the Five Apostles." *NATION* 113 (21 December): 733-34.
On HLM as a gifted denouncer of the philistines; reviews the Free Lance Series, [6, 9, 376, 377, 378, 382], particularly as they bear the stamp of Nietzsche.

794 McFee, William. "Mencken and Menken; or The Gift of Tongues." *BOOKMAN* 54 (December): 361-63.
   Chides HLM for his promotion of an "American" language, when British English is preferable.

795 "New Mutterings in Southern Literature." *CURRENT OPINION* 71 (September): 360-62.
   Summarizes and responds to HLM's "The South Begins to Mutter," *SS* 65 (August 1921): 138-44.

796 Rascoe, Burton. "Reviewing the Reviewer." *FREEMAN* 2 (26 January): 473-74.
   Takes issue with a previous article [787] in which an anonymous reviewer set forth unclear and dubious arguments attacking HLM's position on the situation of the American writer.

797 Ratcliffe, S.K. "Mencken: An English Plaint." *NEW REPUBLIC* 26 (13 April): 191-92.
   PREJUDICES: SECOND SERIES [404] contains some very good writing but becomes a "tiresome spate of ill-temper" (192).

798 Wilson, Edmund. "H.L. Mencken." *NEW REPUBLIC* 27 (1 June): 10-13.
   An important and often cited essay on HLM as an idealist and anti-puritan. Reprinted in [582].

1922

799 Arvin, Newton. "The Role of Mr. Mencken." *FREEMAN* 6 (27 December): 381-82.
   Explains why HLM is not "a true literary critic" (381) but is rather a social critic and a humorist "of a very high order" (382).

800 Cobb, Elizabeth. "The Infallible Three; or Finding America." *BOOKMAN* 54 (February): 603.
   Borrows the "Mencken and Nathan and God" refrain from Berton's famous poem [783] for this "pageant"; by the daughter of humorist Irvin S. Cobb.

801 Lippmann, Walter. "The Near Machiavelli." *NEW REPUBLIC* 31 (31 May): 12-14.
   On HLM's notion of an aristocracy of the mind.

802 McCullough, Arthur F. "A Precursor of Mencken." Baltimore *EVENING SUN* (29 September): 25.
   Compares the iconoclasm of HLM to that of William Cowper Brann of Waco, Texas.

803 "The Visit of Mr. Mencken." *ENGLISH REVIEW* 35 (August): 142-43.
   Expresses hope that HLM's visit to London will benefit British criticism.

804 Walpole, Hugh. "An Open Letter to H.L. Mencken." *BOOKMAN* 55 (May): 225-28.
   Takes issue with HLM for disparaging English novels and literary criticism. See also [117].

1923

805 "American Idealism is Defended by Dr. Mims." Greensboro [NC] *DAILY NEWS* (20 September): 2.
   Professor Edwin Mims of Vanderbilt University sides with Stuart P. Sherman in their critical skirmishes with HLM concerning literature and puritanism.

806 Johnson, Gerald W. "The Congo, Mr. Mencken." *THE REVIEWER* 3 (July): 887-93.
   The South is not a literary "Sahara" [31], but rather a luxuriant "Congo" with color and rhythm.

807 Spingarn, J.E. "The Growth of a Literary Myth." *FREEMAN* 7 (2 May): 181-83.
   Denies that there is a "Croce-Spingarn-Carlyle-Goethe" theory, as HLM suggests in "Criticism of Criticism of Criticism" [39].

1924

808 Hussey, L.M. "A Note Upon An Artist." *SATURDAY REVIEW OF LITERATURE* 1 (22 November): 297-98.

This reviewer of PREJUDICES: FOURTH SERIES [406] finds that there is no way to pin down the "essence" of its author (298).

809 Kallen, H.M. "What Is an Elephant? A Fable for Critics." *NEW REPUBLIC* 41 Supplement (10 December): 1-4.
On the critical battles waging among HLM, Spingarn, Brooks, Babbitt, Eliot, Sherman, and Boyd, encapsulated in CRITICISM IN AMERICA: ITS FUNCTION AND STATUS (NY: Haskell House, 1924; reprinted 1969)

810 Williams, Michael. "Bishops and Brains." *COMMONWEAL* 1 (31 December): 209-11.
Takes exception to remarks made by HLM on the Ku Klux Klan and the Catholic Church in the *AM* 3 (December 1924): 447-48.

1925

811 Bodenheim, Maxwell. "Criticism in America." *SATURDAY REVIEW OF LITERATURE* 1 (6 June): 801-02.
Considers HLM's "candor ... healthy and awakening" but finds him "blind and unreceptive" as a literary critic (802); compares him to Stuart P. Sherman.

812 Chanticleer [pseud]. "Contemporaries: 'This Man, Mencken.'" *INDEPENDENT* 114 (10 January): 45-47.
Beginning with the recently published PREJUDICES: FOURTH SERIES [406], surveys HLM's criticisms of American life and culture, concluding that he "has no humor in him. Even he takes himself seriously" (47).

813 "Federalist: 1925 Model." *SATURDAY REVIEW OF LITERATURE* 2 (12 December): 401, 409.
Reviews AMERICANA 1925 [407], pointing out that HLM is actually conservative although he appears otherwise.

814 Genzmer, George. "Mr. Mencken Triumphant." *NATION* 121 (9 December): 665-65.
Reviews a handful of books by and about HLM and concludes that he is a significant

and powerful force in contemporary
American letters.

815 Hall, Grover C. "E.W. Howe and H.L. Mencken."
Baltimore *EVENING SUN* (24 June): 17.
Howe is "the prophet of the average man,"
HLM of the superman; Howe knows life
first-hand, HLM knows books. But despite
their differences, they also share much in
common.

816 Kelley, William Valentine. "At the Sign of the
Basilisk." *METHODIST REVIEW* 108 (July):
518-27.
Refers to DAMN! A BOOK OF CALUMNY [402]
and the PREJUDICES books [403, 404, 405,
406, 409, 410] to illustrate HLM's ignoble
role as a "venom-squirter" (519).

817 Parshley, H.M. "H.L. Mencken: An Appreciation." *AMERICAN REVIEW* 3 (January-February):
72-84.
Sketch of HLM as critic, writer, and
unique personality. Reprinted as a
pamphlet.

818 Sherman, Stuart P. "Mr. Brownell and Mr.
Mencken." *BOOKMAN* 60 (January): 632-34.
William C. Brownell's THE GENIUS OF STYLE
and HLM's PREJUDICES: FOURTH SERIES [406]
provide a point of departure for a comparison between "the literary aristocracy"
and "the literary proletariat" (632).

819 Walpole, Hugh. "My Dear Mencken." *BOOKMAN* 62
(November): 246-48.
Again the Englishman admonishes HLM for
his criticism of contemporary British
literature; see HLM's response [142].

1926

820 Beach, Joseph Warren. "Pedantic Study of Two
Critics." *AMERICAN SPEECH* 1 (March): 299-306.
Analyzes and compares the styles of HLM
and James Branch Cabell. Reprinted in
Beach's THE OUTLOOK FOR AMERICAN PROSE
(Chicago: University of Chicago Press,
1926).

Articles

821 "Boston Bans April *AMERICAN MERCURY*."
Baltimore *EVENING SUN* (30 March): 1.
   First of a number of articles printed in
   the *SUNPAPERS* through early June covering
   HLM's confrontation with J. Frank Chase
   and the Boston Watch and Ward Society over
   censorship of Herbert Asbury's "Hatrack"
   story.

822 Boyd, Ernest. "Readers and Writers."
INDEPENDENT 117 (30 October): 505.
   HLM's concept of socialism as set forth in
   NOTES ON DEMOCRACY [11] and MEN VERSUS
   THE MAN [4] compared with that of George
   Bernard Shaw.

823 Lippmann, Walter. "H.L. Mencken." *SATURDAY REVIEW OF LITERATURE* 3 (11 December): 413-14.
   Review of NOTES ON DEMOCRACY [11] leads
   to observations on HLM as an "outraged
   sentimentalist." Reprinted in [582].

824 Monroe, Harriet. "Mephistopheles and the
Poet." *POETRY* 28 (July): 210-15.
   Shares HLM's lament that too many editors
   --she names the type "Mephistopheles"--
   encourage the standardization of young
   American minds.

825 Williams, Michael. "Men, the Mob, and Mr.
Mencken." *COMMONWEAL* 3 (10 March): 488-89.
   Defends the common man against HLM's
   attacks.

1927

826 Allen, Frederick Lewis. "These Disillusioned
Highbrows." *INDEPENDENT* 118 (9 April): 378-79.
   On the need to debunk America's over-
   estimated debunkers.

827 "H.L.M. is the Acid Test of Religion, Says
Church Paper." Baltimore *EVENING SUN* (10
January): 17.
   "The Cooperator," Bulletin of the
   Baltimore Federation of Churches, says
   that by their response to HLM's criticisms
   will Christians "Prove Reality of Faith

They Profess or Demonstrate Its Hollowness" (subtitle).

828 Kummer, Frederic Arnold. "Something Must Have Happened to Henry." *BOOKMAN* 65 (June): 408-10.
    Laments HLM's refusal to mellow in middle age as he continues haranguing figures like Edgar Allan Poe and O. Henry.

829 Lewis, Wyndham. "Paleface: Part I." *THE ENEMY* No. 2 (September): 5-30.
    An Englishman examines American ideas on race and religion; the subsections "The Nature of Mencken's Responsibility" and "AMERICANA of Mencken" [407, 408] focus on his approach to the Anglo-Saxon.

830 Pattee, Fred Lewis. "The New Muck-Rake School of Literature." *CHRISTIAN ADVOCATE* 102 (28 April): 523-24.
    Like the muckraking journalists before them, Herbert Asbury and Sinclair Lewis set forth in UP FROM METHODISM and ELMER GANTRY, respectively, those aspects of our culture which are not worth reading about. All this thanks to HLM.

831 Schönemann, Friedrich. "Der amerikanische Anti-Democrat: H.L. Mencken." *DEUTSCHE RUNDSCHAU* 213 (December): 216-18.
    Briefly summarizes HLM's career to date, with particular attention to NOTES ON DEMOCRACY [11]. In German.

832 Simrell, V.E. "H.L. Mencken the Rhetorician." *QUARTERLY JOURNAL OF SPEECH EDUCATION* 13 (November): 399-412.

833 Sinclair, Upton. "Mr. Mencken Calls on Me." *BOOKMAN* 66 (November): 254-56.
    Recalls a meeting with HLM; laments HLM's "little regard for facts" (255) and the fact that he has no real message for the young people who idolize him.

834 Stolberg, Benjamin. "Walter Lippmann, Connoisseur of Public Life." *NATION* 125 (7 December): 639-42.

Commentary on Lippmann's review of HLM's NOTES ON DEMOCRACY [11] leads to a comparison of the two men.

1928

835 Babbitt, Irving. "The Critic and American Life." *FORUM* 79 (February): 161-76.
Blasts HLM and his inadequate literary criticism. Reprinted in the author's ON BEING CREATIVE AND OTHER ESSAYS (Boston: Houghton Mifflin, 1932). Reprinted also in [582].

836 Boyd, Ernest. "Readers and Writers." *INDEPENDENT* 120 (28 January): 91.
In reviewing MENCKENIANA: A SCHIMPFLEXICON [411], the author wonders "if the very shrillness of these cries, their wild hysteria, is not a measure of the success of H.L. Mencken's onslaughts."

837 Ely, Catherine Beach. "The Sorrows of Mencken." *NORTH AMERICAN REVIEW* 225 (January): 23-26.
HLM enjoys being scornful of most of what America is about.

838 Frank, Waldo. "Our Arts, The Rediscovery of America: XII." *NEW REPUBLIC* 54 (9 May): 343-47.
Comments on HLM as rhetorical artist.

839 Harrold, Charles Frederick. "Two Critics of Democracy." *SOUTH ATLANTIC QUARTERLY* 27 (April): 130-41.
Compares HLM to Thomas Carlyle.

840 Jones, Howard Mumford. "Professor Babbitt Cross-Examined." *NEW REPUBLIC* 54 (21 March): 158-60.
Responds to Babbitt's criticism of HLM set forth in [835].

841 Michaud, Régis. "Henry Mencken ou le collectionneur de préjugés." *LES NOUVELLES LITTERAIRES* 7 (9 June): 8.

On the range of American themes covered by HLM's blasts in the PREJUDICES books [403, 404, 405, 406, 409, 410]. In French.

842 Rascoe, Burton. "Those Who Can Criticize." *BOOKMAN* 66 (February): 670-76.
Reviews PREJUDICES: SIXTH SERIES [410], among other works of criticism.

843 Wilson, Edmund. "Literary Politics." *NEW REPUBLIC* 53 (1 February): 289-90.
Categorizes contemporary American critics according to the principles for which they stand, citing HLM and T.S. Eliot as the most formidable ones.

1929

844 Saroyan, William. "The American Clowns of Criticism--Mencken, Nathan, and Haldeman-Julius." *OVERLAND MONTHLY* 87 (March): 77-78, 92-93.
Considering them irresponsible, takes issue with these men's remarks on God and American literature and culture.

1930

845 Collins, Seward. "Criticism in America: The Origins of a Myth." *BOOKMAN* 71 (June): 241-56, 353-64.
Continued in the July issue ("The Revival of the Anti-Humanist Myth," 400-415), this series surveys the critical controversies involving HLM, More, Babbitt, Sherman, and others.

846 Melamed, S.M. "H.L. Mencken's Encyclopaedia of Platitudes." *REFLEX* 6 (May): 3-17.
The "encyclopaedia" is TREATISE ON THE GODS [12]; the "platitudes" concern religion broadly, Jews in particular.

847 Niebuhr, Reinhold. "TREATISE ON THE GODS." *ATLANTIC MONTHLY* 145 (June): 18.
HLM's book [12] "really tells us little more than how one fanatic feels about the other fanatics of a different stripe."

848 Phelps, William Lyon. "As I Like It."
     SCRIBNER'S 88 (August): 205-13.
        Reviews TREATISE ON THE GODS [12],
        admiring the author's spirit but
        disagreeing with his ideas.

849 Williams, Michael. "Mr. Mencken's Bible for
     Boobs." *COMMONWEAL* 11 (2 April): 607-10.
        HLM's friendly yet outspoken Catholic
        antagonist responds to TREATISE ON THE
        GODS [12].

                        1932

850 Gregory, Horace. "Our Writers and the
     Democratic Myth." *BOOKMAN* 75 (August): 377-82.
        On HLM as inheritor of "the Jeffersonian
        ideal of aristocratic libertarianism"
        (377), and on poets Lindsay, Masters, and
        Sandburg as disciples of HLM.

851 Smith, H. Allen. "Depression Exaggerated
     Greatly, Mencken Says." Baltimore *EVENING SUN*
     (25 May): 3.
        Third in a series of United Press inter-
        views inquiring whether "political dis-
        senters in America [have] any pertinent
        suggestions for solution to [the] current
        economic dilemma."

                        1933

852 Maynard, Theodore. "Mencken Leaves *THE
     AMERICAN MERCURY*." *CATHOLIC WORLD* 139 (April):
     10-20.
        Discusses HLM's stamp upon the magazine
        and the *AM*'s stamp upon the country.

853 "Mr. Mencken Leaves the *MERCURY*." *CHRISTIAN
     CENTURY* 50 (18 October): 1292.
        HLM's departure signifies a changing
        social mood. Reprinted in [582].

                        1934

854 Gillis, James M. "Mencken, Moralist!"
     CATHOLIC WORLD 139 (June): 257-66.
        Takes exception to favorable reviews of
        TREATISE ON RIGHT AND WRONG [13] and to

those who praise HLM's approach to ethics and religion.

855 Joad, C.E.M. "Ethical Fireworks." *SPECTATOR* 153 (12 October): 530, 532.
TREATISE ON RIGHT AND WRONG [13] is "facetious without humour ... and serious without scholarship" (530).

1935

856 Hessler, L.B. "On 'Bad Boy' Criticism." *NORTH AMERICAN REVIEW* 240 (September): 214-24.
Denigrates HLM and his "school" of critics, including Burton Rascoe and Ernest Boyd.

857 "Monkey Business." *NATION* 141 (31 July): 118.
Notes the tenth anniversary of the Scopes trial, which the spirit of HLM permeated.

1936

858 Calverton, V.F. "Henry L. Mencken: A Devaluation." *MODERN MONTHLY* 10 (December): 7-11.
Explains why the unchanging HLM is not as popular in the thirties as he was in the twenties.

859 Wilson, Edmund. "Talking United States." *NEW REPUBLIC* 87 (15 July): 299-300.
Reviews the fourth edition of THE AMERICAN LANGUAGE [7] and offers a few philological suggestions of his own.

1937

860 Root, E. Merrill. "Aesthetic Puritans." *CHRISTIAN CENTURY* 54 (25 August): 1043-45.
Compares HLM with other "puritans": Ernest Hemingway, William Faulkner, and Robinson Jeffers.

1938

861 Angoff, Charles. "Mencken Twilight: Another Forgotten Man--That Enfant Terrible of Our Era

Articles

of Nonsense." *NORTH AMERICAN REVIEW* 246 (Winter 1938-39): 216-32.
On the career of the now obsolete HLM.

862 Glicksberg, Charles I. "H.L. Mencken: The Dean of Iconoclasts." *CALCUTTA REVIEW* 67 (April): 13-28.
Defends HLM's literary criticism against those whose opinions have been too easily swayed by their view of his politics, those who have misunderstood his humor and style, and those who believe he does not work from a system of values.

863 Monchak, Stephen J. "H.L. Mencken Rides Again, Rowelling U.S. Newspapers." *EDITOR AND PUBLISHER* 71 (10 September): 9, 14.
Interview with the Sage emphasizes his remarks on journalism.

1939

864 Espy, Willard R. "The Baltimore SUN Goes Down." *NATION* 148 (4 February): 143-46.
On the periodical's diminishing liberalism, largely due to HLM's influence.

865 Minton, Arthur, and Emanuel Bloom. "Are We Like This?" *ENGLISH JOURNAL* (College Edition) 28 (May): 383-93.
Defends American high school and college teachers of English against the attacks levied in the fourth edition of THE AMERICAN LANGUAGE [7].

1940

866 Daniels, Jonathan. "Nonage of an Iconoclast." *SATURDAY REVIEW OF LITERATURE* 21 (27 January): 6.
Favorable review of HAPPY DAYS [15].

867 Owens, Hamilton. "Happy Days." *MARYLAND HISTORICAL MAGAZINE* 35 (March): 81-82.
Reviews the first volume [15] of HLM's autobiography; a subsequent review of NEWSPAPER DAYS [16] was published in the December 1941 issue (444-45). Both essays reprinted in [582].

868 Pritchett, V.S. "Themselves." *NEW STATESMAN AND NATION* n.s. 20 (7 December): 584-85.
Reviews HAPPY DAYS [15] among other autobiographies.

869 Rascoe, Burton. "Mencken, Nathan, and Cabell." *AMERICAN MERCURY* 49 (March): 362-68.
Reviews HAPPY DAYS [15] and books by two of HLM's contemporaries.

1941

870 "Mencken at 61." *TIME* 38 (20 October): 106-08.
Review of NEWSPAPER DAYS [16].

871 Owens, Hamilton. "NEWSPAPER DAYS." *MARYLAND HISTORICAL MAGAZINE* 36 (December): 444-45.
Favorable review, emphasizing HLM's joy in the life of Baltimore.

1942

872 Eastman, Max. "About H.L. Mencken." *AMERICAN MERCURY* 55 (August): 242-47.
Responds warmly to HLM's NEW DICTIONARY OF QUOTATIONS [17], with brief mention of HAPPY DAYS [15] and NEWSPAPER DAYS [16].

1943

873 Cowley, Malcolm. "Mencken and Mark Twain." *NEW REPUBLIC* 108 (8 March): 321-22.
Reviews the DAYS books [15, 16, 18], commenting on their similarity to THE ADVENTURES OF HUCKLEBERRY FINN.

874 Krutch, Joseph Wood. "Mr. Mencken and the Good Old Days." *NATION* 156 (27 March): 456-57.
A backward glance at the impact of HLM upon his time, by way of reviewing HEATHEN DAYS [18].

1946

875 Barzun, Jacques. "Mencken's America Speaking." *ATLANTIC MONTHLY* 177 (January): 62-65.

Mixed opinions on the value and ultimate significance of THE AMERICAN LANGUAGE and its first SUPPLEMENT [7].

876 Gillis, James M. "What Shaw Really Taught." *CATHOLIC WORLD* 163 (September): 481-89.
Considers whether HLM might be an "American G.B.S.," comparing the two men's ideas with particular attention to religion and Christianity.

1947

877 McDavid, Raven I., Jr. "*THE AMERICAN LANGUAGE* ... SUPPLEMENT I." *LANGUAGE* 23: 68-73.
Careful and favorable review of [7]; the author also reviews SUPPLEMENT II in the same periodical, 25 (1949): 69-77. Both reviews reprinted in his DIALECTS IN CULTURE [736].

1948

878 "Mr. Mencken Again." *NEWSWEEK* 31 (5 April): 89-91.
Publication of the second SUPPLEMENT to THE AMERICAN LANGUAGE [7] is the occasion for this personal and historical profile.

1949

879 Bendiner, Robert. "From Mencken to Pegler." *NATION* 169 (27 August): 206-07.
In reviewing the CHRESTOMATHY [413], finds occasion to compare the twenties and the forties, "an era of self-assurance and one of fear," respectively (206).

880 Johnson, Gerald W. "Mencken: Scholar, Wit, One-Man Tornado." New York *HERALD TRIBUNE WEEKLY BOOK REVIEW* 25 (26 June): 1, 10-11.
Considers the impact of HLM as scholar and artist on the occasion of the publication of A MENCKEN CHRESTOMATHY [413].

881 Lardner, John. "Chrestomathy à la Maryland." *NEW YORKER* 25 (9 July): 58-61.

Favorable review of [413] that attempts to analyze the reasons for HLM's popularity with the young intellectuals of the twenties.

1950

882 Francis, Raymond L. "Mark Twain and H.L. Mencken." *PRAIRIE SCHOONER* 24 (Spring): 31-39.
Emphasizes their similarities as iconoclasts and satirists.

883 Manchester, William. "Mencken and the MERCURY." *HARPER'S MAGAZINE* 201 (August): 65-73.

884 ------. "Mencken and the Twenties." *HARPER'S MAGAZINE* 201 (July): 62-72.
Includes drawings "characteristic of the era" by John Held, Jr.

1951

885 Asbury, Herbert. "The Day Mencken Broke the Law." *AMERICAN MERCURY* 73 (October): 62-69.
The author of the "Hatrack" story retells the incident of HLM's confrontation over the story with J. Frank Chase, secretary of Boston's Watch and Ward Society.

1952

886 Smith, Beverly. "The Curious Case of the President's Bathtub." *SATURDAY EVENING POST* 225 (23 August): 25, 91-94.
On HLM's hoax; see [32].

1953

887 "Bouquets for Mencken." *NATION* 177 (12 September): 210-14.
Symposium of comments and recollections on the occasion of HLM's birthday by William Manchester, Harvey Fergusson, Stewart H. Holbrook, H.L. Davis, George Milburn, Gerald W. Johnson, James Branch Cabell, Ruth Suckow, Michael Gold, Thyra Samter Winslow, and Idwal Jones.

Articles

888 Greet, W. Cabell. "George Philip Krapp and Henry L. Mencken." *WORD STUDY* 29 (October): 1-4.
These otherwise dissimilar men were nevertheless "more influential than any others in establishing the linguistic atmosphere in which usage ... is the most important linguistic fact" (1).

1954

889 Angoff, Charles. "The Inside View of Mencken's MERCURY." *NEW REPUBLIC* 131 (13 September): 18-22.

890 Cousins, Norman. "Our Times and the *MERCURY*." *SATURDAY REVIEW* 37 (12 June): 22.
On the magazine's heyday and decline.

1955

891 Cooke, Alistair. "The Baltimore Fox: An Appraisal by a British Journalist of a Writer with an Inimitable Style." *SATURDAY REVIEW* 38 (10 September): 13, 63-64.
Taken from the author's introduction to his soon-to-be-published collection, THE VINTAGE MENCKEN [414].

892 Kemler, Edgar. "The Bright Twilight of H.L. Mencken." *NEW YORK TIMES MAGAZINE* (11 September): 14, 44, 47, 49.
One of HLM's biographers [488] writes of the convalescent years following HLM's stroke; includes a backward glance at his career.

893 Manchester, William. "H.L. Mencken at Seventy-Five: America's Sam Johnson." *SATURDAY REVIEW* 38 (10 September): 11-13.
Discusses parallels and points of difference between the two critic-lexicographers.

894 McKelway, St. Clair. "Thorns Without Roses." *NEW YORKER* 31 (19 November): 229-33.
Cites HLM frequently while reviewing THE VINTAGE MENCKEN [414].

895 Sinclair, Upton. "A Letter." *NEW WORLD WRITING* 8: 280-81.
> Addressed to James T. Farrell, the letter decries his "revival" in a previous essay [665] of HLM's "lies" about the socialist.

1956

896 Bode, Carl. "In Memoriam." *SOCIETY FOR THE HISTORY OF THE GERMANS IN MARYLAND: REPORT 29*: 7-73.
> Obituary reviewing HLM's career and place in American life and letters (Reprinted in Bode's HALF-WORLD OF AMERICAN CULTURE: A MISCELLANY, Carbondale: Southern Illinois University Press, 1965). This issue also contains a reminiscence by A.E. Zucker (68) and a poem by H.F. Manchester (69).

897 Hackett, Francis. "Chicago's Opportunity." *NEW REPUBLIC* 134 (25 June): 21-22.
> The city did not become the national literary capital as HLM had prophesied in 1920.

898 Hazlitt, Henry. "Mencken: A Retrospect." *NEWSWEEK* 47 (20 February): 90.
> The man who succeeded HLM as editor of the AM recalls his views on economics.

899 Horchler, R.T. "Beleagured [sic] Reputation of a Great Iconoclast." *COMMONWEAL* 64 (27 July): 422-23.
> Cautions against one-sided views of HLM, such as those presented by his own posthumous MINORITY REPORT [416] and the Angoff biography [495].

900 Howe, Irving. "A Comedian Playing Hamlet." *NEW REPUBLIC* 134 (21 May): 17-18.
> A reviewer of MINORITY REPORT [416] expresses disappointment that HLM actually believed everything he said, that "he had absolutely no critical distance from his chosen role" (17).

901 Johnson, Gerald W. "Henry L. Mencken [1880-1956]." *SATURDAY REVIEW* 39 (11 February): 90.

Personal profile occasioned by HLM's demise. Reprinted in [582].

902 Morris, Joe Alex. "The Nimble Axeman." *SATURDAY REVIEW* 39 (26 May): 21.
Reviews MINORITY REPORT [416] favorably.

903 Pickrel, Paul. "Captive Critics." *HARPER'S MAGAZINE* 213 (July): 91-92.
Comments on MINORITY REPORT [416] and compares HLM to Ring Lardner.

904 Yarling, Bass. "Mencken and Politics." *NEW REPUBLIC* 135 (22 October): 20-21.
Mixed review of A CARNIVAL OF BUNCOMBE [415].

1957

905 Angoff, Charles. "Mencken and the Wrong Side." *NEW REPUBLIC* 137 (18 November): 3, 23.
Responds to Gerald W. Johnson's claim [907] that HLM was a defender of freedom by stating that HLM was pro-Nazi. Arthur Schlesinger, Jr., in turn denies Angoff's statement in "Mencken and Prejudice," *NR* 137 (16 December 1957): 23. Angoff then follows up with another letter, "Was Mencken Anti-Semitic?" *NR* 138 (13 January 1958): 3, 23, to which Guy J. Forgue responds with "Mencken Debate," *NR* 138 (17 February 1958): 3, 22-23.

906 Bendiner, Robert. "A Mencken Blunderbuss." *THE REPORTER* 16 (24 January): 42-43.
Reviews A CARNIVAL OF BUNCOMBE [415] and comments on HLM's political opinions.

907 Johnson, Gerald W. "Oh, for Mencken Now." *NEW REPUBLIC* 137 (30 September): 11.
Written on the occasion of the removal of HUCKLEBERRY FINN from New York City's high school reading list. See Charles Angoff's response [905].

1959

908 Cowing, Cedric B. "H.L. Mencken: The Case of the 'Curdled' Progressive." ETHICS 69 (July): 255-67.
Studies the post-World War I period in which the sort of progressivism embodied by HLM declined in strength as that embodied by Franklin D. Roosevelt and his New Deal grew.

909 Forgue, Guy. "La carrière de H.L. Mencken et les critiques." ETUDES ANGLAISES 12 (April-June): 112-23.
Summary of HLM's career and critical reception over the years before and since his death. In French.

910 Kloefkorn, Johnny L. "A Critical Study of the Work of H.L. Menchen [sic] As Literary Editor and Critic of the The American Mercury" EMPORIA STATE RESEARCH STUDIES 7 (June): entire issue.
Includes valuable list of authors published or reviewed in the AM as part of an argument that with this magazine, unlike with the SS, HLM's interest in the belles lettres was on the decline.

911 "Mencken on Tape." TIMES LITERARY SUPPLEMENT [London] 13 (March): 142.
This review of the Angoff biography [495] stirred several responses from R.P. Harriss, who asserted that HLM's former assistant editor at the AM distorted his boss's views on such topics as Germany, England, Jews, and blacks. See "Was H.L. Mencken Anti-Semitic?--No," Baltimore AMERICAN 7 June 1959, sec. AL, p.7; "He Derided Life and Made It Gay," Baltimore AMERICAN 21 June 1959, sec. AL, p. 5; and "H.L. Mencken," a letter to the editor, TLS 3 July 1959, p. 399.

1960

912 Babcock, C. Merton. "Profiles of Noted Linguists: Henry Louis Mencken." WORD STUDY 36 (December): 1-4.

Articles

On the significance of HLM's unflagging interest in American English.

913 Fitzgerald, Stephen E. "The Mencken Myth." SATURDAY REVIEW 43 (17 December): 13-15, 71.
Profiles the man who often seemed "a tangle of paradoxes" (13).

914 Weintraub, Stanley. "Apostate Apostle: H.L. Mencken as Shavophile and Shavophobe." EDUCATIONAL THEATRE JOURNAL 12 (October): 184-90.
Analyzes the transformations in HLM's views of George Bernard Shaw.

1961

915 Bloom, Robert. "Past Indefinite: The Sherman-Mencken Debate on an American Tradition." WESTERN HUMANITIES REVIEW 15 (Winter): 73-81.
The different approaches these critics took to Dreiser illustrate the central conflict in their debate: opposing views on "the moral conceptions which should govern life in America" (74).

916 Forgue, Guy Jean. "Myths About Mencken." NATION 193 (16 September): 163-65.
Attempts to dispel several widely held notions about HLM, particularly concerning his views toward Germany, Jews, and blacks.

917 Lowrey, Burling. "Mr. Mencken's Guided Missiles." NEW REPUBLIC 145 (13 November): 14-16.
On the literary and political views voiced in HLM's correspondence, recently collected by Guy J. Forgue [430].

918 McHugh, Robert. "Dirge for a Vanished Art." SOUTH ATLANTIC QUARTERLY 60 (Summer): 340-44.
Recounts one of HLM's hoaxes, this one involving a series of letters to the editor of the Baltimore ES written anonymously by co-conspirator Holger A. Koppel and signed "An American Mother."

919 Nolte, William. "Criticism With Vine Leaves." *TEXAS STUDIES IN LITERATURE AND LANGUAGE* 3 (Spring): 16-39.
Emphasizing style, surveys HLM's criticism of a wide range of people and topics, including Upton Sinclair, Hall Caine, William Allen White, Calvin Coolidge, democracy, music, the New Thought, and "the Uplift."

1962

920 Martin, Edward A. "The Ordeal of H.L. Mencken." *SOUTH ATLANTIC QUARTERLY* 61 (Summer): 326-38.
Sums up the range of HLM's topics as well as his absorption of others' ideas.

921 McCall, Raymond G. "H.L. Mencken and the Glass of Satire." *COLLEGE ENGLISH* 23 (May): 633-36.
Compares HLM to Jonathan Swift.

922 Rothbard, Murray N. "H.L. Mencken: The Joyous Libertarian." *NEW INDIVIDUALIST REVIEW* 2 (Summer): 15-27.
Quoting heavily from his works, analyzes HLM as an individualist whose chief cause was personal liberty.

1963

923 Babcock, C. Merton. "H.L. Mencken: Of Horse-Laughs and Syllogisms." *ETC.: A REVIEW OF GENERAL SEMANTICS* 19 (January): 427-33.
Takes HLM's notion that "One horse-laugh is worth ten thousand syllogisms" as a point of departure, discussing his rhetoric and several comments he made on the subject.

924 Bruccoli, Matthew J. "The First Printing of THE ARTIST." *MENCKENIANA* 8 (Winter): 4-7.
Corrects some incorrect bibliographic information on HLM's play [20].

925 Dolmetsch, Carl Richard. "Forging the Mencken Myth." *BOOKS* [Williamsburg, VA] (June): 1-2.
Bibliographic essay on books published on HLM since his death in 1956.

Articles

1964

926 Babcock, C. Merton. "Mark Twain, Mencken and 'The Higher Goofyism.'" *AMERICAN QUARTERLY* 16 (Winter): 587-94.
An able discussion of the satirists' similarities and differences.

927 Davidson, Wilbur L., Jr. "H.L. Mencken, the *SMART SET*, and the Expatriate Movement." *WILLIAM AND MARY REVIEW* 2 (Spring): 71-84.

928 LeVot, André E. "H.L. Mencken and F.S. Fitzgerald: A Family Quarrel." *MENCKENIANA* 9 (Spring): 6-8.
Sketches the reasons the novelist outgrew HLM.

929 Martin, Edward A. "H.L. Mencken's Poetry." *TEXAS STUDIES IN LITERATURE AND LANGUAGE* 6 (Autumn): 346-53.
HLM's early work in this genre (VENTURES INTO VERSE [1]) contributed to his development as a prose stylist, especially as evidenced in his essay "In Memoriam: W.J.B." [82]. Reprinted in [582].

930 McDavid, Raven. "American English." *COLLEGE ENGLISH* 25 (February 1964): 331-37.
Surveys the development of HLM's attitude toward the National Council of Teachers of English through the various editions of THE AMERICAN LANGUAGE and SUPPLEMENTS I and II [7], speculating on what his opinions might be on NCTE's current concern with American English. Reprinted in [736].

931 ------. "Mencken Revisited." *HARVARD EDUCATIONAL REVIEW* 34 (Spring): 211-25.
On the field of linguistics at the time of and since THE AMERICAN LANGUAGE [7]. Reprinted in LANGUAGE AND LEARNING (New York: Harcourt, 1966) and in [736].

932 Nolte, William H. "GBS and HLM." *SOUTHWEST REVIEW* 49 (Spring): 163-73.

A comparison of satirists Shaw and HLM by way of the latter's remarks on the former and his work.

933 ------. "H.L. Mencken and the American Hydra." *NEW INDIVIDUALIST REVIEW* 3 (Autumn): 37-46.
In-depth analysis of HLM's "Puritanism as a Literary Force" [33].

934 ------. "Mencken on Prose Fiction." *TEXAS QUARTERLY* 7 (Autumn): 139-53.
On HLM's "concept of the novel" (140), particularly as delineated in his book reviews written for the *SS* and the *AM*.

935 Owens, Hamilton. "The *SUNPAPERS'* History." *MENCKENIANA* 12 (Winter): 3-4.
HLM served as general editor of Gerald W. Johnson's history of the newspaper written in celebration of its centennial. The following pages reprint several letters that passed between HLM and Johnson during the project. See also [14].

936 Wycherley, H. Alan. "Mencken and Knopf: The Editor and His Publisher." *AMERICAN QUARTERLY* 16 (Fall): 460-72.

1965

937 Boller, Paul F., Jr. "Purlings and Platitudes: Mencken's Americana." *SOUTHWEST REVIEW* 50 (Autumn): 357-71.
History of the "Americana" department from the *SS* through the *AM*.

938 *MARYLAND ENGLISH JOURNAL* 4 (Fall).
This issue contains a number of brief articles on HLM:
Albert W. Dowling, "H.L. Mencken and the Polytechnic," 23-26
Richard H. Hart, "Poe and Mencken at the Pratt Library," 29-30
"HLM Holdings at the Talbot County Free Library," 42, 44

        "HLM Among the Marylandia at the
        McKeldin Library, University of
        Maryland," 65
        James Walt, "Tale of Another Liberal's
        Progress," 56-57, 59-60, 62

939 Nolte, William H. "The Sex Uproar."
    MENCKENIANA 16 (Winter): 3-7.
        On what HLM had to say about the topic,
    especially as it appears in American
    literature.

940 Pederson, Lee A. "The Mencken Legacy." *ORBIS*
    14 (June): 63-74.
        Praises McDavid's abridgement of THE
    AMERICAN LANGUAGE [7], comparing portions
    of it with the fourth edition and with
    SUPPLEMENTS I and II.

941 Stenerson, Douglas C. "Mencken's Early
    Newspaper Experience: The Genesis of a Style."
    AMERICAN LITERATURE 37 (May): 153-66.
        ... developed during his tenure with the
    Baltimore *HERALD*.

                1966

942 Dolmetsch, Carl Richard. "H.L. Mencken as a
    Critic of Poetry." *JAHRBUCH FR AMERIKASTUDIEN*
    11: 83-95.
        Refutes the widely disseminated view
    (largely HLM's own doing) that America's
    foremost ally of the *belles lettres* was a
    bad judge of poetry. In English.

943 McDavid, Raven I., Jr. "The Impact of Mencken
    on American Linquistics." *MENCKENIANA* 17
    (Spring): 1-7.
        Lecture delivered 21 October 1965 at
    EPFL. Reprinted in [582].

944 Morrison, Joseph L. "Mencken and Odum: The
    Dutch Uncle and the South." *VIRGINIA QUARTERLY*
    REVIEW 42 (Autumn): 601-15.
        On HLM's support for North Carolina
    sociologist Howard W. Odum.

945 Motsch, Markus F. "A Dose of *Kultur*."
    MENCKENIANA 19 (Fall): 8-11.

HLM's enthusiasm for people and things German led him to read and write often of German music, literature, philosophy, and language. Reprinted in slightly different form [1016].

946 Rubin, Louis D., Jr. "H.L. Mencken and the National Letters." *SEWANEE REVIEW* 74 (Summer): 723-38.
What begins as a review of THE AMERICAN SCENE: A READER [420] develops into a thorough discussion of HLM as a stylist and a literary critic, with particular attention to "The National Letters" [52].

947 Stenerson, Douglas C. "The 'Forgotten Man' of H.L. Mencken." *AMERICAN QUARTERLY* 18 (Winter): 686-96.
HLM and George Jean Nathan began the *AM* with the aim of addressing the middle-class individualist whom Social Darwinist William Graham Sumner had called "the forgotten man." Reprinted in [582].

948 Stoddard, Donald R. "Mencken and Dreiser: An Exchange of Roles." *THE LIBRARY CHRONICLE* [University of Pennsylvania] 32 (Spring): 117-36.
When they met in 1908, Dreiser played the role of advisor as HLM ghosted a series of articles for Dreiser's *DELINEATOR*; by the time of A BOOK OF PREFACES in 1917 [401], the tables had turned.

1967

949 Angoff, Charles. "The Mystique of the *SMART SET*." *LITERARY REVIEW* 11 (Autumn): 59-60.

950 Babcock, C. Merton. "Mencken's Shortest Way with Academic Non-Dissenters." *UNIVERSITY COLLEGE QUARTERLY* 12 (January): 28-32.
HLM had little use or respect for teachers or formal education.

951 Brien, Alan. "Mudlark Maestro." *NEW STATESMAN* 74 (6 October): 431-32.

Scans the range of HLM's invective, noting that its success lay largely in his prose style.

952 Christian, Henry A. "Ten Letters to Louis Adamic." *PRINCETON UNIVERSITY LIBRARY CHRONICLE* 28 (Winter): 76-94.
Includes the text of one from HLM while editor of the *AM*; mentions HLM elsewhere throughout the article.

953 Dolmetsch, Carl Richard. "Mencken as a Magazine Editor." *MENCKENIANA* 21 (Spring): 1-8.
Lecture delivered 13 October 1966 at EPFL. Reprinted in [582].

954 Lawson, Lewis A. "Portrait of a Culture in Crisis: Modern Southern Literature." *TEXAS QUARTERLY* 10 (Spring): 143-55.
Uses HLM's "Sahara of the Bozart" [31] as a launching point for a discussion of post-Civil War Southern letters.

955 McDavid, Raven I., Jr. "Mencken's Onomastics." *ORBIS* 16 (June): 93-100.
HLM's chapter on "Proper Names in America" in his AMERICAN LANGUAGE [7] posed special challenges to the author when he prepared his abridgement.

1968

956 Bauer, Harry C. "Grand Master of the Word Art." MENCKENIANA 27 (Fall): 6-12.
HLM will be remembered less for his ideas than for his style.

957 Blodgett, Harold W. "Mencken in Retrospect." *UNION COLLEGE SYMPOSIUM* 7 (Spring): 18-24.
Succinct survey of HLM's work, prose style, and impact on the author's own generation, with a glance at the authors who influenced the Sage.

958 Boller, Paul F., Jr. "American Absurdities." *MENCKENIANA* 25 (Spring): 1-4.

On the "Americana" department of the *SS* and the *AM*; also discussed in his QUOTESMANSHIP: THE USE AND ABUSE OF QUOTATIONS FOR POLEMICAL AND OTHER PURPOSES (Dallas, TX: Southern Methodist University Press, 1967).

959   Jacobs, Bradford. "H.L.M.'s Constitution." Baltimore *EVENING SUN* (12 January): A 26.
      Compares the recent Constitutional Convention's proposals with HLM's "A Proposed New Constitution For Maryland" [355] and finds striking similarities.

960   Johnson, Gerald W. "Upton Sinclair: Not To Be Dismissed." Baltimore *SUNDAY SUN* (1 December): K1.
      Compares the two Baltimoreans, who despite their different political views nevertheless respected each other's "courage and vigor." Partially reprinted in *MENCKENIANA* 29 (Spring 1969): 11.

961   Litz, Francis E. "De Translatione." *MENCKENIANA* 25 (Spring): 7-8.
      Corrects mistaken information about HLM's edition of THE CHARLANTRY OF THE LEARNED [392] caused by an inaccuracy on the title page. In English.

962   Long, Robert Emmet. "B & D: Nathan and Mencken as Maury Noble." *FITZGERALD NEWSLETTER* no. 40 (Winter): 303.
      Argues that the character of Noble in THE BEAUTIFUL AND THE DAMNED is modelled not after George Jean Nathan but rather HLM.

963   Morrison, Joseph L. "Colonel H.L. Mencken, C.S.A." *SOUTHERN LITERARY JOURNAL* 1 (December): 42-59.
      HLM was much more pro-South than he is usually credited with being.

964   Nolte, William H. "The Smart Set: Mencken for the Defense." *SOUTH DAKOTA REVIEW* 6 (Autumn): 3-11.
      On HLM's hopes for the *SS* and their fulfillment.

Articles

965 Ruland, Richard. "Mencken and Cabell." *CABELLIAN* 1: 13-20.
> Covers their personal and professional relations, particularly noting HLM's defense of JURGEN before the censors.

966 Taylor, K. Phillip. "H.L. Mencken: Rhetorical Critic of Presidents." *TODAY'S SPEECH* 16 (November): 27-30.
> Covers HLM's remarks on presidential rhetoric made during his tenure with the *AM*, from 1924 to 1933. See also Stephen B. Voigt's letter to the editor 17 (May 1969): 104, which refutes Taylor's assertion that HLM advocated an aristocratic form of government.

1969

967 Adler, Betty. "*AMERICAN MERCURY* Pseudonyms." *MENCKENIANA* 31 (Fall): 15.
> Here and in subsequent notes, HLM's bibliographer traces the actual authorship of several *AM* articles to Adolphe E. Meyer, Emerson Field Price, and Morris Fishbein. See *MENCKENIANA* 34 and 35 (Summer and Fall 1970): 11 and 15, respectively. See also an earlier note on Kenneth Chafee McIntosh, *MENCKENIANA* 25 (Spring 1968): 16.

968 Castagna, Edwin. "Loud and Clear: H.L. Mencken the Communicator." *MENCKENIANA* 30 (Summer): 1-8.
> Lecture delivered 29 October 1968 at the University of Iowa.

969 Durham, Frank. "Mencken as Midwife." *MENCKENIANA* 32 (Winter): 2-6.
> On HLM's contributions to a Southern literary revival, with emphasis on the work of DuBose Heyward and Julia Peterkin.

970 Iversen, Anders. "Democratic Man, the Superior Man, and the Forgotten Man in H.L. Mencken's NOTES ON DEMOCRACY [1]." *ENGLISH STUDIES* 50 (August): 351-62.
> Attempts "to point out some of the characteristics of [HLM's] political

criticism and journalism, and to show that what ailed him as a thinker was ... the irrelevance of some of his chief ideas and concepts ... " (352).

971 Stenerson, Douglas C. "Short-Story Writing: A Neglected Phase of Mencken's Literary Apprenticeship." *MENCKENIANA* 30 (Summer): 8-13.

972 Walt, James. "Mencken and Conrad." *CONRADIANA* 2 (Winter 1969/1970): 9-21.
Followed by "Conrad and Mencken: Part II" 2 (Spring 1969/1970): 100-10.

973 Wilson, Edmund. "The Aftermath of Mencken." *NEW YORKER* 45 (31 May): 107-15.
A survey of HLM's ideas by way of brief reviews of recent books on him. Reprinted in Wilson's THE DEVILS AND CANON BARHAM: ESSAYS ON POETS, NOVELISTS, AND MONSTERS (New York: Farrar, Straus, and Giroux, 1973).

1970

974 Arnett, Earl. "Mencken and Jazz." *MENCKENIANA* 36 (Winter): 1-2.

975 Babcock, C. Merton. "A Vocabulary on Hysterical Principles." *MENCKENIANA* 36 (Winter): 5-7.
On HLM's diction, so characteristic as to be generally known as "Menckenese."

976 ------. "The Wizards of Baltimore: Poe and Mencken." *TEXAS QUARTERLY* 13 (Autumn): 110-15.
Both men "were prowling practitioners of the black arts, blasphemous profaners of the sacred groves, and bedeviled head-hunters running amuck in the American literary jungle" (110).

977 "Baltimore's Bad Boy: A Great and Beneficent Force." *TIMES LITERARY SUPPLEMENT* [London] (4 September): 973-74.
In reviewing Bode's MENCKEN [532], touches on aspects of HLM not thoroughly discussed by the biographer.

Articles

978 Barrick, Nancy D., and Ernest O. Brown. "Mencken, the Negro and Civil Rights." *MENCKENIANA* 35 (Fall): 4-7.

979 Brod, Donald F. "Mencken on Scopes: Significance and 'Buffooneries.'" *QUILL* 58 (December): 22.
   HLM's coverage of the famous trial included consideration of "the forces in conflict, of the environment in which the antagonistic ideas grew, and of the possible consequences of the outcome."

980 Caldwell, John. "The International Dramatic Critiques' Anti-Playwriting Association." *MENCKENIANA* 36 (Winter): 3-5.
   Corrects some mistaken facts in NEWSPAPER DAYS [16] on HLM's acquaintance with drama critic Glenmore "Stuffy" Davis.

981 Demouy, Jane Krause. "Mencken and Nietzsche: The Journalist and the Mystic." *MARYLAND ENGLISH JOURNAL* 9 (Fall): 35-46.
   Illustrates how HLM misrepresented his "teacher" (36) in THE PHILOSOPHY OF FRIEDRICH NIETZSCHE [3].

982 LaBelle, Maurice M. "H.L. Mencken's Comprehension of Friedrich Nietzsche." *COMPARATIVE LITERATURE STUDIES* 7 (March): 43-49.
   ... was "superficial," according to the author. HLM "was not really influence by Nietzsche but found in him a kindred spirit" (49). Critiques THE PHILOSOPHY OF FRIEDRICH NIETZSCHE [3].

983 Lora, Ronald G. "The Politics of a Conservative Libertarian." *MENCKENIANA* 34 (Summer): 4-11.
   On viewing HLM's "political thought ... in a context larger than that of politics" (6).

984 Wycherley, H. Alan. "H.L. Mencken vs the Eastern Shore: December 1931." *BULLETIN OF THE NEW YORK PUBLIC LIBRARY* 74 (June): 381-90.
   Recounts HLM's battles in print over the Maryland Eastern Shore lynchings of 1931.

1971

985   Bready, James H. "Reading Mencken's Mail."
      Baltimore SUNDAY SUN MAGAZINE (24 January):
      4-5, 7.
         One of a number of articles that appeared
      in various U.S. newspapers announcing the
      release of HLM's correspondence on the
      fifteenth anniversary of his death; he had
      donated this material to the New York
      Public Library and put it under time-lock.

986   Bonner, Thomas C. "Mencken as Whangdoodle: One
      Aspect of H.L. Mencken's Style." MARKHAM
      REVIEW 3 (October): 14-17.
         ... that of reducing people and ideas
      to absurdities.

987   Duke, Maurice. "THE REVIEWER: A Bibliographical Guide to a Little Magazine." RESOURCES
      FOR AMERICAN LITERARY STUDY 1 (Spring): 58-97.
         Introductory essay mentions HLM's "Sahara
      of the Bozart" [31] and his advice for the
      founders of the Virginia magazine. List
      of articles includes several for which HLM
      is either author or subject.

988   Fullinwider, S.P. "Mencken's American
      Language." MENCKENIANA 40 (Winter): 2-7.
         A rather ingenious psychoanalysis of HLM
      approached through his diction and usage.

989   Grinder, R. Dale. "H.L. Mencken: Notes on a
      Libertarian." LIBERTARIAN ANALYSIS 1 (Fall):
      43-51.
         Traces HLM's development as a Social
      Darwinist.

990   Kellner, Bruce. "HLM and CVV [Carl Van
      Vechten]: Friendship on Paper." MENCKENIANA 39
      (Fall): 2-9.

991   Nolte, William H. "Mencken, Faulkner, and
      Southern Moralism." SOUTH CAROLINA REVIEW 4
      (December): 45-61.

992   ------. "Mencken on Art, Order, and the
      Absurd." MENCKENIANA 37 (Spring): 1-7.

Lecture delivered 12 September 1970 at EPFL.

993 Schoettler, Carl. "Debunking the Debunker: Miserly, Mean, Mealy-Mouthed, Say Neighbors of H.L. Mencken." Baltimore *EVENING SUN* (29 September): F20, F2.
> See also the responding editorial, "HLM Would Wink," page A12 of the same issue.

1972

994 Adler, Betty. "Evolution of a Menckenite." *CABELLIAN* 4 (Spring): 99-103.
> Personal letter from the author to the editor of the *CABELLLIAN* telling of her work on various HLM bibliographical projects.

995 Cheslock, Louis. "THE JEWEL MERCHANTS, AN OPERA: A Case History." *CABELLIAN* 4 (Spring): 68-84.
> The author gives background and reprints letters involved in his adaption of Cabell's play for opera, in which he had HLM's assistance.

996 Cooney, Charles F. "Mencken's Midwifery." *MENCKENIANA* 43 (Fall): 1-4.
> On HLM's assistance to the early writing career of novelist and NAACP leader Walter White.

997 Levin, James B. "National Convention Reporter." *MENCKENIANA* 41 (Spring): 9-12.
> HLM's political reporting is very much worth reading, but should be given careful attention: some of his inaccuracies and ambiguities can be misleading.

998 Manglaviti, Leo M.J. "Faulkner's 'That Evening Sun' and Mencken's 'Best Editorial Judgment.'" *AMERICAN LITERATURE* 43 (January): 649-54.
> With the lifting in 1971 of the veil HLM had deliberately lowered at his death over a collection of his papers came more precise information regarding his role in the formation of various writers than had

previously been recognized. Manglaviti thus examines the now available typescript of the version (one of four) of Faulkner's short story published by the *AM* in March 1931.

999 ------. "Markham and Mencken." *THE MARKHAM REVIEW* 3 (February): 38-39.
Overview of the few encounters Mencken had with aging poet Edwin Markham.

1000 Muller, Herbert J. "Reconsideration: H.L. Mencken." *NEW REPUBLIC* 166 (12 February): 31-32.
HLM's writing is still valuable today; reviews PREJUDICES: A SELECTION [418].

1001 Pons, Xavier. "H.L. Mencken et la biologie." *CALIBAN* 8: 105-22.
On HLM's comments on science, biology in particular; and on the influence of Darwin in his social and economic commentary. In French.

1002 Shapiro, Edward S. "The Southern Agrarians, H.L. Mencken and the Quest for Southern Identity." *AMERICAN STUDIES* 13 (Fall): 75-92.
Good background on the "Sahara of the Bozart" [31] uproar.

1003 Stenerson, Douglas C. "Baltimore: Source and Sustainer of Mencken's Values." *MENCKENIANA* 41 (Spring): 1-9.
Lecture delivered at EPFL 11 September 1971.

1004 Turaj, Frank. "Mencken and the Nazis: A Note." *MARYLAND HISTORICAL MAGAZINE* 67 (Summer): 176-78.
HLM's pro-Germanism should not be confused with pro-Nazism.

1005 West, James L.W., III. "F. Scott Fitzgerald's Contributions to THE AMERICAN CREDO." *PRINCETON UNIVERSITY LIBRARY CHRONICLE* 34 (Autumn): 53-58.
Although the author lists a dozen items which Fitzgerald indicated were his contributions to the CREDO [8], HLM

bibliographer Betty Adler remarks that this is unlikely: *MENCKENIANA* 45 (Spring 1973): 16.

1006 Williamson, Chilton, Jr. "Commonsense Politics." *MENCKENIANA* 43 (Fall): 4-11.

1007 Wycherly, H. Alan. "'Americana': The Mencken-Lortimer Feud." *COSTERUS* 5 : 227-36.
Amusing account of the antagonism provoked by the *AM* in George Horace Lortimer, long-time editor of the *SEP*, particularly over the department entitled "Americana" [118].

1973

1008 Bauer, Harry C. "The Glow and Gusto of H.L. Mencken's So and So's." *MENCKENIANA* 47 (Fall): 19-23.
On HLM's habit of punching with two fists--that is, of using at least two words linked by "and" to get his point across.

1009 Cairns, Huntington. "Mencken, Baltimore, and the Critics." *MENCKENIANA* 45 (Spring): 1-9.
Lecture delivered 16 September 1972 at EPFL.

1010 Christian, Henry A. "'What Else Have You in Mind?': Louis Adamic and H.L. Mencken." *MENCKENIANA* 47 (Fall): 1-12.
On HLM's assistance to the slavic writer's early career.

1011 Douglas, George H. "Mr. Mencken on Liberty." *FREEMAN* 23 (December): 709-18.

1012 Evitts, William J. "The Savage South: H.L. Mencken and the Roots of a Persistent Image." *VIRGINIA QUARTERLY REVIEW* 49 (Autumn): 596-611.
HLM's writing on the region was primarily responsible for the anti-Southern sentiment that grew during the twenties and is yet alive and well.

1013 Jansen, Edward K. "Mencken on Ibsen: Even Mencken Nods." *MENCKENIANA* 47 (Fall): 13-18.
Takes issue with the critique of the dramatist HLM gives in his introduction to the Modern Library edition of ELEVEN PLAYS OF HENRIK IBSEN [390].

1014 Johnson, Gerald W. "Mencken and the Art of Boob Bumping." *NEW REPUBLIC* 168 (19 May): 7-8.
HLM would have been disappointed by Richard Nixon's ultimate failure to conceal completely his political maneuvers.

1015 Miles, Elton. "Mencken's *MERCURY* and the West." *SOUTHWESTERN AMERICAN LITERATURE* 3: 39-48.
Lists HLM's contributions, chiefly by way of publication in the *SS* or the *AM*, to the careers of several western American writers of the day, both known and little known.

1016 Motsch, Markus F. "H.L. Mencken and German Kultur." *JOURNAL OF GERMAN-AMERICAN STUDIES* 6 (Fall): 21-42.
A slightly different version of an article printed first in *MENCKENIANA* called "A Dose of *Kultur*" [945].

1017 Novak, Michael. "On Loving Anglo-Americans." *COMMONWEAL* 98 (9 March): 6, 23.
HLM's "The Anglo-Saxon" [65] serves as springboard for commentary on Anglo-Saxon Americanism and ethnocentricity.

1018 Olivar-Bertrand, R. "Mencken's This World Satire." *CONTEMPORARY REVIEW* 223 (October): 202-06.
A sampling of HLM's satire, particularly as it touched upon politics and religion.

1019 Powell, Arnold. "Mencken and the Absurdists." *MENCKENIANA* 46 (Summer): 3-8.
Compares HLM's burlesques to the later theater of the absurd.

1020 Reynolds, Robert D., Jr. "Robert Rives LaMonte: Mencken's 'Millionaire Socialist' Collaborator." *MENCKENIANA* 48 (Winter): 2-4.
Background on the writing of MEN VERSUS THE MAN [4].

1021 Salzman, Jack. "Conroy, Mencken, and *THE AMERICAN MERCURY*." *JOURNAL OF POPULAR CULTURE* 7 (Winter): 524-28.
Fills in historical background on Depression writer Jack Conroy's professional debt to HLM.

1022 Scheideman, J.W. "H.L. Mencken Portrayed in Fiction." *NOTES AND QUERIES* n.s. 20: 142-43.
Lists a handful of fictional characters based on the historical HLM.

1023 Shutt, James W. "H.L. Mencken and the Baltimore *EVENING SUN* Freelance [sic] Column." *MENCKENIANA* 48 (Winter): 8-10.

1024 Turaj, Frank. "H.L. Mencken's Philosophical Skepticism." *MENCKENIANA* 48 (Winter): 12-16.
Compares HLM to Thomas Henry Huxley.

1025 Williams, William H.A. "Realism and Iconoclasm: H.L. Mencken as Drama Critic." *MENCKENIANA* 46 (Summer): 8-12.
HLM's early writing offers clues to the attitudes that shaped his subsequent work.

1026 Woolf, H.B. "Mencken as Etymologist: 'Charley Horse' and 'Lobster Trick.'" *AMERICAN SPEECH* 48 (Fall/Winter): 229-38.

1974

1027 Eastman, John. "HLM's Voice for Posterity." *MENCKENIANA* 51 (Fall): 9-11.
On the Caedmon recording of Donald Howe Kirkley's interview with HLM.

1028 Hart, Richard. "The Mencken Industry." *MENCKENIANA* 52 (Winter): 3-14.
In his lecture of 15 September 1974 at EPFL, former head of the library's Humanities Department describes the establish-

ment and updating of the HLM collection. A "must see" for the newcomer to HLM studies looking for a good bibliographical survey.

1029 Jerome, W.P. "A Baltimore Episcopalian." *MENCKENIANA* 51 (Fall): 7-9.
HLM was much less an atheist than he claimed to be.

1030 Matheson, Terence J. "H.L. Mencken's Reviews of Sinclair Lewis' Major Novels." *MENCKENIANA* 51 (Fall): 2-7.
Reprinted in *SLN* 7-8 (1975-76): 7-10.

1031 "Mencken's Baltimore." Special Supplement, Baltimore *SUNDAY SUN* (8 September): 40 pages.
Includes an introduction by John Dorsey and excerpts from HLM's comments on various aspects of the city.

1032 Wingate, P.J. "H.L. Mencken on Watergate." *MENCKENIANA* 50 (Summer): 4-5.
Speculates that the Sage would be more forgiving than thunderous were he around to comment on modern-day political shenanigans.

1975

1033 Anderson, Fenwick. "Mencken's Animadversions on Journalism." *MENCKENIANA* 53 (Spring): 6-8.
Highlights HLM's criticisms of the profession.

1034 Bauer, Harry C. "Iteration in HLM's Idiom Attic." *MENCKENIANA* 55 (Fall): 2-6.
On HLM's characteristic diction, with special attention given the CHRESTOMATHY [413].

1035 Burr, John R. "H.L. Mencken: Scientific Skeptic." *MENCKENIANA* 54 (Summer): 1-8.
Approaches the debate over whether HLM was a genuine skeptic by distinguishing among varieties of skepticism.

1036 Douglas, George H. "Mencken's Critics in the Twenties." *MENCKENIANA* 53 (Spring): 1-5.

Surveys those responses to HLM by his early contemporaries that are still worth reading.

1037 Johnson, Gerald W. "Reconsideration--H.L. Mencken." *MENCKENIANA* 56 (Winter): 1-3.
People usually associate the right qualities with HLM when they think of him, but for the wrong reasons. Reprinted from the *NR* 173 (27 December 1975): 32-33.

1038 Karp, Laurence E. "The Fundamentalist and the Iconoclast: H.A. Kelley and H.L. Mencken." *NEW ENGLAND JOURNAL OF MEDICINE* 292 (6 February): 297-99.
The story of HLM's relationship to the noted doctor includes a number of issues--chiefly that of theology--on which they disagreed, despite their mutual professional respect.

1039 Shephardson, D.E. "In the Prime of His Time." *AMERICAN HISTORY ILLUSTRATED* 9 (January): 10-19.
An overview of HLM's career and influence.

1040 Shyre, Paul. "Mencken on Stage." *MENCKENIANA* 56 (Winter): 4-8.
The story behind Shyre's one-man, off-Broadway production, BLASTS AND BRAVOS: AN EVENING WITH H.L. MENCKEN.

1976

1041 Banks, Dean. "H.L. Mencken and 'Hitlerism,' 1933-1941: A Patrician Libertarian Besieged." *MARYLAND HISTORICAL MAGAZINE* 71 (Winter): 498-515.
A thorough discussion of HLM's views--never expressed in print--of Nazism.

1042 Bauer, Harry C. "Mulling Over Mencken's *MERCURY*." *SERIALS LIBRARIAN* 1 (Fall): 13-21.
Discusses the birth and life of the *AM*, noting its reception among readers and librarians during the years of HLM's editorship.

1043   Fitzpatrick, Vincent. "The Elusive Butterfly's Angry Pursuer: The Jamesian Style, Mencken, and Clear Writing." *MENCKENIANA* 59 (Fall): 13-17.
        Examines HLM's prose style in the light of his remarks on that of Henry James.

1044   ------. "Mencken, Dreiser, and the Baltimore *EVENING SUN*." *MENCKENIANA* 60 (Winter): 1-5.
        On HLM's use of the paper to defend and promote the novelist.

1045   Gross, Dalton. "H.L. Mencken and George Sterling: Mencken in San Francisco Bohemia." *MENCKENIANA* 58 (Summer): 3-7.
        On HLM's association with the poet.

1046   Hobson, Fred C. "Mencken's Blighted Violet: The Brief Career of Frances Newman." *MENCKENIANA* 60 (Winter): 6-9.
        On HLM's assistance to yet another Southern writer.

1047   Lippman, Theo, Jr. "H.L. Mencken and Press Criticism." *MENCKENIANA* 59 (Fall): 2-13.
        Lecture delivered at EPFL in September 1976.

1048   Metcalfe, Howard E. "Oil the Pearly Gates: Here Comes Mencken!" *MENCKENIANA* 57 (Spring): 2-8.
        On HLM's love for the King James Bible despite his disdain for Christianity.

1049   Moseley, Merritt W., Jr. "H.L. Mencken and the First World War." *MENCKENIANA* 58 (Summer): 8-15.

1977

1050   Bode, Carl. "H.L. Mencken in Washington." Washington *STAR* (27 February): H4.
        Tells of HLM's fondness for the city and its politicians; of his experiences there connected with friend Marion Bloom; and of his humiliation in December 1934 by President Roosevelt at a dinner of the Gridiron Club.

Articles

1051 Dannelley, Paul. "Mencken and Music."
MENCKENIANA 63 (Fall): 4-13.
    Lecture delivered Fall 1976 in Wichita, Kansas. Includes reminiscences by HLM's friend and publisher, Alfred A. Knopf.

1052 Emblidge, David. "H.L. Mencken's IN DEFENSE OF WOMEN." *MENCKENIANA* 61 (Spring): 5-10.
    Critical and bibliographical essay occasioned by Octagon Press's reissuing of the book [6].

1053 Epstein, Joseph. "Rediscovering Mencken." *COMMENTARY* 63 (April): 47-52.
    Analyzes the impact of HLM's career and suggests a few contemporary writers who approximate his role, though not his influence.

1054 Fitzpatrick, Vincent. "Wink Your Eye at Some Homely Girl: Misogyny and Mencken." *MENCKENIANA* 64 (Winter): 4-10.
    Attempts to separate the strands of HLM's complex attitude toward women.

1055 Jones, Carlton. "Mencken's Union Square: Then and Now." *MENCKENIANA* 61 (Spring): 1-3.
    On HLM's neighborhood.

1056 Kenyon, Nellie. "Mencken's Night Visit to the Holy Rollers." Baltimore *SUNDAY SUN* (18 September): D1, D3.
    One of the journalists covering the Scopes "Monkey" trial of 1925 tells of her experience escorting HLM to a fundamentalist revival near Dayton, Tennessee; the meeting led to HLM's essay "The Hills of Zion" [81].

1978

1057 Amrhine, Kenneth W. "The Sage and the Pulp." *MENCKENIANA* 68 (Winter): 4-6.
    As editors of the *SS*, HLM and George Jean Nathan founded companion periodicals of second-rate, sensational fiction in order to subsidize their primary magazine

venture. These were the *PARISIENNE*, *SAUCY STORIES*, and *BLACK MASK*.

1058 Dorsey, John. "The Centennial Mencken Volume: A Work in Progress." *MENCKENIANA* 67 (Fall): 7-13.
Explains the rationale behind the collection of essays the editor subsequently published [578].

1059 Downey, Charlotte. "How Mencken Taps the Resources of Language for His Humor and Satire." *MENCKENIANA* 65 (Spring): 2-12.

1060 Fecher, Charles A. "Researching a Book on Mencken." *MENCKENIANA* 68 (Winter): 9-14.
Background on MENCKEN: A STUDY OF HIS THOUGHT [577].

1061 Goulden, Joseph C. "Mencken and Politics: Adventures of a Menckeniana Collector." *MENCKENIANA* 67 (Fall): 2-7.
Address delivered at EPFL 9 September 1978.

1062 Jervey, Edward D. "H.L. Mencken and American Methodism." *JOURNAL OF POPULAR CULTURE* 12 (Summer): 75-87.
On HLM's attitudes toward the Methodist Church in particular and organized religion in general.

1063 Miller, Jim. "HLM and the Conventions of 1904." *MENCKENIANA* 66 (Summer): 3-10.
Sketches HLM's first journalistic experience of political convention coverage.

1064 Rubin, Louis D., Jr. "That Wayward Pressman Mencken." *SEWANEE REVIEW* (Summer): 474-80.
Review of A GANG OF PECKSNIFFS [423] leads to commentary on HLM as a master journalist and prose stylist; raises questions about the man as yet unanswered by biographers.

1065 Sandler, Gilbert. "Ben Hecht and H.L. Mencken: Exit Laughing." *MENCKENIANA* 65 (Spring): 12-16.

On the personal and professional
interactions of the two writers and
"lovable rogues" (13).

1066 Sedgwick, Ellery, III. "HLM, Ellery Sedgwick,
and the First World War." *MENCKENIANA* 68
(Winter): 1-4.
The grandson of the former *AtlM* editor
describes the amiable debate between HLM
and Sedgwick concerning Germany.

1067 White, Ray Lewis. "Mencken's Lost Review of
WINESBURG, OHIO." *NOTES ON MODERN AMERICAN
LITERATURE* 2 (Spring): 11.
Reprints HLM's comments (first published
in the Chicago *AMERICAN* 28 June 1919) on
Anderson's novel to make the point that
the critic received the book favorably.

1979

1068 Anderson, Fenwick. "Black Perspectives in
Mencken's *MERCURY*." *MENCKENIANA* 70 (Summer):
2-6.
On the *AM*'s coverage between 1924 and
1933 of racial issues.

1069 Clausen, Christopher. "Mencken and the Bible
Belt." *MENCKENIANA* 70 (Summer): 7-11.
Claims that HLM's assertion of the
South's inferiority was founded on his
"perception of the root problem as being
not genetic but religious" (8).

1070 Epstein, Joseph. "H.L. Mencken: The Art of
Point of View." *MENCKENIANA* 71 (Fall): 2-11.
Address delivered at EPFL 8 September
1979. Slightly revised version published
the following year [1086].

1071 Fitzpatrick, Vincent. "Dreiser, Mencken, and
the *AMERICAN MERCURY* Years." *DREISER NEWS-
LETTER* 10 (Fall): 13-16.

1072 Flora, Joseph M. "James Branch Cabell's
Tribute to H.L. Mencken and Their Era."
MENCKENIANA 72 (Winter): 1-7.

Discusses Cabell's remarks on HLM and the twenties in his SOME OF US: AN ESSAY IN EPITAPHS (1930).

1073 Hagemann, Edward R. "THE SMART SET." *LIBRARY REVIEW* [University of Louisville, KY] 28 (May): 24-29.
Lists the names of those published in the *SS* during HLM's tenure first as book review editor, then as co-editor with Nathan, from 1908 to 1923 (less two issues missing from the University of Louisville's recently acquired *SS* collection).

1074 Mason, Franklin. "Wharton Over Mencken." *MENCKENIANA* 72 (Winter): 12-13.
Sketches HLM's attitude toward the novelist, within an editorial occasioned by the U.S. Postal Service's choice of Wharton over HLM for a commemorative stamp. Reprinted from the Baltimore *ES*, 26 November 1979.

1075 Meyer, Adolphe E. "Mencken and the Pedagogues." *MENCKENIANA* 69 (Spring): 4-8.
On HLM's views of American education, by one who also criticized the same within the pages of the *AM*.

1076 Niemtus, Laurice. "H.L. Mencken." *LIBRARY REVIEW* [University of Louisville, KY] 28 (May): 3-23.
The author interviews linguist David W. Maurer who knew HLM for many years and contributed material to his AMERICAN LANGUAGE [7]; Maurer also assisted Raven I. McDavid, Jr., in abridging the work.

1077 Nolte, William H. "The Enduring Mencken." *MISSISSIPPI QUARTERLY* 32 (Fall): 651-62.
Reviews the major HLM scholarship and criticism complete to date, lamenting the lack of a truly penetrating critical biography.

1078 ------. "Mencken on the South." *MENCKENIANA* 69 (Spring): 1-4.

For HLM "the South epitomized the flaws of American democracy" (1).

1079 Welshko, Thomas G. "The Free Lance (I)." *Menckeniana* 69 (Spring): 9-12.
First article in a series on HLM's Baltimore *ES* column, which ran from 1911 to 1915. Subsequent articles: 70 (Summer 1979): 11-14; 83 (Fall 1982): 9-12.

1980

1080 Ayd, Joseph D. "H.L., Where Are You? A Celebration of Henry Mencken on the Centennial of His Birth." *ENGLISH JOURNAL* 69 (September): 32-37.

1081 Barrick, Mac E. "Child-Lore in Mencken's Baltimore." *SOUTHWEST FOLKLORE* 4 no. 3-4 (Summer-Fall): 93-99.
Looks to HAPPY DAYS [15] for information on the typical play of children in turn-of-the-century urban American settings.

1082 Bode, Carl. "Mencken and Maryland (University That Is)." *MARYLAND MAGAZINE* 13 (Winter): 38-39.
While writing a series of *SUNPAPERS* articles on the University of Maryland in Spring 1937, HLM came to like and respect its new president, H.C. Byrd.

1083 Bready, James H. "Mencken's Baltimore: A Visitor's Guide." *MENCKENIANA* 75 (Fall): 11-13.
Explains what happened to the HLM haunts that no longer exist and how to find those that do.

1084 "Disturber of the Peace." *MD: MEDICAL NEWSMAGAZINE* 24 (September): 69-72, 77.
Reviews HLM's career and gives passing attention to several of his chief literary and ideological stances.

1085 Dorsey, John. "H.L. Mencken at 100: What We Celebrate." Baltimore *SUNDAY SUN MAGAZINE* (7 September): 6-7.

On the occasion of HLM's Centennial, the author recapitulates HLM's place in the American life of his day. Followed by numerous photographs on pages 9, 12, 18, 20, 21, 23-27, 30-41.

1086 Epstein, Joseph. "H.L. Mencken for Grown-ups." *ENCOUNTER* [United Kingdom] 55 (August-September): 29-35.
Slightly revised version of an address first printed in *MENCKENIANA* [1070].

1087 Fecher, Charles A. "Mencken and Goethe." *MENCKENIANA* 75 (Fall): 43-47.

1088 *FRAGMENTS* 18 (July-September): 1-11.
Entire issue is devoted to HLM in recognition of his centennial. Contains:
Sydney A. Mayers, "Mencken's Nathan"
Kenneth W. Amrhine, "Henry L. Mencken and the Polytechnic"
Alice Davis Tibbetts, "H.L.M. and the Single Tax"
Patricia Aller, "The Sage of Baltimore"
Irving Starer, "The Economics of H.L.M."
Sheila York Fontana, "The Science of Mencken"
Glenn A. Duffy, "God and Mencken"
Jack Schwartzman, "H.L. on Hell"
Corinne Anderson, "A Woman on Mencken on Women"
Oscar B. Johannsen, "Politics: The Life-Long Fascination of H.L. Mencken"
Jodi Jennings, "Projections of Mencken: A Parable"
Cyril Polansky, "The Importance of H.L.M."
Robert A. Scharf, "What Mencken Believed"
George Deller, "A Minority Report"
Joseph T. McKaharay, "The Enthusiast"
Sydney Mayers, "Criticizing the Critics"
Lora L. Montalto, "A Man Possessed: Mencken in Love"

1089 Harriss, R.P. "Scotus/Germanicus: Gerald W. Johnson and H.L. Mencken." *MENCKENIANA* 76 (Winter): 4-11.
 Background on the personal and professional friendship between the two newspapermen, by a *SUNPAPERS* journalist who knew them both.

1090 Hobson, Fred. "Mencken's 'Poet Born': John McClure of Oklahoma." *MENCKENIANA* 75 (Fall): 40-43.
 On HLM's admiration for a little-known poet, journalist, and Westerner-turned-Southerner.

1091 Kanigel, Robert. "Did H.L. Mencken Hate the Jews?" *MENCKENIANA* 73 (Spring): 1-7.
 Reprinted from the Baltimore *JT* (8 June 1979); surveys a controversy that goes at least as far back as the first World War. See Gwinn Owens's response [1095]. Theo Lippman also responded in the Baltimore *SUN*, 17 June 1979, with "Anti-Semitic Mencken."

1092 Mason, Franklin. "Ring Lardner, Fitzgerald and Mencken in Baltimore." *MENCKENIANA* 73 (Spring): 9-10.
 Reprinted from the Baltimore *ES* (11 January).

1093 McDavid, Raven I., Jr. "H.L. Mencken and the Linguistic Atlas Project." *MENCKENIANA* 73 (Spring): 7-9.
 On HLM's untiring promotion of American English as a discipline unto itself.

1094 Mitchell, Henry. "A Mencken Pilgrimage." Washington *POST* (12 September): F1, F6.
 Discusses HLM's ideas on such subjects as Germany, politics, and journalism; mentions his friendship with Washington singer Gretchen Hood.

1095 Owens, Gwinn. Mencken and the Jews, Revisited." *MENCKENIANA* 74 (Summer): 6-10.
 Responds to a previous article on HLM's alleged anti-Semitism [1091]. Reprinted from the Baltimore *JT*, 9 May 1980.

1096 Poitras, Jean-Maurice. "Fabula Menckeniana."
     MARYLAND STATE MEDICAL JOURNAL 29 (September):
     30-32.
     A few remarks by Poitras on HLM's
     attitude toward medicine serve as intro-
     duction to the text of a radio broadcast
     which HLM gave in April 1934 (printed in
     the Baltimore *SUN* 28 April); here, HLM
     draws a parallel between a sick man's
     dependence upon "amateur healers" (31)
     and the nation's dependence upon
     Roosevelt's economic remedies.

1097 Rasmussen, Frederick N., and Vincent
     Fitzpatrick. "Years of Respect: The H.L.
     Mencken-Hamilton Owens Correspondence."
     MENCKENIANA 75 (Fall): 58-65.

1098 Von Hoffman, Nicholas. "Celebrating Mencken."
     SATURDAY REVIEW 7 (September): 29-32.
     Though an iconoclast, HLM was also a
     conservative.

1099 Welshko, Thomas G. "Stirring Up the Animals."
     MENCKENIANA 75 (Fall): 51-58.
     Discusses HLM's political views as a by-
     product of the values he inherited.

1100 Westlake, Neda M. "'Larval Stage of a
     Bookworm.'" *MENCKENIANA* 75 (Fall): 17-21.
     Of particular interest to book collectors
     is this description of the books HLM
     owned and discussed in his HAPPY DAYS
     chapter of the same name [15]. See the
     "Correction," *MENCKENIANA* 76 (Winter
     1980): 12-13.

1101 Wilson, Robert A. "Collecting H.L. Mencken."
     AMERICAN BOOK COLLECTOR n.s. 1 (September-
     October): 19-20, 22.
     On the rewards, pitfalls, and challenges
     involved.

                          1981

1102 Fitzpatrick, Vincent. "Gratitude and Griev-
     ances: Dreiser's Inscriptions to Mencken."
     DREISER NEWSLETTER 12 (Fall): 1-16.

Articles

On the light shed on their relationship by the inscriptions they wrote one another in books they exchanged. Revised and reprinted in [582].

1103 Gershenowitz, Harry. "Mencken and Frederick Jackson Turner." *MENCKENIANA* 78 (Summer): 14-16.
Points out where HLM was both correct and incorrect in his assessment of the American historian.

1104 Kilpatrick, James L. "The Writer Mencken." *MENCKENIANA* 79 (Fall): 2-10.
Lecture delivered 12 September 1981 at EPFL.

1105 Knopf, Alfred A. "H.L. Mencken, George Jean Nathan, and the *AMERICAN MERCURY* Venture." *MENCKENIANA* 78 (Summer): 1-10.
Responds to Dolmetsch's "inadequate" (1) version of the story [556]. Slightly different version of Knopf's article printed in the Baltimore *ES*, 22-25 June 1981.

1106 Lippmann, Theo, Jr. "Why are Mencken's Papers Under Wraps?" Baltimore *SUNDAY SUN* (27 September): K3.
Editorial lamenting the fact that eight months have passed since HLM's second collection of time-lock papers were released, yet scholars are still unable to review the material. This is one of a dozen or so articles on the subject published in various newspapers during the months preceeding and succeeding the 25th anniversary of HLM's death.

1107 Love, Glen A. "Stemming the Avalanche of Tripe: Or, How H.L. Mencken and Friends Reformed Northwest Literature." *THALIA* 4 (Spring/Summer): 46-53.
Turning the genteel tradition on its head in the Northwest.

1108 McDavid, Raven I., Jr. "Webster, Mencken, and Avis: Spokesmen for Linguistic Autonomy."

CANADIAN JOURNAL OF LINGUISTICS/LA REVUE CANADIENNE DE LINGUISTIQUE 26 (Spring): 118-25.
Reminisces briefly on his personal and professional association with fellow linguists HLM and Wally Avis and compares their contributions to the study of English with that of Noah Webster.

1109 Martin, Edward A. "H.L. Mencken and Equal Rights for Women." GEORGIA REVIEW 35 (Spring): 65-76.
Corrects misleading notions set forth in some HLM biographies and critical studies on HLM's various attitudes toward women; also reevaluates IN DEFENSE OF WOMEN [6] and the changes made in its revised edition of 1922.

1110 Nardini, Robert F. "H.L. Mencken's VENTURES INTO VERSE [1]." SOUTH ATLANTIC QUARTERLY 80 (Spring): 195-205.
Background and analysis.

1111 Ryan, William F. "H.L. Mencken and E. Haldeman-Julius: 'Why Do You Ask ... ?'" MENCKENIANA 79 and 80 (Fall and Winter): 11-16, 2-11.

1982

1112 Burgan, John S. "Studying the Mencken Papers." MENCKENIANA 81 (Spring): 6-9.
Speculates on the publications that might be expected to result from the previous year's release of a set of papers HLM left to the care of EPFL.

1113 Cheslock, Louis. "Mencken, Music, and the Saturday Night Club." Edited by Carol Fitzpatrick. MENCKENIANA 83 and 84 (Fall and Winter): 13-16, 13-16.
Excerpts from Cheslock's notes, with which he wrote MENCKEN ON MUSIC [419].

1114 Gershenowitz, Harry. "Mencken and Weismann." MENCKENIANA 82 (Summer): 3-6.
Explains how the nineteenth-century German biologist's theories came to

influence HLM's ideas on Social Darwinism.

1115 Kempton, Murray. "A Very Great Whale Indeed." *MENCKENIANA* 83 (Fall): 1-7.
Lecture delivered at EPFL 11 September 1982.

1116 Nardini, Robert F. "Mencken and the 'Cult of Smartness.'" *MENCKENIANA* 84 (Winter): 1-12.
On HLM's potent influence on writers, intellectuals, youth, and others of his day.

1117 West, Walter C. "H.L Mencken Letters in the University of North Carolina Collection." *MENCKENIANA* 81 (Spring): 1-3.
The opening of the HLM-Hanes correspondence is the occasion for this sketch of HLM's friendship with Fred, DeWitt, and Betty Hanes.

1983

1118 Ainto, Russell, and Charles Crupi. "Mencken Lecture 1983." *MENCKENIANA* 87 (Fall): 1-9.
Delivered at EPFL in September. The authors of the play MENCKEN AND SARA give background and a synopsis.

1119 Byron, Gilbert. "H.L. Mencken Versus the Eastern Shore." *MENCKENIANA* 86 (Summer): 13-16.
The story of the love-hate relationship between HLM and one part of his native Maryland.

1120 Havard, William C. "The Journalist as Interpreter of the South." *VIRGINIA QUARTERLY REVIEW* 59 (Winter): 1-21.
HLM's "Sahara" essay [31] had its impact not only on Southern novelists but also on such journalists as Gerald W. Johnson and W.J. Cash.

1121 Manglaviti, Leo M.J. "Mencken and Joyce: Hands Across the Waters." *MARKHAM REVIEW* 12 (Spring): 43-45.

HLM published two DUBLINERS stories in the May 1915 issue of the *SS*, three years before Margaret Anderson began serializing ULYSSES in the *LITTLE REVIEW*.

1122 Moseley, Merritt. "H.L. Mencken, American Stylist." *REVUE FRANCAISE D'ETUDES AMERICAINES* 8 (November): 405-14.
Introduces readers to HLM's prose style, particularly as it expanded typical American usage. In English.

1123 Price, G. Jefferson, III. "Israel Took Edge Off Mencken's Cynicism." Baltimore *SUNDAY SUN* (17 July 1983): A2.
Summarizes HLM's remarks on Israel and the Jews made after his visit to the Holy Land in 1934 [25].

1124 Reynolds, Robert D., Jr. "H.L. Mencken: Medical Champion and Human Body Pessimist." *MENCKENIANA* 85 (Spring): 8-15.
On HLM's interest in medicine, particularly as he shared it with some of the "millionaire socialists" of the early twentieth century.

1125 Vass, Mary Miller, and James L.W. West III. "The Composition and Revision of Mencken's TREATISE ON THE GODS" [12]. *PAPERS OF THE BIBLIOGRAPHICAL SOCIETY OF AMERICA* 77: 47-61.
Thoroughly examines the process by which HLM's work of religious inquiry went from his typewriter into its first published form (1930) and later into a revised edition (1946). Includes comments on the book's content, style, and reception by readers. Very useful for a close-up view of HLM at work.

1126 Wingate, P.J. "The Philosophy of H.L. Mencken." *MENCKENIANA* 87 (Fall): 14-16.
Address delivered to the American Philosophical Society, Philadelphia, November 1982. Retells the story of HLM's "bathtub hoax" [32] as an illustration of HLM's belief that people do not really want truth. Because the first page of

Wingate's manuscript was inadvertently omitted from this issue, it appears in MENCKENIANA 88 (Winter 1983): 5-6.

1984

1127 Hahn, H. George. "Twilight Reflections: The Hold of Victorian Baltimore on Lizette Woodworth Reese and H.L. Mencken." SOUTHERN QUARTERLY 22 (Summer): 5-21.
Examines the social and cultural climate which produced these two distinctly different writers. First published in the MH 11 (Spring 1980): 29-37.

1128 Kazin, Alfred. "Mencken's Ghost: The American Language at Election Time." NEW REPUBLIC 191 (22 October): 32-37.
On the occasion of University of Chicago Press's reissuing of Moos's A CARNIVAL OF BUNCOMBE [415], summarizes HLM's views of politics and politicians; notes the differences in modern politics' manipulation of language.

1129 Martin, Edward A. "On Reading Mencken." MENCKENIANA 91 (Fall): 1-10.
Address delivered 8 September 1984 at EPFL. A revised version appears in the SewR 93 (Spring 1985): 243-50.

1130 Riggio, Thomas P. "Of the 'Black Horse Cavalry of Humor': Mencken's Contributions to THE DELINEATOR." MENCKENIANA 90 (Summer): 1-5.
Reprints specimens of early (1910) HLM humor which first appeared in the magazine edited by Dreiser.

1131 Schwartz, Gerald. "The West as Gauged by H.L. Mencken's AMERICAN MERCURY." MENCKENIANA 89 (Spring): 1-14.
Essay followed by a bibliography of AM's coverage of the West.

1132 Thimmesch, Nick. "H.L. Mencken Wrote Here." MENCKENIANA 92 (Winter): 1-3.

Surveys HLM's career, with attention to the role played by 1524 Hollins Street, his lifetime home.

1133 Watson, Ritchie D., Jr. "Sara Haardt Mencken and the Glasgow-Mencken Literary Entente." *ELLEN GLASGOW NEWSLETTER* 20 (April): 6-17.
Examines Sara Haardt's role in HLM's changing attitude toward the Southern novelist. Reprints letters exchanged among the three from 1928 to 1942.

1134 Wingate, P.J. "H.L. Mencken--Man of Letters." *MENCKENIANA* 90 (Summer): 7-12.
Address delivered before the Quill and Grill Club of Wilmington, Delaware; emphasizes HLM's correspondence.

1135 ------. "The Many Mr. Menckens." *MENCKENIANA* 92 (Winter): 8-9.
Attempts to dispel the popular notion that HLM was only a debunker.

1136 ------. "Mencken, Mark Twain, and Shaw." *MENCKENIANA* 92 (Winter): 10-14.

1985

1137 Cheslock, Louis. "The Saturday Night Club Diary." *MENCKENIANA* 94 (Summer): 1-9.
Excerpts from an account kept by HLM's friend of thier weekly musical festivities, donated in 1981 to EPFL by Cheslock's widow. Further excerpts appear in nos. 95, 96, and 97 of *MENCKENIANA*.

1138 Dudden, Arthur Power. "The Record of Political Humor." *AMERICAN QUARTERLY* 37: 50-70.
Appraises HLM's place among the best humorists to come out of nineteenth- and twentieth-century American politics. A wide look at the subject, useful for historical context.

1139 Fecher, Charles A. "Mencken and the Archbishop." *MENCKENIANA* 93 (Spring): 2-6.

With the release of a set of HLM's papers in 1981 came new information concering a controversy waged in 1934 between the editors of the *SUNPAPERS* (in which Hitler had been compared to St. Ignatius Loyola) and many Baltimore Catholics, whose chief spokesman was Archbishop Michael J. Curley. This article first appeared in slightly different form in the Baltimore *CaR*, 19 March 1982.

1140 Gershenowitz, Harry. "Mencken's Misinterpretation of Shaw's Position on Evolution." *MENCKENIANA* 93 (Spring): 7-10.

1141 ------. "A Triangle of Forces: Mencken, Teachers College [Columbia University, New York City] and Horace Mann." *MENCKENIANA* 96 (Winter): 1-3.

1142 Riggio, Thomas P. "Dreiser and Mencken: In the Literary Trenches." *AMERICAN SCHOLAR* 54 (Spring): 227-38.
Good coverage of their personal and professional relationship.

1143 Scruggs, Charles W. "Finding Out About This Mencken: The Impact of A BOOK OF PREFACES [401] on Richard Wright." *MENCKENIANA* 95 (Fall): 1-10.
Lecture delivered at EPFL 14 September 1985.

1144 Wormser, Baron. "Poem to the Memory of H.L. Mencken." *MENCKENIANA* 93 (Spring): 12-13.

1145 Young, Stephen A. "The Mencken-[Sinclair] Lewis Connection." *MENCKENIANA* 94 (Summer): 10-16.

1986

1146 Amrhine, Kenneth W. "The Day Mencken was Arrested." *MENCKENIANA* 98 (Summer): 10-12.
On the publication of Herbert Asbury's "Hatrack" story in the *AM*.

1147 Duberman, Jason D. "H.L. Mencken and the Wowsers." *AMERICAN BOOK COLLECTOR* n.s. 7 (May): 3-14.
Recapitulates the 1926 drama played out between HLM and J. Frank Chase over the *AM* publication of Herbert Asbury's "Hatrack" story.

1148 Gershenowitz, Harry. "Mencken and Nicholas Murray Butler." *MENCKENIANA* 100 (Winter): 14-16.
HLM shared with the Columbia University president (1902-1946) a belief in Social Darwinism.

1149 Hohner, Robert A. "'The Woes of a Holy Man': Bishop James Cannon, Jr. and H.L. Mencken." *SOUTH ATLANTIC QUARTERLY* 85 (Summer): 228-38.
Discusses the unlikely friendship between HLM and the controversial Methodist clergyman, and their agreement or disagreement on several topics.

1150 Poitras, Jean-Maurice. "Leonard Keene Hirshberg and Henry Louis Mencken." *MENCKENIANA* 97 (Spring): 1-7.
Background on HLM's collaboration with Dr. Hirshberg on a series of articles entitled "What You Ought to Know About Your Baby" [102], written for the *DELINEATOR* at the request of its editor, Theodore Dreiser, between 1908 and 1909.

1151 Schrader, Richard J. "But Gentlemen Marry Brunettes: Anita Loos and H.L. Mencken." *MENCKENIANA* 98 (Summer): 1-7.

1152 Wingate, P.J. "Mencken, Shaw, and Honorary Degrees." *MENCKENIANA* 98 (Summer): 8-9.

1987

1153 Kazin, Alfred. "Mencken and the Great American Boob." *THE NEW YORK REVIEW OF BOOKS* (26 February): 8-11.
This review of MENCKEN AND SARA, A LIFE IN LETTERS [444] and DREISER-MENCKEN LETTERS [442] is an expanded version of an article first published in *MENCKENIANA*

Articles

99 (Fall 1986): 108, which compares HLM's America with our current one.

1154 Williams, Harold A. "HLM and the Great Fire." *MENCKENIANA* 102 (Summer): 2-8.
Compares HLM's account in NEWSPAPER DAYS [16] of the Baltimore Fire of 1904 to the actual facts.

I. MENTIONS

1909

1155 Courtney, W.L. ROSEMARY'S LETTER BOOK: THE RECORD OF A YEAR. London: Andrew Melrose.
On the flyleaf of HLM's copy he cites page 159 as the first place he was ever mentioned in a book of criticism, so far as he knows. The discussion is of his PHILOSOPHY OF FRIEDRICH NIETZSCHE [3].

1918

1156 Van Vechten, Carl. THE MERRY-GO-ROUND. New York: Knopf.
Several references to HLM in connection with literary and musical topics. See index.

1920

1157 Spingarn, Joel Elias. "American Criticism Today." THE NATION AND ATHENAEUM [London] 27 (17 April): 82-84.
Placing HLM in the contemporary scene, the author considers him "the most raucous and the most untenable" of critics (84).

1923

1158 Bechhofer, C.E. [Carl Eric Bechhofer Roberts]. THE LITERARY RENAISSANCE IN AMERICA. London: William Heinemann.
Several references to HLM. See index.

1927

1159 Conrad, Joseph. "Joseph Conrad's American Notes--and Thoughts on Life: A Final Installment from the Author's Private Letters." WORLD'S WORK 53 (February): 445-54.
One of HLM's best-loved novelists voices mixed feelings about his American advocate, pages 452-54.

1928

1160 Harrison, Henry Sydnor. "Last Days of the Devastators." *YALE REVIEW* 18 (September): 88-103.
Mentions HLM's PREJUDICES books [403, 404, 405, 406, 409, 410] and his AMERICANA [407, 408] as being part of the current "debunking" vogue in American literature.

1931

1161 Blankenship, Russell. AMERICAN LITERATURE AS AN EXPRESSION OF THE NATIONAL MIND. New York: Henry Holt. Reprint. New York: Cooper Square, 1973. See index.

1162 Tobin, A.I., and Elmer Gertz. FRANK HARRIS: A STUDY IN BLACK AND WHITE. Chicago: Madelaine Mendelsohn. Reprint. 1970.
Quotes HLM frequently on the author and editor. See index.

1932

1163 Lewisohn, Ludwig. EXPRESSION IN AMERICA. New York: Harper and Brothers.
Whenever he leaves the topic of music, HLM is "intellectually lost" (446). See index for various references.

1933

1164 Hazlitt, Henry. THE ANATOMY OF CRITICISM: A TRIALOGUE, 45-49. New York: Simon and Schuster.
Stages a conversation on HLM as a critic. See index for other references.

1165 Van Doren, Carl. AMERICAN LITERATURE: AN INTRODUCTION, 76-78. Los Angeles: U.S. Library Association.
Brief sketch of HLM.

1166 ------. SINCLAIR LEWIS: A BIOGRAPHICAL SKETCH. With a Bibliography by Harvey Taylor. New York: Doubleday, Doran and Company.

Mentions

> The first half of the book mentions HLM
> several times in connection with the
> novelist's development; see index.

1936

1167 ------. THREE WORLDS. New York and London: Harper and Brothers. See index.

1941

1168 Cargill, Oscar. INTELLECTUAL AMERICA: IDEAS ON THE MARCH. New York: Macmillan. See index.

1947

1169 Gunther, John. INSIDE U.S.A. New York and London: Harper and Brothers.
> Gives HLM passing notice in several places. See index for references.

1170 Hyman, Stanley Edgar. THE ARMED VISION: A STUDY IN THE METHODS OF MODERN LITERARY CRITICISM. New York: Vintage Books. Reprint. 1948, 1955. See index.

1949

1171 Elias, Robert H. THEODORE DREISER: APOSTLE OF NATURE. New York: Knopf.
> Frequent mention of HLM; see index.

1951

1172 Cowley, Malcolm. EXILE'S RETURN: A LITERARY ODYSSEY OF THE 1920s. New York: Viking Press. Reprint. Harmondsworth, Eng.: Penguin, 1976. See index.

1952

1173 Glicksburg, Charles I. AMERICAN LITERARY CRITICISM 1900-1950. New York: Hendricks House.
> Contains many references to HLM in the introduction and in various essays by such contemporaries as Joel Elias Spingarn, Stuart P. Sherman, Paul Elmer

More, Irving Babbitt, and Granville Hicks. Also reprints HLM's "Footnote on Criticism" [57]. See index.

1954

1174 Hubbell, Jay B. THE SOUTH IN AMERICAN LITERATURE, 1607-1900. Durham, NC: Duke University Press.
Touches upon HLM's support of Southern writers despite his disparaging "Sahara of the Bozart" [31]. See index.

1957

1175 Lynes, Russell. THE DOMESTICATED AMERICANS, 220-21. New York: Harper and Row. Reprint. 1963.
Briefly retells the story of the bathtub hoax [32].

1176 Schlesinger, Arthur M., Jr. THE AGE OF ROOSEVELT. 3 vols. Boston: Houghton Mifflin, 1957-1960.
HLM and his politics are mentioned in all volumes, though less so in Volume 2. See index for references.

1177 Wilson, Elena, ed. EDMUND WILSON: LETTERS ON LITERATURE AND POLITICS, 1912-1972. Introduction by Daniel Aaron. Foreword by Leon Edel. New York: Farrar, Straus and Giroux. Reprint. 1973, 1974, 1977. See index.

1961

1178 Goldman, Eric F. RENDEZVOUS WITH DESTINY: A HISTORY OF MODERN AMERICAN REFORM. New York: Knopf.
Though an antagonist of American "progressivism," HLM was in a sense one kind of twenties-era reformer. See index.

1179 Johnson, Gerald W. THE MAN WHO FEELS LEFT BEHIND, 118-20. New York: William Morrow.
A brief look back at the useful role HLM played as American critic *par excellence*.

1962

1180 Angoff, Charles. "George Jean Nathan: A Candid Portrait." *ATLANTIC MONTHLY* 210 (December): 45-48.
  Remarks on differences of opinion and contrasting personality traits between Nathan and HLM.

1181 Gelb, Arthur and Barbara. O'NEILL. New York: Harper and Row. See index.

1963

1182 Meyer, Karl E. "The Culture Machine." *NEW STATESMAN* 65 (11 January): 38.
  Suggests that Dwight Macdonald, author of AGAINST THE AMERICAN GRAIN, is a modern-day HLM in his disdain for American culture.

1183 Schwab, Arnold T. JAMES GIBBONS HUNEKER: CRITIC OF THE SEVEN ARTS. Stanford, CA: Stanford University Press.
  On HLM's admiration for and association with the American critic. See index.

1964

1184 Miller, James E., Jr. F. SCOTT FITZGERALD: HIS ART AND HIS TECHNIQUE. New York: New York University Press. Reprint. 1967.
  Refers often to HLM's influence on Fitzgerald, with particular attention to the former's "The National Letters" [52] and the latter's THE BEAUTIFUL AND THE DAMNED. See index.

1965

1185 Clark, Emily. INGENUE AMONG THE LIONS: THE LETTERS OF EMILY CLARK TO JOSEPH HERGESHEIMER. Edited by Gerald Langford. Austin: University of Texas Press.
  Numerous references to HLM by the editor of the Richmond *REVIEWER*, a short-lived literary magazine significant to the Southern renascence. See index.

1186 Hicks, Granville. PART OF THE TRUTH. New York: Harcourt, Brace, and World.
Tells of his work on an article for the AM (February 1927) concerning the role of clergymen in the first World War. See index.

1187 Logan, Andy. THE MAN WHO ROBBED THE ROBBER BARONS. New York: W.W. Norton.
Comments chiefly on HLM as co-editor with Nathan of the SS; see index.

1188 Paul, Sherman. EDMUND WILSON: A STUDY OF LITERARY VOCATION IN OUR TIME. Urbana: University of Illinois Press.
Refers often to the way HLM's values touched Wilson's world and the lives of his dramatic creations. See index.

1189 Starrett, Vincent. BORN IN A BOOKSHOP: CHAPTERS FROM THE CHICAGO RENASCENCE. Norman: University of Oklahoma Press.
The author's early attempts to publish in the SS won him several lively rejection letters from HLM; touches on the critic's admiration for Chicago's literati in the first two decades of the century. See index.

1966

1190 Angoff, Charles. "Concerning the Little Magazines." Symposium. CARLETON MISCELLANY 7 (Spring): 9-16.
Gives a passing glance at the SS and the AM.

1191 Rogers, Katharine M. THE TROUBLESOME HELPMATE: A HISTORY OF MISOGYNY IN LITERATURE. Seattle and London: University of Washington Press.
Remarks briefly on HLM's ideas on women, chiefly drawn from his DEFENSE [6]. See index.

1192 Wycherley, H. Alan. "Fitzgerald Revisited." TEXAS STUDIES IN LITERATURE AND LANGUAGE 8 (Summer): 277-83.

Takes issue with HLM's praise for THIS
SIDE OF PARADISE; notes that Fitzgerald
could get bad work published in the *SS*
but not in the *AM*.

1967

1193 Ford, Corey. THE TIME OF LAUGHTER. Boston:
Little, Brown.
Includes brief references to HLM and
partially reprints an HLM-Nathan parody
which the author first published in
VF, using the pseudonym John Riddell.
See index.

1194 Miller, William J. HENRY CABOT LODGE: A
BIOGRAPHY. New York: James H. Heineman.
Various references to the statesman's
friendship with HLM; see index.

1195 Montagu, Ashley. THE ANATOMY OF SWEARING.
New York: Macmillan. Reprint. New York:
Collier Books, 1973.
Mentions briefly HLM's THE AMERICAN
LANGUAGE [7], with special attention to
American use of the word "bloody." See
index.

1196 Morrison, Joseph L. W.J. CASH: SOUTHERN
PROPHET. New York: Knopf.
Besides corresponding with the journalist
and publishing some of his work in the
AM, HLM influenced him with his preju-
dices and unique style. See index.

1197 Tarrant, Desmond. JAMES BRANCH CABELL: THE
DREAM AND THE REALITY. Norman: University of
Oklahoma Press.
Claims that despite his usual critical
acumen, HLM did not always understand
the novelist's work fully. See index.

1968

1198 Bier, Jesse. THE RISE AND FALL OF AMERICAN
HUMOR. New York: Holt, Rinehart and Winston.
See index.

1199 Kellner, Bruce. CARL VAN VECHTEN AND THE IRREVERENT DECADES. Norman: University of Oklahoma Press. See index.

1200 Pickett, Calder M. ED HOWE: COUNTRY TOWN PHILOSOPHER. Lawrence and London: University Press of Kansas, 1968.
Contains references to their association and to HLM's admiration for the novelist. See index.

1969

1201 Sawey, Orlan. BERNARD DeVOTO. New York: Twayne. See index.

1202 Wagner, Philip M. "The Wages of Literature--II." Philadelphia EVENING BULLETIN (3 March): n.p.
Includes sales history of HLM's books; this section reprinted in MENCKENIANA 31 (Fall 1969): 14.

1970

1203 Frank, Charles P. EDMUND WILSON. New York: Twayne.
Occasionally compares the two critics, and mentions HLM briefly in various other contexts. See index.

1204 Morrison, Joseph L. "Found: The Missing Editorship of W.J. Cash." NORTH CAROLINA HISTORICAL REVIEW 47 (Winter): 40-50.
HLM published in the AM some of the journalist's work while Cash served as editor of the Cleveland PRESS, including the 1929 article "The Mind of the South," which was eventually expanded into the landmark book of the same name.

1971

1205 Bruccoli, Matthew J., comp. PROFILE OF F. SCOTT FITZGERALD. Columbus, OH: Charles E. Merrill.
Essays by the compiler, John Kuehl, and G. Thomas Tanselle and Jackson R. Bryer touch on HLM's influence on Fitzgerald as

well as his reactions to TENDER IS THE
NIGHT and THE GREAT GATSBY. See pages
24, 50, 59, 66, 70, 78-79, and 96.

1206 Kriegel, Leonard. EDMUND WILSON. Carbondale:
Southern Illinois University Press.
How the young journalist and critic did
and did not take after HLM, whom he
admired early in his career. See index.

1207 Kuehl, John, and Jackson R. Bryer, eds. DEAR
SCOTT/DEAR MAX: THE FITZGERALD-PERKINS
CORRESPONDENCE. New York: Charles Scribner's
Sons. Reprint. London: Cassell, 1973.
Writer and editor often mention HLM to
one another; see index.

1208 "Theodore Dreiser: Apostle of Naturalism."
MD: MEDICAL NEWSMAGAZINE 15 (July): 111-17.
HLM as the novelist's friend and apolo-
gist; quotes the eulogy he wrote for
Dreiser.

1209 Van Deusen, Marshall. J.E. SPINGARN. New
York: Twayne.
Occasionally compares the literary
critic's theories with those of HLM.
See index.

1210 Williams, Harold A. BODINE: A LEGEND IN HIS
TIME. Baltimore: Bodine and Associates.
See pages 28, 35, 56, 67, 68, 77, and 80
for mention of HLM and Sara Haardt, whom
SUNPAPERS photographer Aubrey Bodine
frequently shot. See also HLM's 75th-
birthday portrait in the "Photography"
section of the book.

1972

1211 Ashby, LeRoy. THE SPEARLESS LEADER: SENATOR
BORAH AND THE PROGRESSIVE MOVEMENT IN THE
1920'S. Urbana: University of Illinios Press.
Quotes HLM's opinions of the Idaho
senator and of progressivism several
times. See index.

1212 Bruccoli, Matthew J., ed. AS EVER, SCOTT FITZ
--LETTERS BETWEEN F. SCOTT FITZGERALD AND HIS
LITERARY AGENT HAROLD OBER, 1919-1940.
Philadelphia and New York: J.B. Lippincott.
Frequent mention of HLM, Nathan, the *AM*,
and the *SS*. See index.

1213 Forgue, Guy Jean, and Raven I. McDavid, Jr.
LA LANGUE DES AMERICAINS. Paris: Aubier
Montaigne.
References to HLM and his AMERICAN
LANGUAGE [7] occur on pages 13, 14, 18,
31, 43, 131, 136, 140, 155-56, 165-66,
192, 198, 200, and 254. In French.

1973

1214 Boorstin, Daniel J. THE AMERICANS: THE DEMO-
CRATIC EXPERIENCE. New York: Random House.
See index.

1215 Fabre, Michel. THE UNFINISHED QUEST OF
RICHARD WRIGHT. New York: William Morrow.
Refers to the novelist's discovery of HLM
and his subsequent sense of literary
possibility. See index.

1216 Lundquist, James. SINCLAIR LEWIS. New York:
Frederick Ungar.
Touches briefly on HLM's reception of
BABBITT and MAIN STREET and on the
critic's influence over the novelist.
See index for references.

1217 Starr, Kevin. AMERICANS AND THE CALIFORNIA
DREAM, 1850-1915. New York: Oxford University
Press.
HLM unwittingly disappointed troubled
poet George Sterling, who committed
suicide soon afterward. See index.

1974

1218 Blotner, Joseph. FAULKNER: A BIOGRAPHY.
2 vols. New York: Random House.
HLM is mentioned often as an admirer and
publisher (in the *AM*) of the Southern
writer; see index. See also the author's

revised, condensed, and updated version in one volume (New York: Random House, 1984).

1219 Fain, John Tyree, and Thomas Daniel Young, eds. THE LITERARY CORRESPONDENCE OF DONALD DAVIDSON AND ALLEN TATE. Athens: University of Georgia Press. See index.

1220 Flanagan, John T. EDGAR LEE MASTERS: THE SPOON RIVER POET AND HIS CRITICS. Metuchen, NJ: Scarecrow Press, 1974. See index.

1221 Loos, Anita. KISS HOLLYWOOD GOOD-BY. New York: Viking Press.
Pages 12, 35, 64, 88, and 191 mention HLM.

1222 Lundquist, James. THEODORE DREISER. New York: Frederick Ungar.
Several passing references to HLM's views of the man and his writing. See index.

1223 Stegner, Wallace. THE UNEASY CHAIR: A BIOGRAPHY OF BERNARD DeVOTO. Garden City, NY: Doubleday.
Frequent mention of HLM, the *AM*, and the "Hatrack" case; see index.

1975

1224 Burke, John. ROGUE'S PROGRESS: THE FABULOUS ADVENTURES OF WILSON MIZNER. New York: G.P. Putnam's Sons.
Friend HLM thought Mizner a wit in the Twainian tradition, and the editor published him in the *SS*. See index.

1225 Fairlie, Henry. "The Language of Politics." *ATLANTIC MONTHLY* 235 (January): 25-33.
Speaks of HLM's use of William Graham Sumner's term, "the Forgotten Man."

1226 Ford, Hugh. PUBLISHED IN PARIS: AMERICAN AND BRITISH WRITERS, PRINTERS, AND PUBLISHERS IN PARIS, 1920-1939. New York: Macmillan. See index.

1227 Going, William T. ESSAYS ON ALABAMA LITERA-
TURE. University, AL: University of Alabama
Press.
A few remarks on HLM within a discussion
of Sara Haardt and Zelda Sayre Fitzgerald; see index. First published in
the AlR, January 1970.

1228 Hakutani, Yoshinobu, and Lewis Fried, eds.
AMERICAN LITERARY NATURALISM: A REASSESSMENT.
Heidelberg: Carl Winter.
HLM is mentioned in connection with E.W.
Howe, Frank Norris, and Richard Wright.
See index.

1229 Harris, Leon. UPTON SINCLAIR: AMERICAN REBEL.
New York: Thomas Y. Crowell.
Refers often to the friendship and
disagreements between the socialist and
HLM. See index.

1230 Stegner, Wallace, ed. THE LETTERS OF BERNARD
DeVOTO. Garden City, NY: Doubleday.
The literary critic mentions HLM several
times in letters to others. See index.

1231 Tashjian, Dickran. SKYSCRAPER PRIMITIVES:
DADA AND THE AMERICAN AVANT-GARDE, 1910-1925.
Middletown, CT: Wesleyan University Press.
HLM's conservatism annoyed avant-garde
artists and literati, especially when the
AM published Ernest Boyd's "Aesthete:
Model 1924" in its first issue, December
1923. See index.

1232 Whittemore, Reed. WILLIAM CARLOS WILLIAMS:
POET FROM JERSEY. Boston: Houghton Mifflin.
The poet and HLM shared an enthusiasm for
American language despite their differ-
ences on other issues. See index.

1976

1233 Gillon, Adam. "Joseph Conrad: Polish Cosmo-
politan." In CONRAD AND SHAKESPEARE AND
OTHER ESSAYS, 13-39. New York: Astra Books.
Refers to the novelist's dislike of HLM's
attention to his Slavic origins.

Mentions

1234 Heymann, C. David. EZRA POUND, THE LAST ROWER: A POLITICAL PROFILE. New York: Viking Press. See index.

1235 Pullar, Philippa. FRANK HARRIS: A BIOGRAPHY. New York: Simon and Schuster.
Quotes often from the letters of the writer and publisher to friend HLM. See index.

1236 Vonnegut, Kurt, Jr. "Opening Remarks." In THE UNABRIDGED MARK TWAIN. Edited by Lawrence Teacher. Philadelphia: Running Press.
See pages xiv-xv, where the novelist compares HLM to Twain, particularly in their mutual gift for using the American vernacular.

1977

1237 Loos, Anita. CAST OF THOUSANDS. New York: Grosset and Dunlap.
The Hollywood actress and novelist frequently mentions her good friend the magazine editor. See index.

1978

1238 Berg, A. Scott. MAX PERKINS: EDITOR OF GENIUS. New York: E.P. Dutton.
Mentions HLM and George Jean Nathan in connection with the *SS*. See index.

1239 Blair, Walter, and Hamlin Hill, eds. AMERICA'S HUMOR: FROM POOR RICHARD TO DOONESBURY. New York: Oxford University Press.
Several pages on HLM's association with James Stevens, author of the "Paul Bunyan" stories, among other brief references. See index.

1240 Kazin, Alfred. NEW YORK JEW. New York: Knopf. See index.

1241 Lundén, Rolf. "Theodore Dreiser and the Nobel Prize." *AMERICAN LITERATURE* 50 (May): 216-29.
The novelist wrote to HLM to ask his assistance in winning the award.

1979

1242 Drake, William. SARA TEASDALE: WOMAN AND POET. San Francisco: Harper and Row. See index.

1243 Evans, Elizabeth. RING LARDNER. New York: Frederick Ungar.
Quotes HLM's views of the writer and his very American language.

1244 Haugen, Einar. IBSEN'S DRAMA: AUTHOR TO AUDIENCE. Minneapolis: University of Minnesota Press.
HLM was an appreciative if not always penetrating critic of the playwright. See index.

1245 Karl, Frederick R. JOSEPH CONRAD: THE THREE LIVES. New York: Farrar, Straus and Giroux.
Cites the novelist's response to the admiration HLM had for him. See index.

1246 Webster, Grant. THE REPUBLIC OF LETTERS: A HISTORY OF POSTWAR AMERICAN LITERARY OPINION. Baltimore and London: Johns Hopkins University Press.
HLM is mentioned in connection with critics Frederick J. Hoffman and Edmund Wilson. See index.

1980

1247 Benediktsson, Thomas E. GEORGE STERLING. Boston: G.K. Hall.
On the mutual admiration between the poet and HLM, who published him in the *AM*. See index.

1248 Greene, Suzanne Ellery. BALTIMORE: AN ILLUSTRATED HISTORY. Woodland Hills, CA: Windsor Publications. See index.

1249 Margolis, John D. JOSEPH WOOD KRUTCH. Knoxville: University of Tennessee Press.
On HLM's contribution to the writer's professional start, among other topics. See index.

1250 Marsden, George M. FUNDAMENTALISM AND
     AMERICAN CULTURE: THE SHAPING OF TWENTIETH-
     CENTURY EVANGELICALISM, 1870-1925. New York
     and Oxford: Oxford University Press.
          Cites HLM's disdain for fundamentalism,
          especially as revealed in "In Memoriam:
          W.J.B." [82]. See index.

1251 Nagel, James. STEPHEN CRANE AND LITERARY
     IMPRESSIONISM. University Park and London:
     Pennsylvania State University Press. See
     index.

1252 Peplow, Michael W. GEORGE S. SCHUYLER.
     Boston: G.K. Hall.
          Numerous references to HLM's friendship
          with the black writer; see index.

1253 Ryan, Frank L. THE IMMEDIATE CRITICAL RECEP-
     TION OF ERNEST HEMINGWAY. Washington:
     University Press of America.
          See pages 10, 50, 51, and 52 for a few of
          HLM's remarks on the novelist's work.

1254 Steel, Ronald. WALTER LIPPMANN AND THE
     AMERICAN CENTURY. Boston and Toronto: Little,
     Brown.
          Several references to the fellow journ-
          alist, whom Lippmann admired. See index.

1255 Wilson, Edmund. THE THIRTIES: FROM NOTEBOOKS
     AND DIARIES OF THE PERIOD. Edited with intro-
     duction by Leon Edel. New York: Farrar,
     Straus, and Giroux. See index.

                        1981

1256 Baker, Carlos, ed. ERNEST HEMINGWAY: SELECTED
     LETTERS, 1917-1961. New York: Charles
     Scribner's Sons.
          HLM is mentioned--usually unfavorably--in
          a number of the novelist's letters to
          others. See index.

1257 Bruccoli, Matthew J. SOME SORT OF EPIC
     GRANDEUR: THE LIFE OF F. SCOTT FITZGERALD.
     New York and London: Harcourt, Brace,
     Jovanovich.

Refers to HLM, Sara Haardt, and the AM. See index.

1258 Hall, Donald, ed. THE OXFORD BOOK OF AMERICAN LITERARY ANECDOTES. New York and Oxford: Oxford University Press.
Cites anecdotes about HLM and fellow literati Theodore Dreiser, Richard Wright, Sinclair Lewis, and Sherwood Anderson. See index.

1259 Long, Terry L. GRANVILLE HICKS. Boston: Twayne.
On the critic's unfavorable view of HLM; see index.

1260 Martin, Ronald E. AMERICAN LITERATURE AND THE UNIVERSE OF FORCE. Durham, NC: Duke University Press.
See especially his chapter on Theodore Dreiser.

1261 Mintz, Lawrence E. "American Humor in the 1920s." THALIA: STUDIES IN LITERARY HUMOR 4 (Spring and Summer): 26-32.

1262 Perry, John. JACK LONDON: AN AMERICAN MYTH. Chicago: Nelson-Hall. See index.

1263 Primeau, Ronald. BEYOND SPOON RIVER: THE LEGACY OF EDGAR LEE MASTERS. Austin: University of Texas Press.
On the mutual admiration between poet and critic. See index.

1264 Vitelli, James R. RANDOLPH BOURNE. Boston: Twayne. See index.

1982

1265 Curtis, James. BETWEEN FLOPS: A BIOGRAPHY OF PRESTON STURGES. New York: Harcourt, Brace, Jovanovich.
Pages 25-26 comment on the playwright's fascination with HLM's thought, style, and respect for language.

1266 Nast, Lenora Heilig, Laurence N. Krause, and R.C. Monk, eds. BALTIMORE: A LIVING RENAISSANCE. Baltimore: Historic Baltimore Society. Includes brief remarks by HLM on writing; see index.

1983

1267 Douglas, George H. EDMUND WILSON'S AMERICA. Lexington: University Press of Kentucky. Contains several references to Wilson's statements on HLM. See index.

1268 Fowler, Douglas. S.J. PERELMAN. Boston: Twayne.
Like many other newspaper wits of the early twentieth century, Perelman consciously imitated HLM. See index.

1269 Gomes, Peter J. "Pilgrims and Puritans: 'Heroes' and 'Villains' in the Creation of the American Past." PROCEEDINGS OF THE MASSACHUSETTS HISTORICAL SOCIETY 95: 1-16.
"Mencken made sport of the Puritans and their heirs but spoke not a word about the Pilgrims" (16).

1270 Hussman, Lawrence E., Jr. DREISER AND HIS FICTION: A TWENTIETH-CENTURY QUEST. Philadelphia: University of Pennsylvia Press.
Notes that the novelist first encountered Nietzsche's thought through HLM; also mentions HLM's reactions to some of Dreiser's work. See index.

1271 Marling, William. DASHIELL HAMMETT. Boston: Twayne.
Refers briefly to the publishing of his early work in HLM and Nathan's BLACK MASK. See index.

1984

1272 Elledge, Scott. E.B. WHITE: A BIOGRAPHY. New York and London: W.W. Norton.
On the fascination the younger humorist had for the older. See index.

1273 Flake, Carol. REDEMPTORAMA: CULTURE, POLITICS AND THE NEW EVANGELICALISM. Garden City, NY: Anchor Press.
Brief look at the Scopes trial and HLM's comments on Bryan and fundamentalism. See index.

1274 Lee, Lawrence, and Barry Gifford. SAROYAN: A BIOGRAPHY. New York: Harper and Row.
Refers briefly to the writer's indignation expressed when the AM began to accept his submissions only after he was known. See index.

1275 Richardson, H. Edward. JESSE: THE BIOGRAPHY OF AN AMERICAN WRITER, JESSE HILTON STUART. New York: McGraw-Hill.
Yet another young poet proud to have his work published in the AM. See index for references.

1276 Roulston, Robert. "Something Borrowed, Something New: A Discussion of Literary Influence on THE GREAT GATSBY." In CRITICAL ESSAYS ON F. SCOTT FITZGERALD'S THE GREAT GATSBY, 54-66. Edited by Scott Donaldson. Boston: G.K. Hall.
Briefly weighs HLM's influence on the writing not only of this book but also of Fitzgerald's earlier THIS SIDE OF PARADISE and THE BEAUTIFUL AND THE DAMNED.

1277 Torrey, E. Fuller. THE ROOTS OF TREASON: EZRA POUND AND THE SECRET OF ST. ELIZABETHS. New York: McGraw-Hill.
Includes several references to the poet's friendship with HLM and quotations from their letters. See index.

1985

1278 Hertzberg, Hendrik. "Chicken McMencken." NEW REPUBLIC 192 (8 April): 30-33.
Unfavorable review of THE LIBERAL CRACK-UP and its author, R. Emmett Tyrrell, Jr., a self-appointed but unconvincing modern HLM.

1279 Kempf, James Michael. THE EARLY CAREER OF MALCOLM COWLEY: A HUMANIST AMONG THE MODERNS. Baton Rouge and London: Louisiana State University Press.
  The two critics viewed American democracy and culture differently. See index.

1280 "Playboy Interview: John Huston." PLAYBOY 32 (September): 63-65, 68-70, 72, 178-80, 182.
  The noted American filmmaker credits HLM with exercising a great deal of influence over him while a young writer in the 1920s and 1930s.

1281 Putzel, Max. GENIUS OF PLACE: WILLIAM FAULKNER'S TRIUMPHANT BEGINNINGS. Baton Rouge and London: Louisiana State University Press.
  Mentions HLM a handful of times, particularly in connection with the story "That Evening Sun," first published in the AM. See index.

1282 Saunders, Richard. AMBROSE BIERCE: THE MAKING OF A MISANTHROPE. San Francisco: Chronicle Books.
  On the writer's acquaintance with HLM and critic Percival Pollard. See index.

1986

1283 Hermann, Dorothy. S.J. PERELMAN: A LIFE. New York: Putnam.
  Passing reference to HLM as a strong influence on the young newspaper humorist, particularly through the AM. See index for references.

1284 Lingeman, Richard. THEODORE DREISER: AT THE GATES OF THE CITY, 1871-1907. Vol. 1. New York: G.P. Putnam's Sons. See index.

1285 McCrum, Robert, William Cran, and Robert MacNeil. THE STORY OF ENGLISH. New York: Viking Press.
  Cites HLM's philological work often; see index.

1286 Vanderbilt, Kermit. AMERICAN LITERATURE AND THE ACADEMY: THE ROOTS, GROWTH, AND MATURITY OF A PROFESSION. Philadelphia: University of Pennsylvia Press. See index.

1287 Wilson, Edmund. THE FIFTIES: FROM NOTEBOOKS AND DIARIES OF THE PERIOD. Edited with an introduction by Leon Edel. New York: Farrar, Straus, and Giroux. See index.

1288 Yoseloff, Thomas, ed. THE MAN FROM THE MERCURY: A CHARLES ANGOFF MEMORIAL READER. Teaneck, NJ; London and Toronto: Fairleigh Dickinson University Press and Associated University Presses.
Introduction contains frequent mention of HLM.

1987

1289 Donald, David Herbert. LOOK HOMEWARD: A LIFE OF THOMAS WOLFE. Boston and Toronto: Little, Brown; London: Bloomsbury.
Gives brief attention to the attraction HLM had for the novelist. See index.

J. DISSERTATIONS

The following is a list of dissertations written to satisfy the requirements of the Ph.D. degree at various American universities. For master's theses and foreign dissertations, consult the Adler bibliography and its Supplements [459, 465, 473]. Some works have been revised and published as books; consult appropriate author in Section F.

1957

1290 Dolmetsch, Carl Richard. A HISTORY OF *THE SMART SET MAGAZINE*, 1914-1923. University of Chicago.

1959

1291 Nolte, William H. THE LITERARY CRITICISM OF H.L. MENCKEN. University of Illinois at Urbana-Champaign.

1292 O'Brien, Adrian Philip. A CRITICAL STUDY OF THE EDITORIALS OF HENRY LOUIS MENCKEN IN THE *AMERICAN MERCURY* FROM JANUARY 1924 TO DECEMBER 1933. St. John's University.

1293 Thoma, George N. A STUDY OF THE RHETORIC IN H.L. MENCKEN'S ESSAYS, 1917-1927. University of Chicago.

1960

1294 Pickett, Roy G. H.L. MENCKEN'S RHETORICAL BATTLE. University of Iowa.

1295 Ruland, Richard Eugene. A USABLE PAST IN THE CRITICISM OF BABBITT, MORE, SHERMAN, AND MENCKEN. University of Michigan.

1296 Singleton, M.K. A HISTORY OF *THE AMERICAN MERCURY* UNDER THE EDITORSHIP OF HENRY MENCKEN, 1924-1933. Duke University.

1961

1297 Stenerson, Douglas C. A GENETIC HISTORY OF THE PREJUDICES OF H.L. MENCKEN, 1880-1926. University of Minnesota.

1963

1298 Hickman, William. INFLUENCE OF ATTITUDE TOWARD RELIGION UPON THE WRITINGS OF H.L. MENCKEN. University of Pittsburgh.

1965

1299 Simpson, Herbert M. MENCKEN AND NATHAN. University of Maryland.

1967

1300 Remley, David A. THE CORRESPONDENCE OF H.L. MENCKEN AND UPTON SINCLAIR: "AN ILLUSTRATION OF HOW NOT TO AGREE." Indiana University.

1968

1301 Turaj, Frank. H.L. MENCKEN AND AMERICAN LITERATURE. Brown University.

1971

1302 Brown, Barbara Ione Kaufman. THE POLITICAL THOUGHT OF H.L. MENCKEN. Johns Hopkins University.

1303 Grode, Geoffrey. VARIETIES OF ARNOLDIAN THOUGHT IN AMERICAN CRITICISM: JAMES HUNEKER AND H.L. MENCKEN. University of Texas at Austin.

1304 Williams, William H.A., II. H.L. MENCKEN: A CRITICAL STUDY, 1880-1929. Johns Hopkins University.

1972

1305 Hobson, Fred C., Jr. H.L. MENCKEN AND THE SOUTHERN LITERARY RENASCENCE. University of North Carolina at Chapel Hill.

1974

1306 Ryan, Mark B. MENCKEN'S MIND: THE INTELLECTUAL ORIENTATION OF H.L. MENCKEN. Yale University.

1976

1307 Kline, Lawrence Oliver. H.L. MENCKEN'S CONTROVERSY WITH THE METHODISTS WITH SPECIAL REFERENCE TO THE ISSUE OF PROHIBITION. Duke University.

1977

1308 Jones, Daniel C. H.L. MENCKEN: CRITIC OF THE NEW DEAL, 1933-1936. West Virginia University.

1979

1309 Fitzpatrick, Vincent. TWO BEASTS IN THE PARLOR: THE DREISER-MENCKEN RELATIONSHIP. State University of New York at Stony Brook.

1986

1310 Herrin, Roberta Teague. H.L. MENCKEN AS A PHILOLOGIST (AMERICAN ENGLISH, GRAMMAR AND USAGE). University of Tennessee.

K. FORTHCOMING

At this writing, the following works are known to be in progress. Publication dates are tentative, as are some titles.

1988

1311 Bode, Carl. THE EDITOR, THE BLUENOSE, AND THE PROSTITUTE: H.L. MENCKEN'S HISTORY OF THE "HATRACK" CASE. Boulder, CO: Roberts, Rinehart.

1312 DuBasky, Mayo, ed. THE GIST OF MENCKEN. Metuchen, NJ: Scarecrow Press.

1313 Fitzpatrick, Vincent. H.L. MENCKEN. New York: Ungar Publishing.

1989

1314 Fecher, Charles A., ed. THE DIARIES OF H.L. MENCKEN. New York: Knopf.

1315 Hobson, Fred C. Biography of HLM, as yet untitled. New York: Random House.

AUTHOR INDEX

AARON, DANIEL 430, 675, 1181
ABHAU, W.C. 552, 555
ADLER, BETTY 459, 461, 462, 463, 465, 967, 994, 1005
ADLER, ELMER 180
AINTO, RUSSELL 1118
ALDRIDGE, JOHN W. 713
ALLEN, FREDERICK LEWIS 620, 826
ALLER, PATRICIA 1088
AMRHINE, KENNETH W. 1057, 1088, 1146
ANDERSON, CHARLES R. 530
ANDERSON, CORINNE 1088
ANDERSON, FENWICK 1033, 1068
ANDERSON, MARGARET 772
ANDERSON, SHERWOOD 531
ANDOR, JUHASZ 6
ANGOFF, CHARLES 187, 480, 495, 512, 517, 734, 861, 889, 905, 911, 949, 1180, 1190
ARNETT, EARL 974
ARVIN, NEWTON 799
ASBURY, HERBERT 885
ASHBY, LeROY 1211
ASHLEY, PERRY J. 562
AYD, JOSEPH D. 1080
AYD, JOSEPH J. 348

BABBITT, IRVING 582, 835, 1173
BABCOCK, C. MERTON 513, 912, 923, 926, 950, 975, 976
BAKER, CARLOS 1256
BALCH, EMILY CLARK See CLARK, EMILY
BANKS, DEAN 1041
BAROJA, PIO 377
BARRICK, MAC E. 1081
BARRICK, NANCY D. 978
BARZUN, JACQUES 875
BASARAB, STEPHEN 728
BAUER, HARRY C. 956, 1008, 1034, 1042
BAUGH, HANSELL 426
BEACH, JOSEPH WARREN 820
BEARD, CHARLES A. 779
BECHHOFER, C.E. [CARL ERIC BECHHOFER ROBERTS] 1158
BEHRMAN, S.N. 689
BENCHLEY, ROBERT 602
BENDINER, ROBERT 879, 906
BENEDIKTSSON, THOMAS E. 1247
BENTON, THOMAS H. 5
BERANGER, JEAN 730
BERG, A. SCOTT 1238
BETTS, GLYNNE ROBINSON 741
BEWLEY, MARIUS 661
BIER, JESSE 1198
BLAIR, WALTER 1239
BLANCK, JACOB NATHANIEL 452
BLANKENSHIP, RUSSELL 1161
BLEI, FRANZ 6
BLODGETT, HAROLD W. 957
BLOOM, EMANUEL 865
BLOOM, ROBERT 915
BLOTNER, JOSEPH 437, 1218
BODE, CARL 422, 436, 441, 532, 578, 671, 896, 1050, 1082, 1311
BODENHEIM, MAXWELL 811

BOLLER, PAUL F., JR.
937, 958
BONNER, THOMAS C. 986
BOORSTIN, DANIEL J.
673, 1214
BOUDE, KATHERINE S.
466
BOURNE, RANDOLPH 582,
768
BOWDEN, HENRY WARNER
553
BOYD, ERNEST A. 474,
475, 582, 780, 781,
789, 822, 836, 1231
BOYNTON, PERCY HOLMES
582, 589, 621, 782,
789
BRALEY, BERTON 783
BREADY, JAMES H. 985,
1083
BRIEN, ALAN 951
BRIEUX, EUGENE 374
BROD, DONALD F. 979
BROOKS, VAN WYCK 582,
624, 662
BROWN, BARBARA IONE
KAUFMAN 1302
BROWN, ERNEST O. 978
BROWNELL, WILLIAM C.
818
BRUCCOLI, MATTHEW J.
440, 732, 924, 1205,
1212, 1257
BRUSTEIN, ROBERT A.
719
BRYER, JACKSON R. 746,
1205, 1207
BUITENHUIS, PETER 697
BULSTERBAUM, ALLISON
767a
BURGAN, JOHN S. 1112
BURKE, JOHN 1224
BURKE, WILLIAM JEREMIAH
450
BURR, JOHN R. 1035
BUTCHER, FANNY 541
BYRON, GILBERT 1119
BYRON, WILLIAM 754,
1174

CABELL, JAMES BRANCH
380, 426, 431, 615,
887
CABELL, MARGARET
FREEMAN 431
CAIRNS, HUNTINGTON
420, 578, 1009
CALDWELL, JOHN 980
CALVERTON, V.F. 592,
858
CANBY, HENRY SEIDEL
608
CARGILL, OSCAR 684,
1168
CASTAGNA, EDWIN 433,
968
CHANTICLEER 812
CHASE, WILLIAM S. 328
CHENETIER, MARC 438
CHESLOCK, LOUIS 419,
533, 544, 995, 1113,
1137
CHESTERTON, G.K. 344,
616, 625
CHRISTIAN, HENRY A.
952, 1010
CHURCHILL, ALLEN 710
CIVINO, LINDA D. 724
CLARK, EMILY 478, 1185
CLAUSEN, CHRISTOPHER
1069
CLAYTON, BRUCE 757
CLEATON, ALLEN 641
CLEATON, IRENE 641
CLEATOR, P.E. 441
COBB, ELIZABETH 800
COHEN, HENIG 704
COLLIJN, GUSTAF 598
COLLINS, SEWARD 845
COLUM, PADRAIC 431
COMBS, GEORGE HAMILTON
630
CONKLIN, GROFF 634,
692
CONRAD, JOSEPH 1159
COOKE, ALISTAIR 414,
496, 554, 578, 698,
891
COONEY, CHARLES F. 996

COOPER, JAMES FENIMORE 388
COURTNEY, W.L. 1155
COUSINS, NORMAN 890
COWING, CEDRIC B. 908
COWLEY, MALCOLM 670, 692, 873, 1172
CRAN, WILLIAM 1285
CRANDALL, ALLEN 632
CRAWFORD, BILL 27
CRICHTON, KYLE S. See FORSYTHE, ROBERT
CROSS, WILBUR 99
CRUNDEN, ROBERT M. 678
CRUPI, CHARLES 1122
CUNZ, DIETER 659
CURTIS, JAMES 1265

DABNEY, VIRGINIUS 733
DALY, JOSEPH A. 569
DANIELS, JONATHAN 866
DANNELLEY, PAUL 1051
DAVIDSON, DONALD 678, 1219
DAVIDSON, WILBUR L., JR. 927
DAVIS, H.L. 887
DeCAMP, L. SPRAGUE 699
DeCASSERES, BENJAMIN 609, 617
DeKRUIF, PAUL 507
DELLER, GEORGE 1088
DeMELLO, GONZALO G. 20
DEMOUY, JANE KRAUSE 981
DeVOTO, BERNARD 1230
DEWEY, JOHN 191
DiROBILANT, IRENE 610
DOLMETSCH, CARL RICHARD 521, 545, 556, 582, 689, 703, 925, 942, 953, 1290
DONALD, DAVID HERBERT 1289
DONALDSON, SCOTT 1276
DORSEY, JOHN 535, 578, 1031, 1058, 1085
DOUGLAS, GEORGE H. 576, 1011, 1036, 1267

DOWELL, PETER W. 443
DOWELL, RICHARD W. 469
DOWLING, ALBERT W. 938
DOWNEY, CHARLOTTE 1059
DOWNS, ROBERT B. 707
DRAKE, WILLIAM 1242
DREISER, HELEN 492
DREISER, THEODORE 396, 428, 442, 749
DuBASKEY, MAYO 1312
DUBERMAN, JASON D. 1147
DUDDEN, ARTHUR POWER 1138
DUDEK, J.B. 582
DUDLEY, DOROTHY 626
DUFFY, GLENN A. 1088
DUGGAN, MARGARET 440
DUKE, MAURICE 467, 987
DUNLAP, RICHARD L. 536
DURHAM, FRANK 427, 969
DURR, ROBERT ALLEN 501

EASTMAN, JOHN 1027
EASTMAN, MAX 872
EDEL, LEON 550, 1177, 1255, 1287
EDMISTON, SUSAN 724
ELGSTROM, ANNA LENAH 598
ELIAS, ROBERT H. 428, 1171
ELLEDGE, SCOTT 1272
ELY, CATHERINE BEACH 837
EMBLIDGE, DAVID 1052
EPSTEIN, JOSEPH 415, 1053, 1070, 1086
ESPY, WILLARD R. 864
EVANS, BERGEN 654
EVANS, ELIZABETH 1243
EVITTS, WILLIAM J. 1012

FABRE, MICHEL 1215
FADIMAN, CLIFTON 389
FAIN, JOHN TYREE 678, 1219
FAIRLIE, HENRY 1225

FARR, FINIS 716
FARRAR, JOHN 590, 644
FARRELL, JAMES T. 418, 497, 551, 665, 725
FASSETT, JACOB S., JR. 377
FAULKNER, WILLIAM 437
FECHER, CHARLES A. 577, 578, 1060, 1087, 1139, 1314
FENCHAK, PAUL 728
FERGUSSON, HARVEY 887
FETHERLING, DOUG 729
FIELD, EUGENE 783
FINDAHL, THEO 603
FISHBEIN, MORRIS 534
FITZGERALD, F. SCOTT 432, 440, 790, 1211, 1216
FITZGERALD, STEPHEN E. 913
FITZPATRICK, CAROL 1113
FITZPATRICK, VINCENT 473, 557, 582, 1043, 1044, 1054, 1071, 1097, 1102, 1309, 1313
FLAKE, CAROL 1273
FLANAGAN, JOHN T. 1220
FLORA, JOSEPH M. 761, 1072
FOERSTER-NIETZSCHE, ELIZABETH 381
FONTANA, SHEILA YORK 1088
FOOTNER, HULBERT 652
FORD, COREY 1193
FORD, HUGH 1226
FORGUE, GUY JEAN 430, 572, 730, 905, 909, 916, 1213
FORSYTHE, ROBERT [KYLE S. CRICHTON] 635, 645
FOWLER, DOUGLAS 1268
FRANCIS, RAYMOND L. 882
FRANK, CHARLES P. 1203

FRANK, WALDO 642, 838
FREY, CARROLL 447
FREYLIGER, HENRY J. 512
FRIED, LEWIS 1232
FULLINWIDER, S.P. 988

GAFFEY, JAMES P. 737
GALE, STEVEN H. 767a
GALIGAN, EDWARD L. 425
GALINSKY, HANS 703
GARRATY, JOHN A. 545
GAYLE, ADDISON 738
GEISMAR, MAXWELL 658, 677
GELB, ARTHUR 1181
GELB, BARBARA 1181
GENZMER, GEORGE 814
GERBER, PHILIP 722
GERSHENOWITZ, HARRY 1103, 1114, 1140, 1141, 1148
GERTZ, ELMER 1162
GIFFORD, BARRY 1274
GILLIS, ADOLPH 639
GILLIS, JAMES M. 854, 876
GILLON, ADAM 1233
GILMAN, LAWRENCE 774
GINGRICH, ARNOLD 228, 506, 538
GLICKSBURG, CHARLES I. 862, 1173
GOING, WILLIAM T. 1227
GOLD, MICHAEL 651, 887
GOLDBERG, ISAAC 476, 594
GOLDHURST, WILLIAM 679
GOLDMAN, ERIC F. 1178
GOMES, PETER J. 1269
GOODFELLOW, DONALD M. 685
GORDON, CHARLES S. 1
GORKY, MAXIM 379
GOULDEN, JOSEPH C. 424, 1061
GRATTAN, C. HARTLEY 612

AUTHORS

GREENE, SUZANNE ELLERY 1248
GREENE, WARD 660
GREET, W. CABELL 888
GREGORY, HORACE 850
GRIFFIN, JOSEPH 762
GRINDER, R. DALE 989
GRODE, GEOFFREY 1303
GROPPER, WILLIAM 590, 645
GROSS, DALTON 1045
GROUPE DE RECHERCHES ET D'ETUDES NORD-AMERICAINES 755
GRUENING, ERNEST 116
GUNTHER, JOHN 1169

HAARDT, SARA 391, 444
HACKETT, FRANCIS 110, 582, 775, 897
HAGEMANN, EDWARD R. 1073
HAHN, H. GEORGE 1127
HAKUTANI, YOSHINOBU 739, 1228
HALL, DONALD 1258
HALL, GROVER C. 815
HALPER, ALBERT 708
HARRIS, FRANK 587, 776, 791
HARRIS, LEON 1229
HARRISON, GILBERT A. 57
HARRISON, HENRY SYDNOR 1160
HARRISON, JOSEPH B. 567
HARRISS, R.P. 911, 1089
HARROLD, CHARLES FREDERICK 839
HART, RICHARD H. 938, 1028
HARTSHORNE, THOMAS L. 700
HARTWICK, HARRY 640
HATTERAS, OWEN [HLM] 22, 112, 118

HAUGEN, EINAR 560, 1244
HAVARD, WILLIAM C. 1120
HAYS, ARTHUR GARFIELD 604
HAZLITT, HENRY 898, 1164
HEAP, JANE 772
HECHT, BEN 493, 518
HELD, JOHN, JR. 884
HEMINGWAY, ERNEST 1256
HENDERSON, F. C. [HLM] 445, 563
HENSLEY, DONALD M. 709
HERGESHEIMER, JOSEPH 477
HERMANN, DOROTHY 1283
HERRIN, ROBERTA TEAGUE 1310
HERTZBERG, HENDRIK 1278
HESSLER, L.B. 856
HEYMANN, C. DAVID 1234
HICKMAN, WILLIAM 1298
HICKS, GRANVILLE 631, 1173, 1186
HILL, HAMLIN 1239
HILLS, L. RUST 228
HIRSHBERG, LEONARD K. 102
HOBSON, FRED C., JR. 574, 582, 751, 1046, 1090, 1305, 1315
HOFFMAN, FREDERICK J. 667
HOHNER, ROBERT A. 1149
HOLBROOK, STEWART H. 655, 887
HOOPES, ROY 747
HOPKINS, FREDERICK M. 446
HORCHLER, R.T. 899
HOWE, E.W. 376
HOWE, IRVING 900
HUBBELL, JAY B. 1174
HUNEKER, JAMES 387
HUSSEY, L.M. 808

HUSSMAN, LAWRENCE E.,
 JR. 1270
HUSTON, JOHN 1280
HUTCHENS, JOHN K. 519
HUXLEY, A.H. 784
HYMAN, STANLEY EDGAR
 1170

IBSEN, HENRIK 371,
 372, 376, 390
INGE, M. THOMAS 752
ISHILL, JOSEPH 387
IVERSEN, ANDERS 970

JACOBS, BRADFORD 959
JANSEN, EDWARD K. 1013
JARDIN, JEAN 6
JENNINGS, JODI 1088
JEROME, W.P. 579, 1029
JERVEY, EDWARD D. 1062
jh See HEAP, JANE
JOAD, C.E.M. 855
JOHANNSEN, OSCAR B.
 1088
JOHANSON, DONALD 471
JOHNS, BUD 528
JOHNSON, GERALD W. 14,
 490, 582, 806, 880,
 887, 901, 905, 907,
 960, 1014, 1037, 1179
JOHNSON, JAMES WELDON
 582, 771, 880
JOHNSON, MERLE 446,
 452
JOHNSON, RICHARD C.
 468
JONES, CARLTON 1055
JONES, DANIEL C. 1308
JONES, HOWARD MUMFORD
 840
JONES, IDWAL 887

KAGAN, SOLOMON R. 646
KALLEN, H.M. 809
KANIGEL, ROBERT 1091
KARL, FREDERICK R.
 1245
KARP, LAURENCE E. 1038

KAZIN, ALFRED 748,
 1128, 1153, 1240
KELLEY, WILLIAM
 VALENTINE 816
KELLNER, BRUCE 990,
 1199
KELLNER, DORA A. 11
KEMLER, EDGAR 488,
 688, 892
KEMPF, JAMES MICHAEL
 1279
KEMPTON, MURRAY 1115
KENNEDY, ARTHUR
 GARFIELD 233, 448
KENYON, NELLIE 1056
KERR, CAROLINE V. 381
KETCHUM, ROLAND 639
KEUHL, LINDA 546
KILPATRICK, JAMES L.
 1104
KIRBY, THOMAS A. 398
KLINE, LAWRENCE OLIVER
 1307
KLOEFKORN, JOHNNY L.
 910
KNEEBONE, JOHN T. 763
KNOPF, ALFRED A. 379,
 489, 503, 512, 546,
 578, 1105
KNOX, RONALD 627
KOHN, JOHN S. VAN E.
 461
KRAFT, STEPHANIE 735
KRAUSE, LAURENCE N.
 1266
KRETZSCHMAR, WILLIAM A.,
 JR. 736
KRIEGEL, LEONARD 1206
KRONENBERGER, LOUIS
 582, 668, 670
KRUTCH, JOSEPH WOOD
 508, 519, 582, 793,
 874
KUEHL, JOHN 1205, 1207
KUMMER, FREDERIC ARNOLD
 828

LaBELLE, MAURICE M.
 982

AUTHORS

LaMONT, RIVES 4
LANGER, ELINOR 753
LANGFORD, GERALD 1189
LANGFORD, RICHARD E. 691
LARDNER, JOHN 881
LAWSON, LEWIS A. 954
LEARY, LEWIS G. 455, 671
LEE, LAWRENCE 1274
LEMEUNIER, BARBARA SMITH 750
LEVIN, JAMES B. 997
LEVINSON, ANDRE 611
LeVOT, ANDRE. 754, 928
LEWIS, WYNDHAM 829
LEWISOHN, LUDWIG 1163
LINDSAY, VACHEL 438
LINGEMAN, RICHARD 1284
LIPPMAN, THEO, JR. 423, 1047, 1091, 1106
LIPPMANN, WALTER 582, 801, 823
LITZ, FRANCIS E. 392, 961
LOGAN, ANDY 1187
LOGAN, J.D. 565
LOGGINS, VERNON 643
LONG, ROBERT EMMET 962
LONG, TERRY L. 1259
LONGSTREET, STEPHEN 714
LOOS, ANITA 690, 1221, 1237
LORA, RONALD G. 983
LOVE, GLEN A. 1107
LOWREY, BURLING 917
LUNDEN, ROLF 1241
LUNDQUIST, JAMES 1216, 1222
LYNES, RUSSELL 1175

MacAFEE, HELEN 99
MacDONALD, EDGAR E. 752
MacDOUGALL, CURTIS D. 650
MacNEIL, ROBERT 1285
MALONE, KEMP 233
MANCHESTER, H.F. 896
MANCHESTER, WILLIAM 490, 548, 578, 883, 884, 887, 893
MANGLAVITI, LEO M.J. 998, 999, 1121
MANLY, JOHN MATTHEWS 449
MARGOLIS, JOHN D. 1249
MARIANI, PAUL 742
MARLING, WILLIAM 1271
MARSDEN, GEORGE M. 1250
MARTIN, EDWARD A. 580, 582, 920, 929, 1109, 1129
MARTIN, RONALD E. 1260
MASON, FRANKLIN 1074, 1092
MATHESON, TERENCE J. 1030
MATTHEWS, BRANDER 777
MAURER, DAVID W. 7
MAY, HENRY F. 672
MAYERS, SYDNEY A. 1088
MAYFIELD, SARA 522, 529, 539
MAYNARD, THEODORE 852
McCALL, RAYMOND G. 921
McCORMICK, JOHN 711
McCRUM, ROBERT 1285
McCULLOUGH, ARTHUR F. 802
McDAVID, RAVEN I., JR. 7, 582, 704, 736, 877, 930, 931, 943, 955, 1093, 1108, 1213
McELVEEN, J. JAMES 562
McFEE, WILLIAM 794
McHUGH, ROBERT P. 417, 498, 918
McKAHARAY, JOSEPH T. 1088
McKELWAY, ST. CLAIR 894
MELAMED, S.M. 846
MELLOW, JAMES R. 759
MENCKE, JOHANN BURKHARD 392

MENCKEN, AUGUST 394
METCALFE, HOWARD E. 1048
MEYER, ADOLPHE E. 1075
MEYER, KARL E. 1182
MICHAUD, REGIS 595, 841
MILBURN, GEORGE 887
MILES, ELTON 559, 1015
MILLER, JAMES E., JR. 1184
MILLER, JIM 1063
MILLER, WILLIAM J. 1194
MILLETT, FRED BENJAMIN 449, 451
MIMS, EDWIN 805
MINTON, ARTHUR 865
MINTZ, LAWRENCE E. 1261
MITCHELL, HENRY 1094
MITGANG, HERBERT 706
MODERN LANGUAGE ASSOCIATION 457
MODLIN, CHARLES E. 760
MOERS, ELLEN 705
MONCHAK, STEPHEN J. 863
MONK, R.C. 1266
MONROE, HARRIET 824
MONTAGU, ASHLEY 1195
MONTALTO, LORA L. 1088
MOOS, MALCOLM 415, 578
MORAND, PAUL 6
MORE, PAUL ELMER 605, 1173
MORRIS, JOE ALEX 902
MORRISON, JOSEPH L. 944, 953, 1196, 1204
MORTON, BRUCE 439
MOSELEY, MERRITT W., JR. 1049, 1122
MOSS, DAVID 446
MOTSCH, MARKUS F. 945, 1016
MOTT, FRANK LUTHER 701
MUIR, EDWIN 378

MULLER, HERBERT J. 1000
MUNSON, GORHAM 764
MURAIRE, ANDRE 755

NAGEL, JAMES 1251
NARDINI, ROBERT F. 1110, 1116
NAST, LENORA HEILIG 1266
NATHAN, ADELE GUTMAN 509
NATHAN, GEORGE JEAN 5, 8, 10, 22, 109, 112, 118, 123, 124, 480, 500, 582, 583
NELSON, FREDERIC 681
NELSON, RANDY F. 743
NELSON, RAYMOND 744
NEWMAN, FRANCES 426
NIEBUHR, REINHOLD 582, 847
NIEMTUS, LAURICE 1076
NIETZSCHE, FRIEDRICH 9, 373, 381
NOAH, TONY 8
NOLAN, WILLIAM F. 756
NOLTE, WILLIAM H. 421, 464, 571, 573, 578, 919, 932, 933, 934, 939, 964, 991, 992, 1077, 1078, 1291
NOVAK, MICHAEL 1017

OBER, HAROLD 1216
O'BRIEN, ADRIAN PHILIP 1292
O'CONNOR, RICHARD 693
O'HARA, JOHN 499
OLIVAR-BERTRAND, R. 1018
OPPENHEIMER, GEORGE 525
O'SULLIVAN, VINCENT 563, 778
OSZKAR, FEKETE 6
OWENS, GWINN 1095

OWENS, HAMILTON 430, 520, 527, 582, 867, 871, 935

PARKHURST, WINTHROP 786
PARSHLEY, H.M. 817
PARTRIDGE, ERIC 633, 674
PATTEE, FRED LEWIS 584, 618, 830
PATTERSON, GROVE 487
PAUL, SHERMAN 1188
PAYNE, DARWIN 723
PEARCE, EUGENE L. 619
PEDERSON, LEE A. 940
PEGLER, WESTBROOK 647
PEPLOW, MICHAEL W. 1252
PERKINS, MAX 1211
PERPENTIKEL, PETER 10
PERRY, JOHN 1262
PERSON, JAMES E., JR. 758
PHELPS, WILLIAM LYON 848
PHILLIPS, FRANCES L. 377
PICKETT, CALDER M. 1200
PICKETT, ROY G. 1294
PICKREL, PAUL 903
PIPER, HENRY DAN 692
PIZER, DONALD 469, 726
POITRAS, JEAN-MAURICE 1096, 1150
POLANSKY, CYRIL 1088
PONS, XAVIER 1001
PORTER, BERNARD H. 456
POUDER, G.H. 523
POUND, LOUISE 233
POUPARD, DENNIS 758
POWELL, ARNOLD 1019
PRICE, G. JEFFERSON, III 1123
PRIMEAU, RONALD 1263
PRITCHETT, V.S. 868
PULITZER, RALPH 104
PULLAR, PHILIPPA 1235

PUTZEL, MAX 1281

QUINE, W.V. 745

RALBAG, J. HOWARD 653
RASCOE, BURTON 563, 582, 590, 612, 634, 644, 692, 709, 769, 796, 842, 869
RASMUSSEN, FREDERICK N. 557, 1097
RATCLIFFE, S.K. 797
REFERENCE DEPARTMENT, UNIVERSITY OF PENNSYLVANIA LIBRARY 458
REMLEY, DAVID A. 1300
REYNOLDS, ROBERT D., JR. 1020, 1124
RICHARDSON, H. EDWARD 1275
RICKERT, EDITH 449
RIDDELL, JOHN See FORD, COREY
RIGGIO, THOMAS P. 442, 749, 1130, 1142
ROBBINS, JACK ALAN 551, 725
ROBERTS, CARL ERIC BECHHOFER See BECHHOFER, C.E.
RODGERS, MARION ELIZABETH 444
ROGERS, CAMERON 628
ROGERS, KATHARINE M. 1191
ROOT, E. MERRILL 860
ROOT, RAOUL 772
ROSA, ALFRED 734
ROSNER, JOSEPH 686
ROSS, RALPH 721
ROTHBARD, MURRAY N. 922
ROULSTON, ROBERT 1276
RUBIN, LOUIS D., JR. 694, 717, 761, 946, 1064
RULAND, RICHARD 695, 706, 965, 1295

RUSCH, FREDERICK E.
469
RUYL, LOUIS 652
RYAN, FRANK L. 1253
RYAN, MARK B. 1306
RYAN, WILLIAM F. 1111
SABO, WILLIAM J. 555
SALISBURY, WILLIAM 566
SALZMAN, JACK 1021
SAMUEL D. 613
SANDLER, GILBERT 558,
1065
SAROYAN, WILLIAM 542,
844
SAUNDERS, RICHARD 1282
SAWEY, ORLAN 1201
SCHARF, ROBERT A. 1088
SCHEFFANER, HERMAN
GEORGE 588
SCHEIDEMAN, J.W. 1022
SCHLESINGER, ARTHUR M.,
JR. 905, 1176
SCHMAULHAUSEN, SAMUEL
D. 613
SCHMIDT, W.E.F. 568
SCHOETTLER, CARL 993
SCHONEMANN, FRIEDRICH
831
SCHORER, MARK 676
SCHRADER, RICHARD J.
1151
SCHUYLER, GEORGE S.
582
SCHWAB, ARNOLD T. 1183
SCHWARTZ, GERALD 1131
SCHWARTZMAN, JACK 1088
SCRUGGS, CHARLES W.
581, 582, 1143
SEDGWICK, ELLERY, III
1066
SEMPER, I.J. 582, 629
SERGE, RICARD 750
SERGEANT, ELIZABETH
SHEPLEY 582, 599
SHAFER, ROBERT 636
SHAPIRO, EDWARD S.
1002
SHAPIRO, KARL 702

SHAW, ALBERT 156
SHAW, BYNUM 537
SHAW, CHARLES GREEN
606
SHEEAN, VINCENT 514
SHEPHARDSON, D.E. 1039
SHERMAN, STUART P.
582, 585, 596, 770,
818, 1173
SHIVERS, FRANK R., JR.
765
SHUTT, JAMES W. 1023
SHYRE, PAUL 1040
SIEGEL, JOHN 1
SIMON, JOHN 680
SIMPSON, HERBERT M.
1299
SIMRELL, V.E. 832
SINCLAIR, ANDREW 682
SINCLAIR, MARY CRAIG
510
SINCLAIR, UPTON 429,
511, 600, 669, 833,
895
SINGLETON, M.K. 570,
582, 691, 1296
SKLAR, ROBERT 696
SMITH, BERNARD 648
SMITH, BEVERLY 886
SMITH, H. ALLEN 484,
502, 515, 543, 851
SMITH, S. STEPHENSON
479
SPIES, HEINRICH 7, 593
SPILLER, ROBERT E.
397, 677, 720
SPINGARN, JOEL ELIAS
807, 1157, 1173
SPOTSWOOD, CLAIRE MYERS
637
STAGG, HUNTER T. 582
STARER, IRVING 1088
STARR, KEVIN 1217
STARRETT, VINCENT 1189
STEARNS, HAROLD E.
383, 481
STEEL, RONALD 1254
STEGNER, WALLACE 1223,
1230

STENERSON, DOUGLAS C.
540, 582, 941, 947,
971, 1003, 1297
STERNSTEIN, JEROME L.
545
STODDARD, DONALD R.
948
STOLBERG, BENJAMIN 834
STONE, EDWARD 494
STRACHEY, J. ST. LOE
597
STRODE, HUDSON 549
STRUNSKY, SIMEON 622
SUCKOW, RUTH 887
SULLIVAN, MARK 638
SUSHKO, WOLODYMYR 728
SWAN, BRADFORD F. 454
SWANBERG, W.A. 524,
687

TAKAGAKI, MATSUO 601
TANSELLE, G. THOMAS
468, 1205
TARG, WILLIAM 180
TARRANT, DESMOND 1197
TASHJIAN, DICKRAN 1231
TATE, ALLEN 1219
TAYLOR, HARVEY 1170
TAYLOR, K. PHILLIP 966
TAYLOR, WALTER FULLER
640
TAYLOR, WILLIAM E. 691
TEACHER, LAWRENCE 1240
TEBBEL, JOHN 715
THALER, DAVID S. 561
THIMMESCH, NICK 1132
THOMA, GEORGE N. 1293
THURBER, JAMES 504
TIBBETTS, ALIVE DAVIS
1088
TOBIN, A. I. 1162
TORREY, E. FULLER 1277
TRACHTENBERG, STANLEY
559
TULLY, JIM 485
TURAJ, FRANK 1004,
1024, 1301
TURNBULL, ANDREW 432

UNGER, LEONARD 547
UNTERMEYER, LOUIS 483,
586, 773

VAN DEUSEN, MARSHALL
1209
VAN DOREN, CARL 591,
649, 1165, 1166, 1167
VAN DOREN, MARK 649
VAN GELDER, ROBERT 656
VAN ROOSBROECK, GUSTAVE
L. 564
VAN VECHTEN, CARL 431,
491, 1156
VANDERBILT, KERMIT
1286
VARNEY, HAROLD L. 221
VASS, MARY MILLER 1125
VILLARD, OSWALD
GARRISON 205
VITELLI, JAMES R. 1264
VOIGHT, STEPHEN B. 966
VON HOFFMAN, NICHOLAS
1098
VONNEGUT, KURT, JR.
1236

W.G.L. [HLM] 100
WAGNER, PHILIP M. 363,
516, 547, 721, 1202
WAGNER, (WILHELM)
RICHARD 381
WAGNIERE, HARRIET HELMS
734
WALKER, SUSAN 440
WALLACE, DeWITT 512
WALPOLE, HUGH 804, 819
WALT, JAMES 505, 938,
972
WATSON, RITCHIE D., JR.
1133
WAY, BRIAN 740
WEAVER, MIKE 712
WEBSTER, GRANT 1246
WEEKS, EDWARD 718
WEINTRAUB, STANLEY 914
WELLEK, RENE 767
WELSHKO, THOMAS G.
1079, 1099

WERTHEIM, ARTHUR FRANK 727
WEST, HERBERT FAULKNER 453, 526
WEST, JAMES L.W., III 470, 749, 1005, 1125
WEST, WALTER C. 1117
WESTLAKE, NEDA M. 749, 1100
WHITE, RAY LOUIS 531, 1067
WHITEHALL, HAROLD 582
WHITTEMORE, REED 1232
WICKHAM, HARVEY 614
WILLIAMS, GLUYAS 602
WILLIAMS, HAROLD A. 1154, 1210
WILLIAMS, MICHAEL 607, 810, 825, 849
WILLIAMS, WILLIAM CARLOS 666
WILLIAMS, WILLIAM H.A. 575, 1025, 1304
WILLIAMSON, CHILTON, JR. 1006
WILSON, EARL 657
WILSON, EDMUND 486, 550, 582, 663, 688, 788, 798, 843, 859, 973, 1177, 1255, 1287

WILSON, ELENA 1177
WILSON, ROBERT A. 1101
WINGATE, P.J. 579, 766, 1032, 1126, 1134, 1135, 1136, 1152
WINSLOW, THYRA SAMTER 887
WISH, HARVEY 664
WOOD, JAMES N. 382
WOOLF, HENRY BOSLEY 398, 1026
WOOLF, LEONARD 623
WORMSER, BARON 1144
WRIGHT, RICHARD 482
WRIGHT, WILLARD HUNTINGTON 5
WYCHERLY, H. ALAN 936, 984, 1007, 1192

YARDLEY, JONATHAN 731
YARLING, BASS 904
YATES, NORRIS W. 683
YOSELOFF, THOMAS 1288
YOUNG, STEPHEN A. 1145
YOUNG, THOMAS DANIEL 1219

ZADIG, BERTRAND 596
ZUCKER, A.E. 896

SUBJECT INDEX

ADAMIC, LOUIS 952, 1010
ADE, GEORGE 272, 403, 418
ADLER, BETTY 460
AESTHETICS 75, 80, 90, 103, 197, 314, 404, 406, 409, 410, 414, 418, 419, 422, 757, 782, 860, 992, 1231
AGRARIAN MOVEMENT 185, 207, 751, 1002
AIKEN, CONRAD 147, 792
ALCOHOL (See also PROHIBITION) 317, 420, 422, 528, 669, 682
ALLEN, FREDERICK LEWIS 723
AMERICA, AMERICANISM, and AMERICANS 8, 41, 61, 76, 98, 103, 118, 155, 163, 187, 197, 237, 256, 274, 276, 303, 308, 310, 376, 385, 405, 407, 408, 409, 410, 417, 418, 420, 422, 576, 597, 608, 622, 658, 668, 675, 685, 700, 713, 812, 813, 825, 829, 830, 837, 841, 844, 915, 937, 947, 958, 1007, 1017, 1153, 1159, 1160, 1161, 1182, 1214, 1279
AMERICAN FEDERATION OF LABOR 360
AMERICAN MERCURY, THE 124, 195, 524, 539, 556, 565, 594, 600, 604, 610, 651, 701, 708, 710, 718, 724, 732, 734, 762, 821, 852, 853, 883, 889, 890, 898, 910, 937, 947, 953, 967, 1015, 1021, 1042, 1068, 1105, 1131, 1146, 1147, 1186, 1190, 1192, 1196, 1212, 1223, 1257, 1288, 1291, 1292, 1296, 1311
ANATOMY and PHYSIOLOGY 112
ANDERSON, MARGARET 183, 1121
ANDERSON, SHERWOOD 125, 140, 152, 170, 421, 760, 1067, 1258
ANGLO-SAXONS 65, 114, 264, 406, 414, 829, 1017
ANGOFF, CHARLES 734, 1288
ANTHROPOLOGY 166
APOLLINAIRE, GUILLAUME 126
ARCHER, WILLIAM 251
ARKANSAS 330
ASBURY, HERBERT 321, 821, 830, 1146, 1147
ATHEISM and ATHEISTS 88, 94, 410, 653, 1029
AUTOMOBILES 354, 360
AVANT-GARDE, AMERICAN 1231
AVIS, WALLY 1108

BABBITT, IRVING 133, 809, 840, 845, 1173, 1295
BACH, JOHANN SEBASTIAN 325, 419
BALTIMORE (See also MARYLAND) 84, 228,

255

232, 238, 248, 341,
409, 414, 418, 422,
578, 598, 652, 662,
681, 765, 871, 993,
1003, 1009, 1031,
1083, 1092, 1127,
1154, 1248, 1266
BARKLEY, ALBEN W. 369
BARTENDING 98, 410,
422
BEERBOHM, MAX 421
BEETHOVEN, LUDWIG VON
409, 417, 419, 420
BELIEF -- See FAITH
BENET, STEPHEN VINCENT
147
BENNETT, ARNOLD 403
BIERCE, AMBROSE 33,
86, 172, 178, 410,
420, 693, 1282
BIRTH CONTROL 79, 409,
417
BLACKS 112, 230, 251,
314, 370, 417, 419,
421, 422, 581, 582,
763, 911, 916, 978,
1068
BLOOM, MARION 1050
BODE, CARL 719
BODINE, AUBREY 1210
BONAPARTE, CHARLES J.
422
BORAH, WILLIAM E. 1211
BOSTON WATCH AND WARD
SOCIETY -- See CHASE,
J. FRANK (Secretary)
BOURNE, RANDOLPH 757,
1264
BOYD, ERNEST 645, 809,
1231
BRAHMS, JOHANNES 419
BRANN, WILLIAM COWPER
802
BRIEUX, EUGENE 374
BROOKS, VAN WYCK 744,
809
BROUN, HEYWOOD 162
BROWNELL, W.C. 137
BROWNELL, WILLIAM C.
818

BRYAN, WILLIAM JENNINGS
82, 247, 307, 409,
414, 420, 619, 1250,
1273
BUSINESS 303, 776
BUTLER, NICHOLAS MURRAY
1148
BUTLER, SAMUEL 164
BYRD, H.C. 1082

CABELL, JAMES BRANCH
23, 127, 135, 150,
157, 164, 168, 177,
380, 421, 431, 523,
752, 820, 869, 965,
995, 1072, 1197
CAIN, JAMES M. 535,
747
CAINE, HALL 421, 919
CANON, JAMES, JR. 324,
1149
CAPITAL PUNISHMENT 79,
258, 288, 348, 394,
409
CAPITALISM 54, 111,
217, 405
CAPONE, AL 331
CARLYLE, THOMAS 807,
839
CASH, W.J. 751, 1120,
1196, 1204
CATHER, WILLA 125,
140, 158, 379, 421,
722
CATHOLICISM -- See
RELIGION
CAWEIN, MADISON 56,
405
CENSORSHIP 162, 182,
260, 289, 312, 327,
328, 538, 604, 718,
743, 885, 965, 1146,
1147, 1311
CHASE, J. FRANK (See
also "HATRACK" CASE)
604, 821, 885, 1146,
1147, 1311
CHESTERTON, G.K. 421
CHICAGO 110, 275, 897,
1189

SUBJECTS 257

CHILD CARE 102, 351, 1150
CHILDHOOD and ADOLESCENCE 15, 166, 211, 265, 425, 558, 561, 866, 867, 868, 869, 872, 873, 938, 1081, 1088
CHRISTIAN SCIENCE -- See RELIGION
CHRISTIANITY -- See RELIGION
CHRISTMAS 27, 420
CIGARETTE SMOKING 255
CIVIL RIGHTS 213, 221, 260, 261, 365, 370, 417, 604, 905, 978
CLEATOR, P.E. 441
CLEMENS, SAMUEL LANGHORNE -- See TWAIN, MARK
CLERGY -- See RELIGION
COBB, IRVIN S. 800
COLLEGE 266, 294, 356, 417
COMFORT, WILL LEVINGTON 36, 403
COMMUNISM 206, 213, 290, 333
COMSTOCK, ANTHONY 98
COMSTOCKERY -- See PURITANISM
CONGRESS and CONGRESSMEN 326, 383, 417
CONGRESS OF INDUSTRIAL ORGANIZATIONS 360
CONRAD, JOSEPH 30, 78, 105, 125, 132, 140, 401, 409, 418, 421, 422, 972, 1233, 1245
CONROY, JACK 435, 1021
CONTROVERSY 91, 315, 410, 417, 418
COOLIDGE, CALVIN 119, 163, 176, 284, 300, 414, 415, 919
COOPER, JAMES FENIMORE 388, 420
COUGHLIN, CHARLES E. 352
COWLEY, MALCOLM 1279
COX, JAMES M. 286
CRANE, STEPHEN 1251
CREATIONISM 305, 307
CRIME 79, 199, 288, 290, 331, 348
CROCE, BENEDETTO 807
CUBA 271
CULLEN, COUNTEE 147
CURLEY, MICHAEL J. 1139
CURTIS, CHARLES W. 318

DARROW, CLARENCE 307
DARWIN, CHARLES 1001
DAUGHTERS OF THE AMERICAN REVOLUTION 316
DAVIDSON, DONALD 185, 207, 751, 1219
DEATH 51, 88, 91, 313, 404, 410, 414, 420
DeKANSAS, WHITE 46, 403
DEMOCRACY 11, 54, 72, 133, 143, 293, 344, 382, 405, 406, 412, 591, 608, 623, 663, 678, 822, 823, 831, 834, 839, 850, 919, 970, 1078, 1214, 1279
DENTE, M.A.H. 433
DEPRESSION, THE GREAT 337, 851, 1021
DeVOTO, BERNARD 1201, 1223, 1230
DEWEY, THOMAS E. 369
DosPASSOS, JOHN 130, 146
DRAMA 2, 10, 20, 42, 48, 108, 188, 249, 254, 371, 372, 374, 375, 390, 399, 405, 421, 422, 509, 594, 780, 924, 980, 995, 1013, 1019, 1025, 1040, 1118, 1181, 1188, 1244, 1265
DREISER, THEODORE 21, 33, 34, 107, 144,

179, 186, 240, 273,
396, 401, 414, 417,
420, 421, 422, 427,
428, 442, 469, 492,
506, 524, 626, 687,
695, 705, 726, 739,
757, 762, 915, 948,
1044, 1071, 1102,
1130, 1142, 1150,
1153, 1208, 1222,
1241, 1258, 1260,
1270, 1284, 1309
DRESS 112
DUNCAN, ISADORA 160

ECONOMICS 54, 55,
159, 181, 191, 198,
200, 212, 215, 217,
218, 220, 299, 330,
337, 339, 342, 343,
345, 348, 352, 355,
361, 362, 363, 364,
368, 405, 415, 418,
755, 851, 898, 1001,
1088, 1096
EDDY, MARY BAKER 327
EDUCATION 93, 114,
128, 191, 198, 262,
294, 305, 307, 323,
365, 405, 410, 417,
421, 422, 865, 907,
930, 950, 1075, 1141
EINSTEIN, ALBERT 285,
569
ELIOT, T.S. 173, 809,
843
ELLIS, HAVELOCK 56,
388, 405, 417, 421
EMERSON, RALPH WALDO
47, 49, 403, 418,
420, 624
ENGLAND 911
ENOCH PRATT FREE
LIBRARY (Baltimore)
938
ETHICS 13, 264, 326,
344, 854, 855
ETIQUETTE 41, 403, 418
EUGENICS 219, 316, 417
EUROPE 5, 201, 361,
673, 714
EVOLUTION, THEORY OF
305, 306, 307, 537,
699, 979, 1001, 1140
EXPATRIATE MOVEMENT,
THE 927, 1172

FAITH 67, 156, 184,
389, 406
FARMING 68, 215, 406,
418, 420
FAULKNER, WILLIAM 437,
860, 991, 998, 1218,
1281
FIFTIES, THE (1950s)
1287
FISHBEIN, MORRIS 967
FITZGERALD, F. SCOTT
139, 304, 421, 432,
440, 470, 679, 696,
732, 740, 746, 754,
759, 928, 962, 1005,
1092, 1184, 1192,
1205, 1207, 1212,
1257, 1276
FITZGERALD, ZELDA S.
759, 1227
FLETCHER, JOHN GOULD
185
FOOD 417, 421, 612
FORD, HENRY 421
FORGUE, GUY JEAN 436,
725
FRANCE, ANATOLE 421
"FREE LANCE" COLUMN
261, 422, 1023, 1079
FREE LANCE SERIES 6,
9, 376, 377, 378,
382, 793
FREEDOM OF SPEECH --
See CENSORSHIP
FROST, ROBERT 43
FUNDAMENTALISM (See
also PURITANISM) 81,
98, 305, 306, 307,
312, 326, 409, 410,
414, 417, 420, 553,
625, 1038, 1056,
1250, 1273

SUBJECTS

GARLAND, HAMLIN 46, 403
GARRISON, FIELDING H. 646
GERMANY 106, 194, 264, 269, 270, 271, 422, 659, 911, 916, 945, 1004, 1016, 1066, 1094
GILBERT, SIR WILLIAM SCHWENCK 419
GLASGOW, ELLEN 139, 174, 193, 1133
GOETHE, JOHANN WOLFGANG VON 807, 1087
GOLD, MICHAEL 181
GOLDBERG, ISAAC 632
GOODMAN, PHILIP 517
GOVERNMENT 70, 204, 223, 224, 344, 346, 355, 368, 383, 406, 410, 417, 418, 502, 959, 966
GREENE, WARD 174

HAARDT, SARA 391, 444, 517, 522, 535, 539, 681, 1088, 1133, 1153, 1210, 1227, 1257
HALDEMAN-JULIUS, EMANUEL 844, 1111
HAMMETT, DASHIELL 756, 1271
HANES FAMILY 1117
HARDING, WARREN G. 113, 284, 415, 655
HARLEM RENAISSANCE, THE 581, 582
HARRIS, FRANK 56, 188, 405, 1162, 1235
HARRISON, HENRY SYDNOR 46, 403, 427
"HATRACK" CASE 312, 538, 604, 718, 743, 821, 885, 1146, 1147, 1223, 1311
HAUPTMANN, GERHART 421
HAYDN, FRANZ JOSEPH 419
HAZLITT, HENRY 195
HEARST, WILLIAM RANDOLPH 423
HECHT, BEN 150, 729, 1065
HEINE, HEINRICH 596
HEMINGWAY, ERNEST 161, 177, 189, 732, 860, 1253, 1256
HENRY, O. 421, 828
HERBST, JOSEPHINE 753
HERGESHEIMER, JOSEPH 78, 409, 489, 1185
HEYWARD, DuBOSE 761, 969
HICKS, GRANVILLE 1173, 1259
HIRSHBERG, LEONARD KEENE 1150
HITLER, ADOLPH 194
HOAXES 32, 92, 410, 417, 418, 579, 650, 654, 743, 886, 918, 1126
HOFFMAN, FREDERICK 1246
HOLLYWOOD 690, 1221, 1237
HOLMES, OLIVER WENDELL 414
HOOD, GRETCHEN 443, 1094
HOOVER, HERBERT 318, 337, 415
HOWE, E.W. 169, 274, 376, 776, 815, 1200, 1228
HOWELLS, WILLIAM DEAN 40, 403, 421
HUMOR and HUMORISTS 136, 148, 399, 400, 499, 559, 580, 597, 611, 630, 683, 717, 765, 767a, 799, 812, 1059, 1065, 1130, 1138, 1198, 1224, 1239, 1243, 1261, 1268, 1272
HUNEKER, JAMES 29, 58,

SUBJECTS

386, 401, 405, 418,
420, 421, 422, 609,
788, 1183
HUNGER 330
HUXLEY, ALDOUS 127
HUXLEY, THOMAS HENRY 1024

IBSEN, HENRIK 108, 371, 372, 375, 390, 1013, 1244
ICKES, HAROLD 657
ICONOCLASM 378, 488, 589, 643, 657, 685, 694, 695, 697, 707, 727, 802, 826, 828, 836, 856, 882, 899, 976, 977, 1025, 1038, 1084, 1098, 1099, 1199
IMMIGRATION 364
INDIVIDUALISM 3, 639, 922, 947

JAMES, HENRY 792
JEFFERS, ROBINSON 860
JEFFERSON, THOMAS 98, 410
JOHNS HOPKINS HOSPITAL, Baltimore, MD 358
JOHNSON, GERALD W. 120, 433, 520, 935, 1089, 1120
JOHNSON, JAMES WELDON 582
JOHNSON, SAMUEL 893
JOSEPHSON, MATTHEW 126
JOURNALISM 16, 95, 104, 115, 162, 295, 298, 311, 334, 353, 410, 414, 418, 420, 423, 425, 562, 717, 733, 748, 763, 863, 864, 867, 870, 871, 872, 873, 941, 970, 1023, 1033, 1047, 1063, 1064, 1089, 1090, 1094, 1120, 1196, 1204, 1254, 1268

JOYCE, JAMES 1121
JUDAISM and JEWS 25, 181, 338, 846, 905, 911, 916, 1091, 1095, 1123, 1240
JUSTICE -- See CRIME

KELLEY, FRANCIS CLEMENT 737
KELLY, HOWARD A. 433, 1038
KIPLING, RUDYARD 100
KIRKLEY, DONALD H. 423, 680, 1027
KLINE, HENRY BLUE 185
KNOPF, ALFRED A. 384, 393, 517, 710, 936, 1051
KNOPF, BLANCHE 433
KNOX, FRANK 349
KOPPEL, HOLGER A. 918
KRAPP, GEORGE PHILIP 888
KRUTCH, JOSEPH WOOD 145, 201, 1249
KU KLUX KLAN 320, 743, 810

LABOR 296, 360
LaMONT, ROBERT RIVES 422, 1020
LANDON, ALFRED M. 214, 349
LANGUAGE 7, 98, 99, 103, 208, 209, 225, 226, 227, 229, 230, 231, 233, 234, 235, 236, 237, 239, 241, 242, 257, 262, 340, 357, 397, 398, 410, 417, 420, 422, 448, 450, 463, 560, 578, 593, 633, 661, 666, 674, 704, 712, 728, 731, 736, 742, 745, 774, 775, 777, 794, 859, 875, 877, 878, 888, 893, 912, 930, 931, 940, 943, 945, 955, 1026, 1076,

1093, 1108, 1128,
1195, 1213, 1225,
1232, 1236, 1243,
1285, 1311
LANIER, LYLE H. 185
LARDNER, RING 78, 131,
 148, 192, 409, 418,
 731, 903, 1092, 1243
LAW ENFORCEMENT -- See
 CRIME
LAWRENCE, D.H. 182
LEWIS, SINCLAIR 138,
 154, 163, 167, 190,
 329, 421, 514, 580,
 640, 676, 713, 830,
 1030, 1145, 1166,
 1216, 1258
LIBERALISM 284, 297,
 763, 864, 938
LIBERTY 405, 418, 639,
 922, 983, 1011
LINCOLN, ABRAHAM 56,
 149, 405, 414
LINDSAY, VACHEL 28,
 43, 147, 438
LIPPMANN, WALTER 143,
 1254
LITERARY CRITICISM 29,
 39, 46, 52, 57, 58,
 60, 64, 66, 77, 80,
 105, 107, 112, 120,
 121, 122, 173, 175,
 387, 401. 404, 405,
 406, 409, 410, 413,
 414, 417, 418, 420,
 421, 422, 430, 571,
 574, 577, 578, 581,
 582, 584, 585, 587,
 589, 592, 595, 596,
 598, 601, 605, 615,
 616, 618, 620, 621,
 624, 631, 636, 640,
 643, 646, 648, 649,
 656, 658, 661, 662,
 663, 664, 665, 667,
 668, 670, 671, 675,
 676, 677, 679, 694,
 695, 696, 700, 702,
 703, 705, 706, 711,
 717, 720, 721, 722,

725, 726, 727, 731,
732, 738, 739, 740,
744, 746, 747, 748,
749, 752, 754, 756,
757, 758, 761, 762,
767, 768, 769, 770,
771, 772, 773, 778,
779, 780, 781, 782,
784, 785, 786, 787,
789, 790, 791, 792,
793, 795, 796, 797,
799, 803, 804, 805,
806, 807, 808, 809,
811, 812, 814, 815,
816, 817, 818, 819,
820, 828, 831, 835,
840, 841, 842, 843,
844, 845, 856, 860,
862, 893, 896, 897,
909, 910, 914, 915,
917, 919, 923, 927,
928, 932, 933, 934,
939, 942, 945, 946,
948, 952, 953, 954,
965, 969, 971, 972,
973, 976, 987, 991,
992, 996, 998, 999,
1000, 1002, 1010,
1012, 1013, 1015,
1021, 1025, 1030,
1039, 1044, 1045,
1046, 1053, 1065,
1067, 1071, 1073,
1074, 1084, 1090,
1107, 1116, 1131,
1133, 1142, 1143,
1145, 1156, 1157,
1158, 1159, 1160,
1161, 1163, 1164,
1166, 1170, 1171,
1172, 1173, 1174,
1177, 1179, 1181,
1183, 1184, 1185,
1188, 1189, 1192,
1197, 1199, 1200,
1201, 1203, 1205,
1206, 1208, 1209,
1216, 1218, 1220,
1222, 1223, 1227,
1228, 1230, 1231,

SUBJECTS

1233, 1242, 1243,
1244, 1245, 1246,
1247, 1249, 1251,
1252, 1253, 1257,
1259, 1260, 1262,
1263, 1264, 1267,
1270, 1276, 1279,
1281, 1282, 1284,
1286, 1290, 1291,
1294, 1295, 1296
1297, 1301, 1303,
1304, 1305, 1306,
1309, 1313
LODGE, HENRY CABOT
 414, 1194
LOHRFINCK, ROSALIND
 436
LONDON, JACK 403, 1262
LONG, HUEY P. 345
LOOS, ANITA 1151
LORTIMER, GEORGE HORACE
 1007
LOVE 73, 238, 417
LOWELL, AMY 43
LYNCHING 258, 332,
 394, 984
LYTLE, ANDREW NELSON
 185

MacDONALD, DWIGHT 1182
MacLANE, MARY 38, 403
MAGAZINES (GENERAL)
 and MAGAZINE EDITING
 35, 83, 112, 121,
 195, 196, 287, 403,
 409, 422, 987, 1057
MAILER, NORMAN 702
MAN and MEN (TYPES OF)
 63, 71, 91, 405, 406,
 417, 418
MANCHESTER, WILLIAM
 433, 434
MANN, HORACE 1141
MARKHAM, EDWIN 999
MARQUIS, DON 580
MARRIAGE 112, 281,
 292, 406, 417, 681
MARYLAND (See also
 BALTIMORE) 116, 165,
 332, 355, 659, 728,

959, 984, 1119
MARYLAND, UNIVERSITY OF
 356, 938, 1082
MASTERS, EDGAR LEE 43,
 78, 129, 147, 409,
 1220, 1263
MATTHEWS, BRANDER 257
McCLURE, JOHN 1090
McINTOSH, KENNETH
 CHAFFEE 967
McNARY, CHARLES L. 367
McPHERSON, AIMEE SEMPLE
 160
MEAD, MARGARET 166
MEDICINE 26, 358,
 1096, 1124
MEDIEVALISM 691
MENCKE, JOHANN BURKHARD
 392, 961
MENCKENIANA 459, 460
MENDELSSOHN, (JAKOB
 LUDWIG) FELIX 419
METAPHYSICS and
 METAPHYSICIANS 91,
 410
MEYER, ADOLPHE E. 967
MILITARY, U.S. 62,
 405, 414, 420
MIMS, EDWIN 805
MIZNER, WILSON 1224
MONDAY ARTICLES, THE
 283, 284, 415
MONROE, HARRIET 43
MOORE, GEORGE 421
MORALITY 13, 79, 103,
 254, 256, 264, 277,
 322, 409, 419, 420,
 422, 919, 991
MORE, PAUL ELMER 56,
 405, 421, 845, 1173,
 1295
MOTION PICTURES 87,
 153, 259, 328, 410,
 414, 417, 1280
MUSIC 75, 268, 325,
 381, 409, 417, 419,
 421, 443, 919, 945,
 974, 1051, 1113,
 1137, 1156, 1163

NATHAN, GEORGE JEAN
  22, 42, 418, 504,
  508, 517, 538, 556,
  602, 612, 645, 703,
  724, 756, 764, 843,
  869, 947, 962, 1057,
  1073, 1088, 1105,
  1180, 1187, 1193,
  1212, 1238, 1271,
  1299
NAZISM 905, 1004, 1041
NEW DEAL 200, 212,
  218, 220, 339, 361,
  362, 363, 364, 368,
  415, 755, 908, 1308
NEW THOUGHT, THE 919
NEW YORK CITY 74, 84,
  96, 110, 240, 275,
  406, 410, 603, 724,
  727, 1240
NEWMAN, ERNEST 419
NEWMAN, FRANCES 426,
  761, 1046
NIETZSCHE, FRIEDRICH
  3, 106, 373, 378,
  381, 421, 422, 494,
  609, 793, 981, 982,
  1270
NOBEL PRIZE, THE 329,
  1241
NORRIS, FRANK 33, 1228

OBER, HAROLD 1212
ODUM, HOWARD W. 751,
  944
O'HARA, JOHN 716
O'NEILL, EUGENE 1181
OPERA -- See MUSIC
OPPENHEIMER, JAMES 43
OWENS, HAMILTON 1097

PAINE, ALBERT BIGELOW
  136
PAINTING 75, 409
PARIS 714, 1226
PARODIES 586, 602,
  637, 783, 788, 800,
  1193
PATTEE, FRED LEWIS 421
PATTERSON, PAUL 423

PEGLER, WESTBROOK 657,
  879
PERELMAN, S.J. 1268,
  1283
PERKINS, MAX 1207,
  1238
PETERKIN, JULIA 761,
  969
PHELPS, WILLIAM LYON
  421
PHILOLOGY -- See
  LANGUAGE
PHILOSOPHY and
  PHILOSOPHERS 3, 49,
  91, 365, 373, 381,
  410, 421, 422, 577,
  578, 793, 945, 981,
  982, 1126, 1270
PITTSBURGH, PA 90,
  410, 414
POE, EDGAR ALLAN 33,
  47, 145, 403, 417,
  418, 420, 621, 828,
  938, 976
POETRY and POETS 1,
  28, 43, 88, 100, 126,
  147, 173, 176, 180,
  313, 403, 420, 421,
  422, 438, 461, 669,
  929, 942, 983, 999,
  1045, 1090, 1110,
  1144, 1217, 1220,
  1242, 1247, 1263
POLITICS and
  POLITICIANS 72, 111,
  112, 113, 119, 194,
  203, 214, 223, 224,
  246, 247, 283, 284,
  286, 296, 297, 300,
  301, 309, 317, 318,
  319, 321, 336, 337,
  349, 350, 353, 355,
  359, 361, 362, 366,
  367, 368, 369, 381,
  406, 412, 414, 415,
  417, 418, 420, 422,
  424, 577, 578, 588,
  647, 656, 695, 851,
  862, 904, 906, 917,
  959, 960, 966, 970,

997, 1006, 1014,
1018, 1032, 1061,
1063, 1088, 1094,
1099, 1128, 1138,
1176, 1177, 1194,
1225, 1234, 1302,
1304, 1308
POLLARD, PERCIVAL 46,
403, 1286
POOLE, ERNEST 46, 403
POPE PIUS XI 352
PORNOGRAPHY 182
POUND, EZRA 43, 421,
1234, 1277
PRICE, EMERSON FIELD
967
PROFANITY 231, 357
PROGRESSIVISM 908,
1178, 1211
PROHIBITION 69, 205,
278, 317, 336, 337,
406, 510, 511, 655,
669, 682, 1307
PROLETARIANISM 202,
692
PSYCHOLOGY 406, 421
PULITZER PRIZE 311
PURITANISM 33, 38, 44,
65, 69, 79, 103, 107,
114, 182, 254, 263,
282, 291, 328, 401,
406, 409, 410, 417,
421, 589, 614, 768,
779, 788, 1269

QUACKERY 24, 89, 392,
410, 418

RACE 112, 230, 251,
332, 370, 422, 581,
582, 763, 829, 911,
916, 978, 1068
RADIO 335, 352
RANSOM, JOHN CROWE 185
RASCOE, BURTON 709
REESE, LIZETTE
WOODWORTH 421, 1127
RELIGION 12, 25, 59,
67, 81, 256, 267,
312, 315, 320, 324,
327, 338, 344, 352,
405, 406, 409, 414,
417, 418, 419, 420,
422, 627, 629, 653,
737, 810, 827, 829,
844, 846, 847, 848,
849, 854, 855, 876,
1018, 1029, 1038,
1048, 1056, 1062,
1069, 1088, 1091,
1095, 1123, 1125,
1139, 1149, 1186,
1250, 1273, 1298,
1307
REMARQUE, ERICH MARIA
171
RÉPÉTITION GÉNÉRALE
109
RHETORIC -- See STYLE
ROBERTS, ELIZABETH
MADOX 761
ROBINSON, JOSEPH T.
319, 359
ROCKEFELLER, JOHN D.
421
ROGERS, WILL 499
ROOSEVELT, FRANKLIN
DELANO (See also NEW
DEAL) 210, 214, 220,
222, 286, 337, 343,
345, 350, 353, 361,
363, 364, 366, 368,
414, 415, 681, 755,
908, 1050, 1096,
1176, 1308
ROOSEVELT, THEODORE
53, 246, 253, 404,
415, 418, 750
ROSS, HAROLD 504
RUSSELL, BERTRAND 365

SACCO, NICOLA 290
SALTUS, EDGAR 409
SANDBURG, CARL 43, 149
SAROYAN, WILLIAM 1274
SATIRE 20, 499, 580,
597, 635, 649, 691,
882, 921, 926, 932,
1018, 1059
SATURDAY NIGHT CLUB
419, 523, 1113, 1137

SUBJECTS

SCHUBERT, FRANZ PETER 419
SCHUMANN, ROBERT 268, 419
SCHUYLER, GEORGE S. 1252
SCIENCE 279, 347, 1001, 1088, 1114
SCOPES, JOHN THOMAS 81, 82, 305, 306, 307, 409, 414, 420, 508, 537, 553, 660, 699, 763, 766, 857, 979, 1056, 1273
SCOTT, EVELYN 761
SEDGWICK, ELLERY 1066
SEX 37, 85, 97, 403, 404, 409, 410, 939
SHAKESPEARE, WILLIAM 249, 1233
SHAW, GEORGE BERNARD 2, 48, 188, 403, 418, 421, 422, 643, 821, 876, 914, 932, 1136, 1140, 1152
SHERMAN, STUART P. 107, 175, 421, 644, 695, 805, 809, 811, 845, 915, 1173, 1295
SINCLAIR, UPTON 33, 91, 128, 159, 342, 345, 429, 433, 510, 511, 919, 960, 1229, 1300
SKEPTICISM 193, 256, 414, 616, 1024, 1035
SMART SET, THE 421, 508, 539, 556, 594, 634, 689, 692, 701, 703, 724, 753, 756, 762, 764, 910, 927, 937, 949, 953, 964, 1015, 1057, 1073, 1187, 1190, 1192, 1212, 1238, 1290
SMITH, AL 319, 321, 415
SOCIAL CLASS 111
SOCIAL DARWINISM 947, 989, 1001, 1114, 1148

SOCIALISM and SOCIALISTS 4, 45, 91, 128, 159, 217, 342, 345, 410, 422, 510, 511, 822, 1020, 1124, 1229, 1300
SONG -- See MUSIC
SOUTH AMERICA 368
SOUTH (AMERICAN) and SOUTHERNERS 31, 120, 174, 185, 193, 207, 226, 287, 296, 320, 340, 391, 404, 410, 414, 415, 417, 418, 420, 422, 574, 582, 684, 730, 751, 761, 763, 771, 795, 806, 954, 963, 969, 987, 991, 1002, 1012, 1046, 1069, 1078, 1090, 1120, 1133, 1174, 1185, 1196, 1204, 1218, 1227, 1305
SPINGARN, JOEL ELIAS 39, 809, 1173, 1209
SPORTS 370, 414
STERILIZATON -- See EUGENICS
STERLING, GEORGE 313, 669, 1045, 1217, 1247
STEVENS, JAMES 1239
STEVENSON, ROBERT LOUIS 134, 417
STRAUSS, JOHANN 419
STRIBLING, T.S. 761
STUART, JESSE HILTON 1275
STURGES, PRESTON 1265
STYLE 45, 80, 113, 137, 192, 395, 415, 420, 577, 578, 629, 702, 721, 820, 832, 838, 891, 919, 923, 929, 941, 946, 951, 956, 957, 966, 968, 971, 975, 986, 988, 1008, 1034, 1043, 1048, 1059, 1064,

1104, 1122, 1125, 1196, 1293
SUCKOW, RUTH 130, 146, 161, 177
SUDERMANN, HERMANN 403
SUICIDE 91, 313, 410, 1217
SUMNER, WILLIAM GRAHAM 947, 1225
SUNDAY, BILLY 267, 421, 422
SUNPAPERS, BALTIMORE (MD) 14, 395, 424, 520, 864, 867, 935, 1023, 1044, 1089, 1210
SWIFT, JONATHAN 654, 921
SYNGE, JOHN M. 421
SYPHILIS 341

TASSIN, ALGERNON 35
TATE, ALLEN 176, 185, 1219
TAYLOR, GLEN H. 369
TEACHERS COLLEGE (COLUMBIA UNIVERSITY) 1141
TEASDALE, SARA 1242
THIRTIES, THE (1930s) 1226, 1255
THOMPSON, DOROTHY 514
TRUMAN, HARRY S. 369
TURNER, FREDERICK JACKSON 1103
TWAIN, MARK 33, 136, 276, 403, 417, 420, 421, 422, 777, 873, 882, 907, 926, 1136, 1224, 1236
TWENTIES, THE (1920s) 505, 525, 550, 599, 620, 621, 638, 663, 664, 667, 670, 672, 688, 700, 723, 748, 750, 761, 764, 858, 861, 879, 881, 884, 908, 957, 1036, 1072, 1172, 1178, 1211, 1226, 1261

TYRELL, R. EMMETT 1278
UKRANIA 728

VALENTINO, RUDOLPH 87, 410, 414
VAN VECHTEN, CARL 127, 489, 990
VANZETTI, BARTOLOMEO 290
VEBLEN, THORSTEIN 45, 403, 420
VIRGINIA 521

WADE, JOHN DONALD 185
WAGNER, (WILHELM) RICHARD 381, 419
WALLACE, HENRY A. 369, 414
WALPOLE, HUGH 117, 142
WAR 79, 194, 216, 225, 229, 361, 409
WARREN, EARL 369
WARREN, ROBERT PENN 176, 185
WASHINGTON, D.C. 1050
WATCH AND WARD SOCIETY (BOSTON) -- See CHASE, J. FRANK (Secretary)
WAYS, MAX 295
WEBER, F. PARKES 51
WEBSTER, NOAH 1108
WEISMANN, AUGUST 1114
WELLS, H.G. 141, 151, 403, 421
WEST (AMERICAN) and MIDWEST 274, 379, 472, 1015, 1090, 1107, 1131
WHARTON, EDITH 1074
WHITE, E.B. 1272
WHITE, WALTER 996
WHITE, WILLIAM ALLEN 46, 403, 421, 919
WHITMAN, WALT 33, 47, 403, 418, 420, 624
WILDE, OSCAR 421
WILDER, THORNTON 161

SUBJECTS

WILLIAMS, WILLIAM CARLOS   712, 742, 1232
WILLKIE, WENDELL L.   367
WILSON, EDMUND   1188, 1203, 1206, 1246, 1267
WILSON, WOODROW   414, 415, 421
WITCHCRAFT   98, 410
WOLFE, THOMAS   1289
WOMEN   6, 60, 85, 112, 255, 261, 265, 266, 280, 409, 502, 637, 1052, 1054, 1088, 1109, 1191
WOOD, JAMES N.   382
WOODBRIDGE, HOMER   175
WORLD WAR I   264, 269, 270, 757, 1049, 1066, 1186
WORLD WAR II   194
WRIGHT, RICHARD   738, 1143, 1215, 1228, 1258
WRIGHT, WILLARD HUNTINGTON   703
WRITING   50, 80, 180, 192, 202, 302, 329, 395, 404, 420, 508, 560, 600, 665, 692, 744, 767, 787, 796, 824, 971, 1043, 1104

YOUNG, HUGH H.   433
YOUNG, STARK   185

ZEITLIN, JACOB   175